The HERB & SPICE COOKBOOK
A Seasoning Celebration

SHERYL & MEL LONDON

Photography by
The Rodale Press Photography Department

Rodale Press, Emmaus, Pa.

Printed in the United States of America.

Book design: Anita G. Patterson

Recipe on the front cover: *Orange-Ginger Chicken with Sugar Snap Peas, page 128*

Library of Congress Cataloging in Publication Data
London, Sheryl.
    The herb & spice cookbook.

    Includes index.
    1. Cookery (Herbs) 2. Spices. I. London, Mel. II. Title.
III. Title: Herb and spice cookbook.
TX819.A1L66 1986   641.6′57   86-13069
ISBN 0-87857-641-X hardcover

2 4 6 8 10 9 7 5 3 1   hardcover

For All the Herbs:

Herb Brodkin, Herb Schlosser, Herb Klagsbrun,
Herb Abramowitz, and Herb Salkin

and for the Spice in Our Lives:

Tina, Suzanne, and Sally

Other Books by Sheryl and Mel London

The Fish-Lovers' Cookbook
Sheryl and Mel London's Creative Cooking
with Grains and Pasta

By Sheryl London

Eggplant and Squash: A Versatile Feast
Making the Most of Your Freezer
Anything Grows

By Mel London

Getting into Film
Bread Winners
Easy Going
Second Spring
Bread Winners Too (The Second Rising)
Making It in Film

CONTENTS

ACKNOWLEDGMENTS

Some time ago, one of our favorite food writers did an article about her major complaints in the field of cookbooks, over a hundred of which she was asked to review each year. Her major criticism—indeed, her "cardinal sin"—was the custom of publishing cookbooks in which no recipes were tested before being released to the unsuspecting public. She called the habit "intolerable," a comment with which we heartily agree.

Of course, she did excuse the inadvertent error, and both she and we have been guilty of some. We remember with some amusement and chagrin one recipe in which the tomatoes that were reserved never made it back into the mixture according to the directions—and that after three testings and two copy edits. We never claimed to be perfect!

However, in all our years of writing cookbooks for Rodale Press, we can proudly point to the fact that *every* recipe has been tested at least twice and sometimes three times. A recipe received from a "guest" chef or baker is tested by the chef at least once. Then, it is tested by us in our own Fire Island kitchen. And finally, the ultimate testing takes place at Rodale's Test Kitchens, under the supervision of Tom Ney. Even after that, the results are passed out to the editorial staff for a taste test and a rating, which determines whether the recipe stays or goes.

This book is no exception, and so we would like to thank Tom's staff for their dedication, their work, and their reports to us—especially JoAnn Brader, who headed the team this time. A thank you is also extended to the rest of the Test Kitchen staff: Anita Hirsch and Diane Drabinsky. We appreciate, too, the work of Carl Doney, Angelo Caggiano, John P. Hamel, Alison Miksch, Mitchell T. Mandel, Sally Shenk Ullman, and Christie C. Tito, who studied our amateur slides showing what the finished dishes looked like and then translated them into the lovely photographs that fill this book. To stylists, Barbara Fritz and Kay Seng Lichthardt, we also offer our thanks.

And, as always, we express our deepest gratitute to two people who have worked closely with us on so many books: Charles Gerras, our editor, whose calls on Saturday afternoons to see if we were "still slaving away in the kitchen" were a delight and a spur to us, and Camille Bucci, who once again kept track of the recipe count and transformed a mountain of paper into a well-ordered manuscript, never losing her sweetness or her sense of humor through it all.

And finally, thanks go to our "guest chefs" and herb garden experts who graciously contributed their recipes, their stories, and their good wishes.

INTRODUCTION

This is a book that we have wanted to write for a long time.

Throughout the development and testing of all our cookbooks—through the baking of hundreds of different kinds of breads, the creation of innumerable dishes using fish of all names and sizes, working with a great variety of grains and pasta and countless experiments with eggplant and squash, we have used and encouraged others to use fresh herbs and lots of spices. Our interest in herbs and spices has also carried through in our everyday preparation of food and in entertaining guests. Especially as we began to reduce the amount of salt in our recipes and then to eliminate it almost entirely, herbs and spices and citrus became the seasonings most natural to us. And as we continued to experiment with them in our kitchen, we opened up a whole new world of taste and surprising combinations.

The little herb garden we keep in back of our Fire Island home began to expand, and we learned that we could also grow fresh herbs in our city apartment, in small containers, in regular flowerpots, and in flats outside on a rooftop terrace, defying urban blight and polluted soot-filled air. We soon amassed a collection of jars and bottles that read like the manifest from a ship of the old Dutch East India Company. Our friend Rudy, a superb hobby craftsman, mercifully offered to build a prodigious spice shelf to handle the overflow.

Of course, it was not always this way for us. Like most other Americans, our knowledge of herbs and spices has improved dramatically over these past 20 or 30 years. We remember, with some nostalgia, an experience we had soon after the opening of New York's marvelous Four Seasons restaurant, some 25 years ago. One of our friends knew a captain on the staff, and we all dined there one night on a surprising—and expensive—dinner. After dessert and coffee, our captain friend took us on a tour of the kitchen. It was a truly memorable adventure.

There, among the busy white-coated, toque-topped chefs and their countless assistants, who moved the copper cookware deftly from preparation to stove to warmed plates—performing a remarkably timed ballet that produced four or six or eight dishes perfectly finished, decorated, and served at exactly the same time—we saw pots and pots of *fresh herbs* on top of the shelves over the center counter, each one still green and growing in its own dark, rich black earth! We do not remember exactly what we ate that evening, and we certainly don't remember what the bill was, but we still carry the memory of fresh herbs being plucked and minced and scattered and mixed right there in the kitchen of the Four Seasons. The next day we began to collect flowerpots at home and started planting our very first herb garden in the corner of the living room that the city sun visited for a few hours a day. Some were so beautiful, so elegant, that we hated to cut them!

The sense of discovery we experienced was all the more remarkable because we knew full well that the history of herbs and spices went back over 5,000 years. And what seems somehow new in the 1980s is, in fact, as old as the caravan routes across the deserts of Africa, the Crusades, and the explorations of the early Dutch and Portuguese explorers. Indeed, we owe the discovery of the New World to a search by Europeans for new trade routes to the spice centers of Asia.

Now, centuries later, we are thrilled to "discover" herbs and spices that were familiar to the ancient Romans—coriander and cumin, oregano, ginger, cardamom, cloves, caraway, mustard seed, and chervil, among many others. The Roman chef, Apicius, who lived at the dawn of the Christian Era, had access to the spice markets of Asia. He made pepper, cloves, nutmeg, and ginger available to prosperous Roman citizens. (Of course, spices were too expensive for use by the general populace.) Almost every one of his recipes was enhanced with lovage, aniseed, caraway, coriander, and with pepper.

Virtually every spice has been credited with aphrodisiacal qualities. But none of the recipes in this book make any such claims. The Egyptians used spices for food preparation and also for embalming and for cleansing the musty smell of closed rooms. The Barbarian Goths used spices in their religious rites. Histories of the Middle Ages are rife with descriptions of herbal remedies and love potions brewed by witches and folk herbalists. For a fee, poisoners of the day could and did whip up quick-acting fatal herbal concoctions.

But, for the most part, our ancestors used herbs and spices, especially the latter, for a much more practical reason: to disguise the flavor of decaying food. With no refrigeration, and few preservation techniques, keeping meat and other foods fresh over time was impossible.

Of course, in later years, herbs and spices became common everyday adjuncts to home cooking as chefs learned to alter, improve, and expand the taste of other foods. Until the early twentieth century, almost every home kitchen had a mortar and pestle or a spice mill for grinding whole dried spices, since commercially ground spices were not yet available. But, somehow, the use of popular herbs, such as rosemary, basil, tarragon, and oregano, almost disappeared during the 1920s, and they didn't return until well after World War II. Though Sheryl came from a family where experimentation with food and a knowledge of it was presumed, Mel can barely remember a spice (not to mention an herb) ever being used by his mother, except for a tiny touch of garlic for meatballs and spaghetti! For us, it was the discoveries we made through travel that changed our lives and our cooking and eating habits. Today that seems to be happening to more and more people.

In the early sixties, we spent almost five years producing a series of films for Alitalia Airlines around the world, and our home base for the job was Rome. In lovely Italy, originator of so many delicious dishes, we learned even more about what we had been missing in fine flavorings all these years. Though we discovered some great culinary treasures in the more than 40 countries we visited over that five-year period, Italy itself surely taught us more about the use of fresh, seasonal ingredients and the use of herbs and spices than any other place.

We fondly recall a delectable lunch in a Roman restaurant where, for the first time, we feasted on that basil-based masterpiece that is now commonly served all over the United States, pesto! Since language aptitude was never one of our major assets, we were always confused by the two words: *basilica* ("church") and *basilico* ("basil"). That explains why we once asked for "fresh tomatoes with church" at a little trattoria in the Umbria region!

Today, everyone seems to be learning about the use of fresh and dried herbs and the vast array of spices now available to us. The spice shelf has undergone a minor revolution, and fresh culinary herbs are available almost everywhere, whether it be from small personal gardens and flowerpots or from supermarket shelves across the country.

For a variety of reasons, cooks have taken to using these flavorings—albeit tentatively—but sometimes with little knowledge of which flavors marry well, and which do not. We have found that even in the "best" restaurant in town, not every herbal combination is successful, and some are downright disastrous. But, overall, sophistication in the American taste has grown tremendously:

❧ People are beginning to travel more. In fact, there has been an explosion of available itineraries that offer the traveler a chance to sample and to experiment. Where, formerly, visits to Florida and California were considered adventures and a trip to the Caribbean was a journey for the Outward Bound program, many of our friends have now been to China, to Nepal, to Ecuador, and certainly to Europe (several times). Even our sons and daughters have backpacked in England and France while still in their teens.

❧ Interest in fresh foods, in nutrition, and in gardening, both in small plots and in larger areas at home or even in inner-city community gardens, has grown steadily. These gardens are not only devoted to fresh vegetables (that *taste* good), but many also have small patches of fresh herbs.

❧ Cooking schools and cooking lessons have become popular activities among Americans—even the young career-minded set who say they often eat out or just "graze" when they are at home because they're too tired to cook. The sale of cooking instruction video tapes is booming!

• A surge in the popularity of ethnic restaurants and the availability of ethnic ingredients for home cooking has awakened an herb-and-spice interest among Americans of all ages. The proliferation of Japanese, Vietnamese, Chinese, Greek, and even Ethiopian, Thai, Cuban, Haitian, and Indian/Pakistani restaurants in almost all the major cities in the country, has helped us to discover the taste treats that have remained hidden for so many years—except for the adventurous traveler.

There is another bright side to this change in American eating and cooking habits. We firmly believe that using culinary herbs and spices in new and unusual ways can help to make all of us healthier. Bland foods lead to overeating (and most of the food served in this country is bland). Just observe the *amounts* of food piled on buffet plates in restaurants! The taste buds are not satisfied when flavors are muted.

This book shows that herbs and spices can redefine food flavors and provide startling and unusual accents, so that we find satisfaction in the *taste* of foods that are good for us. You need not use the *same* herbs and spices in the same dish, time and time again; just a simple change in seasoning can create an entirely new and unusual dish.

The book is about how to avoid boredom in food tastes. It is about experimentation, about new ways to use the usual, and about encouragement to try the unusual. It is an invitation to take a sensual journey by cooking with flavors that originate in the far-flung corners of the earth—and trying them all without ever leaving home or hearth.

On a more practical level, it is a book about an exciting way to cook. We think that using a few well-chosen minced herbs or a surprise spice can make you look like an absolute genius to your guests. What more can a chef desire?

Sheryl and Mel London
Fire Island, New York

Chapter 1
WHY HERBS & SPICES?

Redolent—fragrant, aromatic, perfumed, scented, ambrosial, savory, sweet-smelling. We started using the word to describe some of the first dishes we created for this book, but it soon became a dominant theme. We looked at one another and laughed because everything was redolent. Everything *smelled* good!

Certainly we are not the first cooks to discover that the word *taste* used by itself is woefully inexact. When we say that something "tastes good," we are actually describing the sum total of several sensations. The tongue tells us whether a food is gritty or slippery or crisp; it also distinguishes sweet and sour, salt and bitter. The tongue reveals how pungent a food is (too much horseradish or chili peppers), or how astringent (a ripe persimmon)—but very little else. The rest of what we call *taste* is actually *smell*.

In *The Physiology of Taste*, Brillat-Savarin wrote extensively on his theory of smell as it relates to taste:

For myself, I am not only convinced that there is no full act of tasting without the sense of smell, but I am also tempted to believe that smell and taste form a single sense, [of] which the mouth is the laboratory and the nose is the chimney; or, to speak more exactly, of which one serves for the tasting of actual bodies and the other for the savoring of gases . . . when the sense of smell is cut off, the taste itself is paralyzed.

Think of the diminished taste food has when you are fighting a miserable head cold. Movement of air in the nasal passages is essential for delivering a true taste sensation. The oenophile, the expert on wine, speaks of the "nose" or bouquet of the wine to help to portray the taste.

We know that many other factors affect the taste of food.

❧ The *geographical location* means a lot. Did you ever wonder why those marvelous dishes you devoured in Seville or Athens don't taste quite as good when you have them in New York or Dallas, even when the restaurants are ethnic and the recipes authentic? Climatic conditions of a region can actually affect how things "taste," since the sense of smell is more acute in a moist atmosphere than in a dry one.

❧ The *temperature* of food counts, too. Sweet and sour tastes are reduced by cold; saltiness is increased. The Italians and the French learned centuries ago to serve both fruit and cheese unchilled and at their tastiest best. Consider the taste of a ripe, luscious melon just out of the refrigerator

1

versus another slice of the very same melon brought to room temperature.

ᕉ The *method or style of preparation,* quite independent from *how* we season our food, affects the final "taste." Think, for example, of fish served raw *(sashimi)* or broiled or steamed—each one markedly different in flavor and texture. How about the ever-popular chicken? The same bird, fried or sauteed or roasted or broiled, will take on a different flavor, aside from the herbs and spices used.

The choice of seasonings can make interesting alterations that enhance the basic taste of the food. Herbs and spices, particularly, have their own individual aromas, and they have the power to effect substantial, usually pleasing, changes in other foods. Properly used, they become the friends of cooks, brightening and adding flavor, encouraging experimentation, and opening new avenues for the adventurous soul.

The range of herbs and spices available today is vast. Spices are the dried parts of tropical plants—the roots, berries, and bark—all grown in the Far East, except for allspice, the one major spice indigenous to the New World. Herbs are the leafy parts of plants or trees, all grown in the temperate zones of the world. There are guidelines, perhaps, but not hard-and-fast rules for using herbs and spices. We are often asked how much dried oregano is equal in flavoring intensity to a given amount of the fresh, and how does one determine the right amount of an herb or spice to use? Like many other home cooks, we can only reply, "Well, it depends . . . "

ᕉ *It depends upon personal taste.* It is the reason that most new Chinese restaurants proclaim on their menus that they can prepare any dish "mild, hot, very hot, or dynamite." Your own preferences will dictate many of the rules you eventually establish.

ᕉ *It depends upon the age of your spices, where they were grown, and how they were processed.* The older the spice, the greater the loss of flavor. The *brand* of spice and whether it is store-bought or ground at home with a mortar and pestle will also affect the intensity of flavor.

ᕉ *It depends upon whether you use fresh herbs or dried.* The difference in flavor will amaze you. Even here, the tastes of the herbs will vary according to the variety grown, the kind of soil used, the amount of sun available, the amount of water given to the plants, and *when* the herb was cut and *how* it was used in a dish.

ᕉ *It depends upon the exposure to air and the oxidation that results in flavor loss for both herbs and spices.* We offer some tips on storage in a later chapter (page 42), but essentially, herbs stay fresh if their roots are immersed in water and if they are stored in the refrigerator; spices should be kept whole rather than ground and in airtight containers in a cool, dark place.

Though we give suggestions throughout the book, the final decision as to dried versus fresh or the amount to use in a selected dish will have to be a personal one. But, however you use them, herbs and spices do illustrate the important role *smell* plays in the taste sensation.

The scientific community is discovering (or rediscovering) another aspect of the aromas of cooking that was familiar to our grandmothers generations ago. The experts recommend an array of pleasant odors — including the smell of herbs used in cooking — to alleviate stress as well as some other physical maladies.

Grandmother probably never had a science course, but she knew all about the soothing appeal of something that smells good as it cooks on the stove. We were told of one wise woman who followed a ritual every evening about 15 minutes before her husband was due home from work. She began to saute some onions. No matter what the menu for that evening, the onions went on the stove to greet the returning husband with a tempting aroma. As he opened the door, the tiredness seemed to leave him and his nose went into the air, "Boy! Something smells good!" The cares of the day were gone for the moment. Even before the tasting, the pleasure was there.

So it is with herbs, and so it is with spices. They let us begin the enjoyment of eating in advance. *Redolent!*

Chapter 2
HERB & SPICE ADVENTURES

Many of the recipes that are handed down from generation to generation give amounts casually in terms of "a pinch" or "a handful" or, even worse, "some." Add some basil. Put in some oregano. Melt some butter. We realized years ago that grandma was probably a much "easier" and instinctive cook than most of us. In addition, at least in the case of our own grandmothers, her stock of recipes was confined to a very few good ones which she repeated over and over again. Finally, she may have withheld explicit instructions deliberately so that the pie or the soup or the turkey could never be duplicated quite the way "grandma used to make." That dish remained the highlight of the holiday visit then, and we still think back to those great flavors with a tinge of nostalgia.

If recipes provided too little information in the old days, we might have *too much* information at our fingertips now. For example, we used to think of basil as basil, and now we find that there are about *150* varieties of the herb. Our own garden on Fire Island now boasts at least four of them. Friends who dropped by last summer were amazed to find an entire section of growing area devoted exclusively to basil plants, some purple, some green; some with tiny leaves, others with large ones.

In *The Basil Book* (New York: Long Shadow Books/Simon & Schuster, 1984), author Marilyn Hampstead delightfully describes about 14 varieties of basil—including Sweet Basil, Licorice Basil, Cinnamon Basil, Dark Opal Basil, and Piccolo Fino Verde Basil, reputed to be the *authentic* pesto basil.

Today we have access to so many herbs, fresh and dried, spices, bottled and in bulk, ground and unground, in sticks, seeds, and bark, plus a whole range of colorful edible flowers, that a lot of cooks are scared off. They fall back on the same old standbys over and over again, and miss out on some of the great culinary pleasures.

At the beginning, let's just go back to the idea that basil is basil. Gradually, we can allow ourselves to discover the less common varieties that might to be fun to try. Work with only a few simple rules for the use of herbs and spices, and a few basic terms you need to know, and soon your hand will begin to reach for them confidently, more and more often as you cook. It will become clear that the use of herbs and spices depends a great deal upon personal taste and upon experimentation without fear.

That is one reason that we are *not* presenting any kind of chart that lists "perfect" combinations, immutable rules that would forever marry sage to pork or poultry with no room for options. We think that sage with pork or poultry is just great. But why not pork with a combination of sweet marjoram and caraway seed? Or pork with anise and orange juice? Or poultry with a lemon and dill stuffing? For each of these, the home chef can create a *new* taste sensation by using just a bit of imagination that will take us past "the rules of the game."

How Much to Use

Employ the same thinking to overcome doubts about how much spice to use or how many herbs to add to the dish. Seasoning amounts cannot be precisely determined to suit every taste, no matter how explicit the recipe. In this book we only *suggest* the amounts. Just use your seasonings sparingly at first; you can always add more later on. Use seasonings that are as *fresh* as possible to get the best results in aroma and in taste.

A Few Herb Terms

Whether you use fresh herbs or dried, there are some terms that you will need to know, and we give their definitions here. A bit further on in this chapter, we also provide a few tips on how to use and prepare fresh herbs, dried herbs, spices, and edible flowers. We also have some comments on the prepared, premixed commercial blends of culinary herbs.

The culinary herbs, those used specifically for cooking, are sometimes referred to as *kitchen herbs*. Here are some other terms:

Pot Herbs—Vegetable plants whose leaves and stems are used for food rather than just for seasoning, for example, dandelion greens, beet tops, and spinach. Incidentally, the word *vegetable* appeared only 200 years ago; before that time, any plant used for cooking in a pot was called a "pot herb."

Salad Herbs—Any herbs used to flavor salads, such as fennel, basil, parsley, or chives.

"Faggot of Herbs"—An English term for a combination of herbs usually thrown on a fire to flavor grilling meats.

Herb Bouquets—Sometimes called *bouquets garnis* are combinations of herbs, fresh as well as dried, used to flavor soups, braised dishes, and stews. Generally they are tied in a package to allow easy removal after cooking and to prevent dispersal of the herbs during the cooking process. The classic bouquet garni consists of:

1 bay leaf
3 sprigs thyme
1 sprig tarragon
2 sprigs parsley

In this book, we use a basic fresh herb bouquet, and we add other herbs for specific dishes:

3 sprigs parsley
2 sprigs thyme
1 bay leaf

For chicken or fish dishes, we add a sprig or two of dill or fennel leaves, lovage or celery leaves, and whole peppercorns. *For lamb,* we add a sprig of rosemary. *For beef or pork,* we like to add a few whole dried cloves or basil.

There are other variations, of course. Sometimes bouquets garnis are wrapped in bay leaves and shaped like cigarettes. These are available commercially (see Mail-Order Sources), and they come in different combinations:

> sage bouquet — pork or poultry
> thyme bouquet — meats and sauces
> tarragon bouquet — poultry and veal

Look at the above list. Surely you can see that there is room for experimentation. Who says that a tarragon bouquet can't be used with fish?

Fines Herbes — A blend of finely minced fresh herbs. The classic blend consists of parsley, chives, tarragon, and chervil in equal amounts. It's traditionally sprinkled over egg and cheese dishes — but we have also used the combination to liven up sauces and soups, with fish, veal, or chicken, and for green salads. Along the way, we have created our own substitutes for the traditional blend; such as mint, basil, thyme, and summer savory. For convenience, you might try some of the prepackaged *dried herb* mixtures.

Fresh Herbs and How to Use Them

We try to use fresh herbs whenever possible to get the truest and the best flav-ors. At one time, fresh herbs were simply not available during the winter months, or any other time, outside of the large metropolitan centers in this country, unless they were homegrown or nurtured in a greenhouse or on sunny windowsills. Today, fresh herbs are available through supermarkets and specialty food shops nearly everywhere. In fact, we are convinced that some herbs are decidedly better *only* when used fresh, for example, basil, borage, parsley, chives, chervil, and cilantro.

When seasoning with herbs, it is best to choose one for the dominant flavoring, adding other milder flavored herbs in smaller amounts as nuance. Keep in mind that the major purpose for using herbs today is to *enhance* the flavor of the food itself, not to disguise it as in former times.

❧ Strip small leaves from the tough stems. Snip the delicate, wispy herbs (chives, dill, fennel leaves) with scissors.

❧ Mince the larger leaf herbs finely. Mincing releases their flavor, something you will discover as you do it.

❧ For *hot* foods, sprinkle on the herbs at the last minute. The heat will help to release their flavor, and their texture and bright green color will remain. Mix in the herbs before serving. If you add fresh herbs earlier, the flavor will be maintained, but some color and texture may be lost. Retain some of the fresh, minced herbs to sprinkle on top for eye appeal.

❧ For *cold* dishes, add fresh herbs several hours or even the night before serving to

(continued on page 10)

Identify the Fresh Herbs

You might have fragrant mint, pungent garlic, or flavorful dill growing wild right in your backyard. Would you recognize these herbs if you saw them? Perhaps your supermarket offers a selection of fresh herbs at the produce counter. If you wanted to buy them, could you pick out basil, or tarragon, or thyme by their appearance? In case you are not sure of what these and other popular herbs look like, we invite you to use these pictures as a convenient reference.

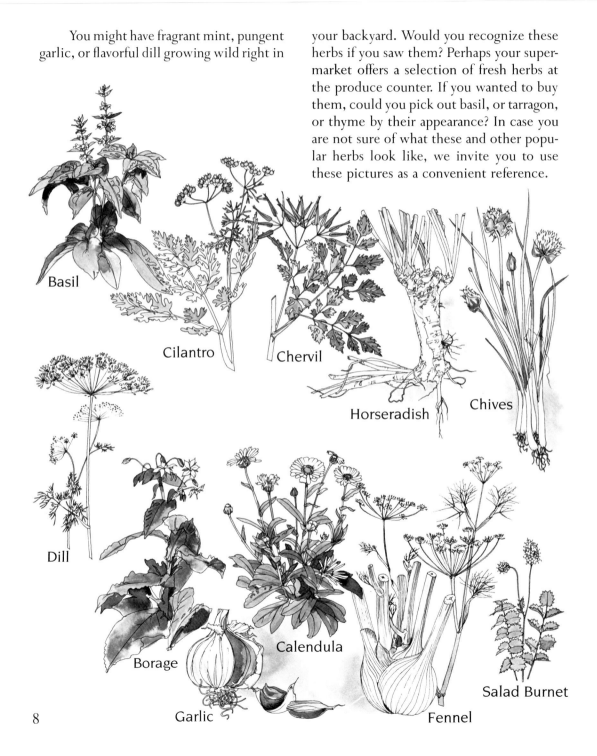

Basil

Cilantro

Chervil

Horseradish

Chives

Dill

Borage

Calendula

Garlic

Fennel

Salad Burnet

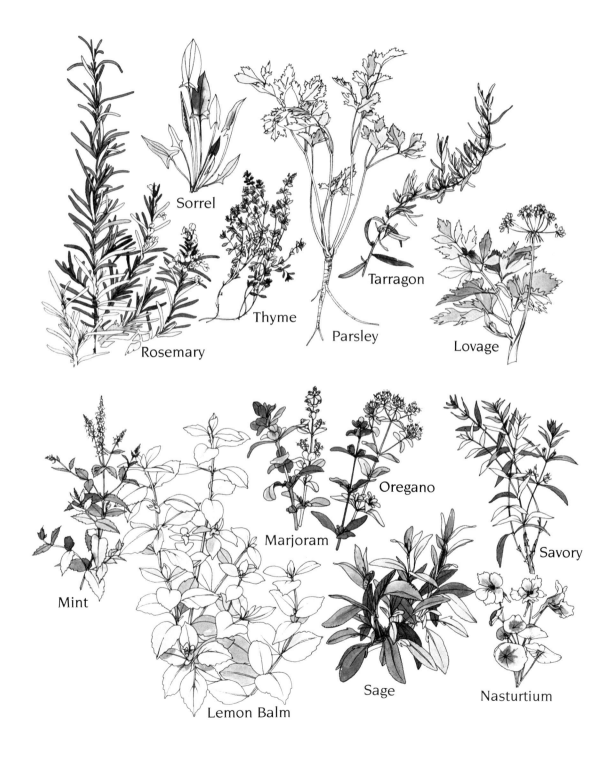

Sorrel

Thyme

Rosemary

Tarragon

Parsley

Lovage

Oregano

Marjoram

Savory

Mint

Sage

Nasturtium

Lemon Balm

develop full flavor and permeate the dish thoroughly.

❧ Our *equivalent* for using fresh herbs in place of dried herbs called for in a recipe: Use three times as much of the fresh. A good rule of thumb is 1 tablespoon of fresh herbs equals 1 teaspoon of crushed, dried herbs. But remember, much depends upon the *kind* of herbs and the proper storage of the dried herbs, so taste as you go.

❧ Use any *leftover* herbs you have snipped or minced to your advantage. (We generally have a teaspoon to a tablespoon too much of parsley or cilantro or dill.)

— Make herb butters (page 256) with excess minced herbs.

— Use excess whole leaves for herb vinegars (page 274).

— Tie parsley stems together and add them to a slow-cooking dish.

Dried Herbs, Savory Spices, and How to Use Them

Those of us who have joined the trend toward eating foods with lower saturated fat content, more whole grains, and reduced sodium have discovered that we can still enjoy flavorful and interesting food. In fact, we have made our cuisine even *more* interesting by introducing a variety of new taste sensations through our expanded knowledge of herbs and spices. All across the country, innovative restaurants are doing the same thing. They increasingly depend on herbs and spices for flavoring instead of on salt.

The average American consumes over 4,000 milligrams of sodium a day (from all sources of food). By comparison, diets that severely restrict sodium recommend about 500 milligrams daily. A teaspoon of salt contains 2,300 milligrams of sodium; a teaspoon of parsley flakes, 5.9 milligrams; cloves, 4.2 milligrams; celery seed, 4.1 milligrams.

Here are some tips on buying and using *dried* herbs and spices.

❧ Buy dried herbs and spices in small quantities whenever possible. Those sealed

---

GOVERN THE GARLIC

❧ For a *hint* of garlic, the mildest intensity, do not peel before adding it to the dish. You can also peel the clove, slit it, and remove the innermost green heart, then use the rest of the clove.

❧ For *stronger* garlic flavor, mince the cloves.

❧ For *strongest* flavor, crush or mash the garlic. It will be two to three times stronger than when it is minced.

A tip: Never brown garlic when you are cooking it or it will become bitter.

in packages and sold at your supermarket or specialty food store, have a shelf life of two to three years. Once you open them at home their intensity diminishes in direct relation to how they are stored.

🌢 Keep dried herbs and spices in a cool, dry place, tightly sealed. When you use them, remove the amount you need, and then close the container quickly.

🌢 Try to purchase the more fragile dried herbs in their whole form (for example, thyme leaves and tarragon leaves). They'll last longer on the shelf, and when you want to use them, you can easily crush them between your fingers to release the flavors before adding them to the dish. (Bay leaf, however, is usually dropped into the cooking pot whole and then removed before serving.)

🌢 As a rule, whole dried spices (for example, cloves, nutmeg, peppercorns, coriander) are more pronounced in flavor than ground or powdered ones. They also tend to keep their flavor for longer periods of time.

🌢 When you use whole dried spices in your cooking, put them in a cheesecloth bag for easy removal later on. Many a tooth has been chipped by a stray peppercorn in a stew.

🌢 We suggest that you grind whole spices in the small amounts that will be needed for a recipe just before using them. The grinding process breaks down the cell walls of the spice and releases the volatiles. The finer the grind, the richer the flavor. If you invest in a good peppermill and a good nut-meg grater, we guarantee that you'll become a convert.

Finally, check your spice supply once a year to make sure each one is still fresh and strong; if the aroma seems weak, replace the spice.

About the Premixed Commercial Blends

Perhaps you have already tried some of the commercial spice blends that the supermarkets sell, since many have been around for a long time. On our shelves, we have always kept several boxes of commercial crab boil, waiting for the September nights on our island when the blue crabs literally cover the bottom of the bay and swim around the dock pilings. Other blends have become basic standbys—chili powder and poultry seasoning, for example. The Chinese five spice powder and the French herbes de Provence are standard combinations for cuisines just now being used with more frequency by American cooks.

Some of the blends may be unique to manufacturers, or a product may be one of the many similar blends, varying slightly from the traditional mixtures. We list below a few of the many blends that are available across the country, an easy timesaving choice for the cook.

One word of warning: *Read the labels carefully.* Be cautious. Commercially prepared herb and spice salts (for example, celery salt and garlic salt) may also contain the chemical MSG (monosodium glutamate) along with plenty of sodium. Look for the commercial blends that omit MSG and advertise on the label that they are now *salt free,* as some of the chili powders do.

Chili Powder—A convenient seasoning for "Tex-Mex" dishes, this blend usually consists of ground hot chili pepper as a basic ingredient, plus ground cumin seed, oregano, and dehydrated garlic. Sometimes cloves and allspice are added. Be sure to check the salt content when purchasing chili powder. Better still, look for a no-salt blend.

Crab Boil or Shrimp Spice—These are quite similar and the blends depend upon the manufacturer. They consist of whole spices, used primarily in the boiling water when cooking seafood. Typically, they include whole peppercorns, bay leaf, mustard and dillseed, hot red pepper, ginger, and sometimes allspice and cloves. This combination is quite similar to mixed pickling spice.

Five Spice Powder (Ng Heung Fun)—A sweetly aromatic Chinese blend consisting of ground spices: star anise, cinnamon bark, fennel seed, whole cloves, and anise pepper.

Poultry Seasoning—This blend of dried herbs consists mostly of sage with undertones of thyme, marjoram, and savory. Depending upon the brand, you may also find rosemary, celery seed, or some spices that are added to the basic herbs.

Quatre Epices—A French "four spice" blend, it includes nutmeg, ginger, cloves, cinnamon, and a bit of pepper.

Herbal Seasoning—Natural foods shops are a particularly good source for premixed "salt-replacement" mixtures. However, we have a personal aversion to the idea of using their major ingredients: dried parsley, dried onion, and garlic powder in that form. We much prefer these herbs in their fresh form and with their true flavors left intact.

Pumpkin Pie Spice—Though this blend was created as a convenience seasoning for pumpkin pies, we find it quite pleasing to use in other ways. You will find it in a few of the non-pumpkin-pie recipes. The mixture consists of cinnamon, nutmeg, cloves, and ginger, a true marriage of the "sweet spices."

Herbes de Provence—This is a pungent mix of dried herbs from the south of France, where many herb varieties grow wild. Their flavors are quite different from the herbs that are grown in this country. The blend consists of wild thyme, lavender flowers, fennel seed, basil, and savory. We find herbes de Provence to be quite versatile; a large clay crock of this blend sits near our cooking space for easy access when fresh herbs are not available.

Curry Powder—We should mention at the outset that serious Indian cooks resent the term *curry powder,* since Indian spice blends are as complex and personal as handwriting or fingerprints. Good Indian cooks prefer to make their own blend of spices for this ancient cuisine. For example, one called *garam masala,* a warm, fragrant blend of spices, is traditionally a blend of cardamom pods, whole cloves, cumin seed, coriander seed, cinnamon, and peppercorns, roasted first and then freshly ground into a powder. The blends are varied and combined according to treasured family recipes. Some versions are now available in the Indian markets or specialty stores under the name of *garam masala.*

Other commercial blends of curry powder contain as many as 20 spices, combined to give what we Westerners consider a characteristic flavor of Indian cooking. These products usually include turmeric, ginger, fenugreek seed, cumin, mustard seed, red and black peppers, and, occasionally, cinnamon and cloves. No matter which blend you use, this is an assertive seasoning, so use it sparingly.

Adventures with Edible Flowers

We found an article from 1960 (it was crumbling in our files) headlined, *"What! Flowers in Cooking?"* The idea was news then, it seemed even a bit bizarre, but after the first reactions, we realized that our mothers and our grandmothers had always used flowers, or close relatives of flowers, in their cooking. After all, it is the lily family that provides garlic, onions, leeks, and chives. The cauliflower, artichokes, broccoli, Brussels sprouts, and bok choy we eat are the floral parts of those vegetables. Tarragon is a charter member of the aster family.

We made our most memorable discovery concerning floral cuisine in Italy, as with so many of our culinary treasures. At a table in a sun-drenched trattoria near the Pantheon in Rome, we were served golden zucchini blossoms, stuffed with mozzarella cheese and anchovies, and deep fried in a light, crisp batter. Where had these miracles of flavor been all of our deprived lives?

Many years later, we would scavenge in our own garden early on a summer morning to pick the dew-kissed male blossoms of our own flourishing zucchini plants. Then we would prepare them in exactly the same way and serve them as a light and delicious Italian luncheon to the delight of appreciative guests. In those days many of our gardening friends would let us pick *their* morning blossoms too, exclaiming, "You can have them. I don't know what to do with them anyway!" They have all changed their tunes. Now they harvest the crop and use the blossoms as we do.

We are pleased to see that this neglected art of cooking with flowers is being revived and expanded. There are *so many* edible flowers—some of them ornamental, some of them vegetable blossoms, some of them the flowers of herbs. Why shouldn't we be cooking with all of them? They have a long and honorable history.

In Confucius's time, chrysanthemums were a common cooking ingredient. The edible blossoms of lilac, nasturtium, and lavender were familiar to Shakespeare's England. And when colonists came to the New World they brought the tradition of cooking with flowers with them.

Throughout the world, rose petals are used to make a delicate jam, to brew into a fragrant tea, and to flavor all kinds of cakes, cookies, and fruit desserts. Sometimes rose petals are candied as violets are. These violets are a common decoration for desserts and other confections in Spain and France. A dazzling amethyst-colored liqueur called *Parfait Amour* is made from violets.

Orange blossoms made into Neroli oil are used as orange-flower water, a flavoring agent. President Eisenhower used the peppery nasturtium, a favorite flower of ours, as a seasoning for soup. Calendula (pot marigold) is known as the "poor man's saffron," since it tints food a deep golden color, just as the more expensive seasoning does.

Many herbs whose leaves or roots are used for seasoning also have edible blossoms. Oregano, thyme, basil, and chives are just a few of these herb flowers. Not only are they beautiful, but their flavors are exquisite, giving any dish a more delicate, perfumed version of the herb leaves.

The aforementioned squash blossoms are a favorite with the Italians, who pluck them, remove their stamens, stuff them, and then deep fry them in a tempura batter.

EDIBLE FLOWERS

By way of introduction to cooking with edible flowers, one of the best ways we know is to gather herb leaves, ornamental flowers, or herb and vegetable flowers, dip them into a tempura batter (recipe on this page), and serve them with Horseradish and Soy Dipping Sauce (page 258). For example, try:

Lemon Balm Leaves
Zucchini Blossoms
Parsley Leaves
Lovage Leaves
Sage Leaves
Mint Leaves
Borage Leaves and Blossoms
Basil Leaves and Blossoms
Cilantro Blossoms

Strew the finished tempura with a few colorful nasturtiums just before serving and stand back so that the compliments don't bowl you over!

Tempura

6 to 8 servings

1   cup rye or whole wheat flour
½   teaspoon baking powder
1   egg, beaten
1   cup milk
1   pound assorted vegetable or
    herb blossoms and leaves
    vegetable oil, for frying

Combine flour and baking powder in a small bowl. Add egg and milk, and stir until well mixed. Let stand for 30 minutes.

Meanwhile prepare vegetables. Then heat oil in a deep fryer (oil should reach 375°F). Dip vegetables into batter, and then lower coated vegetables into hot oil. Cook until batter is browned to your liking. Drain on paper towels.

Serve with Horseradish and Soy Dipping Sauce.

Blue borage flowers impart a delicate cucumberlike flavor to anything they're added to. Day lily buds are favored by oriental cooks, and pansies, with their bright little faces, make a lively decoration when gently pressed on cake frosting or allowed to peer through a clear, lemony molded gelatin.

One word of caution about using flowers as food. We suggest that you avoid using the flowers that are sold in commercial nurseries or in florist shops. Many of them have been sprayed with toxic insecticides. There is also a danger in eating flowers that grow close by our major highways, due to their exposure to lead and other toxic chemicals in automobile exhaust. The best flowers to choose are those grown in your own garden or that of a friend who has not yet discovered the joy of using flowers in cooking and the special flavors they provide.

Throughout this book we try to tempt you with delicious dishes that include edible flowers. *Do* try them. Flowers add unusual flavor to any dish. They add vivid, unexpected color. So we do urge you to not only smell the flowers but to eat them, too. You'll love it!

The Four Pillars of Flavor: Peppercorns, the Capsicums, the Alliums, and Citrus, Et Cetera

Some dinners we have had at the homes of friends, where bountiful platters put before us and rapidly devoured, left us with a faint suspicion that the seasonings had been locked in the cupboard when the meal was being prepared. At such dinners we are likely to consume more food than we usually do and we leave the table feeling uncomfortable and not very happy. There is no doubt in our minds that when the seasoning is right we tend to feel more satisfied with *less* food.

Throughout the book, we use "the four pillars of flavor" quite liberally at times. We think they are invaluable to the home cook, and they make a tasty and effective underpinning for both herbs and spices. Actually, the four are quite familiar to almost everyone and they've been around a long time—so don't be afraid to use them.

A Peppercorn of a Different Color . . .

We've always been charmed by the fact that *black* peppercorns come from berries that are *green* and then dried in the sun, while *white* peppercorns come from berries that have been allowed to ripen to *red,* with the skin and fleshy part then removed. And *both* are from the same plant! Actually, depending upon how they are allowed to ripen, and how they are harvested or dried or peeled, peppercorns are a pungent condiment ranging in color from white or black, to brown or green, or even pink.

❧ We use several kinds of pepper in this book, and we suggest that all of them be *freshly ground* in order to get the freshest flavor. You should invest in a really good pepper mill, if you don't have one, the kind that can vary the grind from fairly coarse to very, very fine.

❧ For milder flavor, use the white peppercorns. You might also use white for aesthetic reasons in light-colored dishes or sauces, where you prefer not to have the little specks of black showing.

❧ Green peppercorns come in various forms: dried so that they can be ground and water packed so that they can be mashed into a puree without the risk of someone's chipping a tooth on a cracked peppercorn. You might also want to substitute mashed green soft peppercorns for cracked black peppercorns in dishes like pepper steak.

The Capsicums—"Sweet, Mild, Hot, Hotter, Hottest, Help!"

The capsicums are now available year round in the marketplace in many forms and colors. They can be purchased fresh, dried, flaked, and powdered. Although neither a true herb nor a spice, these colorful, versatile flavor givers are considered as such.

Chili Peppers—Possibly the most famous of the family, these range in flavor from "small dynamite" to large "sweet." Chilies arouse. They stimulate the flow of gastric juices and saliva, thereby aiding in digestion. They have a very practical function in the hot climates where they are most common to the cuisine: They induce perspiration and then evaporation, which has a cooling effect. Midwestern and Northeastern America are just beginning to learn what this hot spice can do for food. The veritable explosion of

Tex-Mex restaurants in these areas is exposing their patrons to a variety of chili-seasoned dishes.

There are so many types of chilies that identifying them completely would take a volume of its own. Generally, however, chilies that have broader stem tops and rounder tips are the milder varieties, and whether dried or fresh, "the smaller the hotter!" And for some people we know, "the hotter the better!" We have eaten in restaurants in the southern part of Texas where diners take an incendiary mouthful of chilies and, with the tears streaming down their cheeks and invisible flames shooting from their mouths, exclaim "Boy, that's great eatin'! " We had a dear Indian friend from Bombay, who upon eating a chili soup that we did not dare touch for fear of catching fire, would keep muttering through it all, "Hot? This is not hot! Real chili is *hot!*"

We prefer a much more moderate use of chili, and some of you might be still less tolerant and balk at even a few grains of cayenne. When you buy chilies (or grow them) make sure you determine just how hot they are and how much you can use in a recipe without letting the flames get out of control. There is one thing you can be sure of: When you use chili, you sure don't need salt!

The names are beautiful: ancho, serrano, jalapeno, and they vary not only in size but also in color. Don't presume that red chilies are hotter than green ones; this is not necessarily so. Since most chilies, as well as green bell peppers, turn red on the vine as they ripen, the red ones may actually be milder and sweeter than the green (unripe) ones. On the other hand, pale green, or immature, chilies are usually milder than the riper dark green ones. And those dark green chilies that are streaked with light red are infernos. Their seeds are even hotter, so beware. Here are some tips on preparing and using chilies:

🍂 When you prepare fresh chilies for cooking, wear rubber gloves to protect your hands from the irritants of capsicum found inside the chilies.

🍂 Parch and blister the skins, holding one or two chilies over a gas flame or under a broiler, using long tongs. Then place them in a brown paper bag and seal it. After ten minutes open the bag and slip on your gloves. Split the peppers on paper towels, then scrape out the seeds and the interior veins. Cut off the stems and remove the charred skin. Rinse the peppers under cold water and then mince.

🍂 When using dried chilies, rinse off any accumulated dust and soak the chilies in water for one hour to rehydrate them. Use gloves and proceed as with fresh chilies.

🍂 You can add dried chilies, either whole or flaked, directly to food. Cook for at least 30 minutes after adding them to soups or stews.

🍂 If you are using whole chilies, remember to retrieve and discard them before serving the dish. One way to make certain that you can find them again is to tie them in a piece of cheesecloth before adding them to the pot.

Along with the range of fresh and hot chilies, there are two additional members of the capsicum family which are a bit more familiar to most Americans:

Ground Cayenne Pepper—A blend of several ground and dried species of small chilies, usually quite hot. No more than a few grains of cayenne—at most, about ⅛ teaspoon—should be used to enhance the other flavors in the dish.

Paprika—This is a mild, bright red powder, only slightly piquant. It generally comes from California, Hungary, Latin America, or Spain. The Hungarian variety has the fullest flavor, the Spanish and American the brightest color.

The Alliums—Lily and Her Sisters

Perhaps the most universally available of the herbs used for flavoring are the alliums, members of the lily family, of which the onion is the most popular. The alliums are among the most versatile, since they can be used to flavor practically everything, except desserts. They can be eaten raw, pickled, roasted, sauteed, baked with other foods, or eaten as a vegetable. Alliums can be served as condiments, and some of them—like chives—flourish in small herb gardens or in pots. The alliums are indispensable to cooks and, like the other three flavor pillars, we use them lavishly in our recipes—along with many of their colorful and flavorful blossoms, such as lavender chives or white garlic chive blossoms.

The alliums in the list that follows range from delicate to dynamic. We include some of their Latin names as an aid to selecting plants in case you wish to grow them in your own garden:

🌰 Chives (*Allium schoenoprasum*)
🌰 Garlic Chives or Flat Chinese Chives (*A. tuberosum*) They have flat fronds and are mildly garlicky in flavor. These are the only kind of alliums that are *not* cooked, since heat destroys the flavor.
🌰 Garlic (*A. sativum*)
🌰 Bulbing Onions (*A. cepa*)—These are white, yellow, and red skinned; they include tiny white pearl onions and large Bermuda onions.
🌰 Shallots (*A. ascalonicum*)
🌰 Green Onions or Scallions or Spring Onions—These are the young shoots of onions before they form their final mature shapes.
🌰 Elephant Garlic—As the name implies, this garlic has huge cloves; some weigh as much as an ounce. A few years ago they were so hard to get that you had to grow them in your own garden to sample them. Now they are stocked at many gourmet greengrocers around the country. They are milder than other varieties.
🌰 Ramps—Some alliums, such as ramps, grow in the wild. They are extremely strong and found regionally in the South. Ramps have their own loyal following; an annual springtime festival is held in West Virginia to celebrate these powerful alliums.
🌰 Egyptian Walking Onions or Tree Onions—To our knowledge, they are not yet available commercially; we have become familiar with them by growing them in a

corner of our own herb garden. Their fascinating growth habits make them especially interesting. The plant has bulblets on top of the stem, and during the growing season, the stem begins to bend over, letting the bulblet touch the earth and then begin to propagate a new plant. The entire plant can be eaten—bulblets, hollow stems, and all. The hollow stems can be stuffed. If you grow them, save some bulblets for pickling and replanting.
🌰 Welsh Onions (*A. fistulosum*)—These have coarse, hollow stems.
🌰 Leeks (*A. porrum*)
🌰 Rocambole or Sand Leek (*A. scorodoprasum*)—This allium has bulbs somewhat smaller than garlic and the leaves can be eaten as well. It is used widely by French-Canadian cooks.
🌰 Gigantic decorative alliums (*A. moly*)— If you have an herb or vegetable garden, you may want to grow these strictly for decorative purposes, since they are *not* used for cooking. They grow 4 to 5 feet tall and their flowers can be cut and used for table decorations.

Citrus, Et Cetera—"Lemon-Aids" and Other Flavor Helpers

Especially (but not exclusively) for those of us who are on salt-free diets or who want to cut down on salt, the acidic properties of citrus juices, the aromatic peels of lemons, oranges, or limes, vinegars, yogurt, buttermilk, and sour cream are life savers. They add character, interest, and fragrance while also helping to underscore and brighten the natural flavors of many foods. The proper use of these flavor aids can also help to blend and to build the natural essence of those foods.

For example, there is no doubt that extra flavor can be coaxed out of most fruits when we touch them with a small amount of lemon, lime, or orange juice or rind. Think of what our salads gain from the addition of a dressing made of an acid-oil combination. Indeed, most vegetables, salads, fish, chicken, and lamb can profit from a bit of citrus or a marinade bath in yogurt, herbal buttermilk, vinegar, or citrus juices. You'll find that we use many of these ingredients in our recipes, but here are a few additional tips:

❧ Lemon juice or vinegar added to the poaching liquid for fish helps to keep the fish white and firm.

❧ Lemon juice added to the cooking water acts as a mild bleach for celery.

❧ Lemon juice sprinkled on fresh fruit helps to prevent the fruit from discoloring when exposed to the air.

❧ Lemon juice added to the cooking water prevents artichokes from discoloring.

❧ Lime juice or lemon juice, when used as a marinade, will "cook" raw fish. This is the principle behind "seviche."

❧ Although orange juice is less acidic than other citrus and vinegar, its sweetness helps to cut the fatty taste of duck and pork, while complementing their essential flavors.

❧ The range of vinegars is very, very wide—from mild white wine vinegar, to French red wine vinegar, dark Italian balsamic vinegar, apple cider vinegar, rice vinegars, a choice of herb vinegars that go from basil to tarragon. Our shelf bulges with a great variety, some of which we have made ourselves. All of them are fun to try.

Chapter 3
GROWING YOUR OWN HERBS

Back in the sixties, Simon and Garfunkel were instrumental in making America newly aware of herbs as they sang of "parsley, sage, rosemary, and thyme." It was then that we also became aware of a return to the simpler pleasures and an alliance with the earth, as people across the country again began to grow their own fresh vegetables and a large variety of fresh herbs in a movement that continues to this very day. Sparked by these new gardens and the fresh yield that came from them, a new and experimental interest in cooking also took hold, and that, too, is still with us and growing rapidly. The trend is toward lighter food, more nutritious ingredients, indeed a vast and vital change in our entire diet.

For the committed gardener, for the sometime gardener, for the tender of small pots in a city apartment, growing herbs can be a rewarding experience. Best of all, it's easy. And if you never understood what the word *fresh* can mean before, just try growing herbs and using them in your cooking, harvested only a few minutes before you need them! Now you'll begin to understand why we were so impressed by the herb pots at the Four Seasons many years ago.

Those concerned about results will be glad to know that the rate of success in growing herbs is quite high. And for those intrigued by scope and variety, herb growers have a never-ending assortment from which to choose. If you select carefully, the contrasting foliage of herbs, the distinctive and the complementary range of grays and greens, make for a decorative enrichment. Add to that the bonus of attractive and edible flowers that top some varieties, as well as edible seeds that can be used as seasoning.

Herbs require very little maintenance, whether grown indoors or outside. They have a remarkable resistance to pests, they use very little water or fertilizer, and they flourish in almost every climate across the country.

If you decide to try growing herbs, and we certainly hope you do, remember that there are dozens of varieties and the easiest way to distinguish one from the other is to determine their botanical Latin names. We give those names in the chart that begins on page 25; you'll also find them in the seed catalogs and on the tag identifications at your local greenhouse or nursery. Use them to choose the variety you like best. Even professional herbalists differ on the count for any given variety. For thyme alone, for example, some say there are 27 different varieties, some say as many as *200!* Just take your time. Ask questions. And don't be afraid to experiment. Many of the people who visited our island herb garden (page 35) went away with fresh herbs for the evening meal, but some also took cuttings and grew their own plants—some in pots, others in gardens. We guarantee that if you do the same, the first time that you choose a leaf from one of your plants and crush it between your fingers to let the aroma drift up to your nose, the first time that you *taste* the difference between a fresh, homegrown herb as compared to the store-bought or dried ones, you'll begin to realize just what a satisfying experience the whole process can be.

Growing Herbs Indoors on Your Windowsill

Choosing the Site

🌿 Herb plants do best near a south window with lots of sun, at least 5 to 6 hours a day.

🌿 If you have no window that receives sun for that period of time, give the plants 12 to 16 hours of combined cool white and daylight fluorescent illumination, or use grow lights.

🌿 On cold winter nights, draw draperies or shades to keep the plants from getting chilled.

Choosing the Containers

🌿 Use clay flowerpots, 5 inches across at the inside top rim, about 5 inches high.

🌿 The number of pots, of course, will depend upon the size of your windowsill. If you need more room, try hanging some

of the pots or use the hanging shelves that can be purchased at local hardware stores or nurseries.

🌿 At the bottom of each pot, add 1 inch of broken pot shards, stones, or broken charcoal for drainage.

Preparing the Soil

🌿 Each 5-inch pot will hold 1 quart of soil, filled to within ½ inch of the top.

🌿 To make the proper mixture of soil, use a 1-pound coffee can as a measure. In a large plastic garbage container, combine and mix well 5 cans of potting soil or a good, clean garden soil, 3½ cans perlite, vermiculite, or coarse builders' sand, and ½ cup of cottonseed meal. Fill each pot with the mixture to within ½ inch of the top.

Choosing the Crops

🌿 For the choice of herbs for your indoor garden, see the chart that begins on page 25.

Watering and Feeding

🌿 Use lukewarm water and measure ½ cup for each 5-inch pot. Water once or twice a week, depending upon the dryness of the soil.

🌿 For feeding, use half-strength soluble fish emulsion fertilizer (an excellent source of nitrogen, though the odor may be disagreeable to some), ½ teaspoon per quart of water. Use ½ cup of this solution per clay pot every two to three weeks.

The Harvest

🌿 Snip with scissors from the outside edges of the plants. New leaves will spring up from the center.

Growing Herbs Outdoors

Choosing the Site

🌿 There is an herb that is "right" for every garden spot—almost any kind of soil, and moist or dry, sunny, and even shady locations. Therefore, you can choose herbs that fit your site, once you know the needs of each herb. These sites can include your vegetable garden, rock garden, flower border, or containers just outside the kitchen door.

🌿 Some herbs are tall, while others form squat bushes or low mounds. Keep this in mind when choosing a site. You may also want to consider the color of the flowers or blossoms in making your plans.

Preparing the Soil

🌿 Light, sandy soil is best for herbs, one of the reasons that they do so well near the sea. For a 75-square-foot garden, dig in thoroughly:

— 5 pounds garden lime.
— 5 pounds bone meal.
— either 100 pounds of compost or a 6-cubic-foot bale of peat moss and a 25-pound bag of dried cow manure.

Choosing the Crops

🌿 Though your garden path may be paved with good intentions, you can easily get carried away by romantic or intriguing herbal names—fenugreek, for example. Be forewarned! The fenugreek you plant will probably remain unharvested, since there is very little call for it in the kitchen.

🌿 Plan your herb garden according to your own tastes and needs. Then experiment, if you'd like. Perhaps you want to try a few added varieties of the same herb or a few new kinds of herbs each year. For example:

— If you like Chinese or Mexican food, grow cilantro.
— Chervil is rarely available, even in most gourmet produce markets, since it is very perishable once cut. Grow some to have when you want it readily available.

In our own case, we switched varieties one year because of a visit from a knowledgeable friend. We had just begun our garden (it was in the time before the trees grew too tall to let the sun come in), and the herbs were flourishing. Sally Darr, formerly with *Gourmet* magazine, and now the chef and co-owner with her husband, John, of New York's well-known three-star restaurant La Tulipe, dropped by one summer day. Wandering through the paths of the garden, she bent to clip a leaf of tarragon, crushed it between her fingers, held it to her practiced nose, and turned to exclaim, "But this is Russian tarragon! Can't you get the *French?*" We never realized that there *was* a difference. And, indeed there is! The next year we were growing *French* tarragon and everything we cook with it tastes better than with the Russian, there is no doubt.

Watering and Feeding

ᵉ⁂ Water thoroughly once a week.

ᵉ⁂ Feed with fish emulsion (dilute according to directions on label) once every three weeks during growing season.

The Harvest

ᵉ⁂ The same instructions hold for outdoors as for indoors. Snip with scissors from the outside leaves of the plants and new leaves will spring up in the center.

ᵉ⁂ Keeping the herbs in constant use also keeps the seeds from forming and gives the leaves the best flavor.

ᵉ⁂ On the other hand, you may want to use the seeds of the fennel or coriander or dill plants, for example. They are delicious. In that case, allow part of the plants to "go to seed," pick the seeds, and then let them dry before you use them.

A Chart for Growers of Herbs

Like all plants, herbs require basic growing conditions that meet their individual personalities and habits. We have grown each of the culinary herbs listed here, either in one or both of our gardens on the island, or on our terrace in the city. For one who is just starting out, we also include the plans for both island gardens, which you may use as guidelines for your planting. If you've never grown herbs before, just adapt the designs to your own growing areas; make the plots larger or smaller as you wish.

To make the task even simpler, we also include a code for each herb, to indicate whether it grows well in full sun, partial sun, or in the shade, and whether it is an annual, a perennial, or a biennial. Just check the codes and match them to your growing area before selecting the varieties.

ALL-PURPOSE HERB CHART

○ **Annual.** Will not winter over. Must be planted early.

□ **Perennial.** Lasts many years; can be started from transplants or seeds. As plants mature, cuttings may be taken and rooted for new plants.

◩ **Tender Perennial.** Will winter over only in warm areas; not hardy outdoors below 20°F. In colder climates, plants may be moved indoors during the winter months and then brought outdoors again in the spring.

■ **Biennial.** Plant will produce leaves during the first year; blooms in second year. Seeds must be sowed early in the season for maximum growth.

❀ **Edible Flowers.**

❧ **A Rampant Grower.** This herb plant needs to have its roots confined so that it doesn't take over the whole garden.

✸ **Full Sun.**

☆ **Partial Sun.**

✴ **Shade.**

HERB	BOTANICAL NAME	GENERAL TIPS	CULINARY USE	HARVEST AND PRESERVATION
Basil, Sweet Bush basil: Also called dwarf basil. Bushy plant with leaves ¼ inch long. Strongest flavor. Grows about 12 inches tall. Dark opal basil: Bronze/purple leaves. Flavor similar to sweet basil. Ornamental with food. Fine-leaf basil: Small leaves, compact size. Grows about 15 inches tall. ○ ✸ or ☆	*Ocimum basilicum* *O. minimum* *O. basilicum* 'Purpurascens' *O. basilicum* var. *feinum*	Start seeds indoors 1 month before transplanting or buy transplants. Set outdoors about the same time as tomatoes. Pinch tops to encourage bushy leaf growth and to keep flowers from forming. Fine-leaf and dwarf varieties can grow nicely in a pot.	Use in pesto sauces and herb vinegars, and with tomatoes and onions.	Every 2 to 3 weeks, cut 2 inches from central stem for a continuous fresh supply until frost. Preserve by pureeing and freezing in ice cube trays.

(continued)

ALL-PURPOSE HERB CHART—*Continued*

HERB	BOTANICAL NAME	GENERAL TIPS	CULINARY USE	HARVEST AND PRESERVATION
Borage ○ ✿ ✾ or ✦	*Borago officinalis*	Seed directly. Will self-seed.	Use young leaves raw where flavor of cucumber would be pleasant. Blossoms can be used in salads, pasta, or vinegars.	Clip a few leaves as needed without stripping all leaves.
Burnet, Salad ☐ ✾ or ✦	*Sanguisorba minor*	Grow from seed. Grows from a central rosette in a spreading fashion. Has a long season in the garden.	Use leaves in salads.	Cut the outside leaves, since the new growth comes up from the central core.
Chervil Classic culinary herb. Feathery leaves. Grows about 12 inches tall. ○ ✦	*Anthriscus cerefolium*	Good container plant. Seeds need light for best germination. Press into soil and don't cover seeds. Grows best in cool weather. Do not allow plant to flower.	Best when used fresh. Delicate licorice and parsleylike flavor. Goes well with soups, vegetables, fish, or chicken. Prime ingredient in classic fines herbes.	Harvest leaves only. Does not preserve well.
Chives Hollow grasslike leaves, lavender blossoms. Grows about 12 inches high.	*Allium schoenoprasum*	Start transplants or sow seed early. Dig up and divide clumps in fall. Lavender blossoms appear in summer.	Medium onion flavor. Can be used with anything. Add last to preserve color and texture. Use garlic chives raw. Mild garlic flavor.	Clip leaves with scissors close to ground, but do not cut entire plant down. Cut outside leaves first.

HERB	BOTANICAL NAME	GENERAL TIPS	CULINARY USE	HARVEST AND PRESERVATION
Garlic chives: Sometimes called broad-leaf or Chinese chives. Has flat blades, white blossoms. ☐ ✿ ✪ or ✫	*A. tuberosum*		Blossoms of both varieties are edible.	
Cilantro Also called culantro, leaf coriander, or Chinese parsley. Grows about 2 feet high. ◯ ✪ or ✫	*Coriandrum sativum*	Start from seed in late spring. New plants can be started every 3 weeks. Needs darkness to germinate.	The slightly fringed, delicate-textured leaves have a distinctive and pungent, aromatic flavor. Use them fresh in Oriental, Mexican, and Latin American dishes.	Cut leaves only. Does not taste as good when dried. Fresh seed in soft stage has even more intense flavor than leaves.
Cress, Garden Not to be confused with watercress. Varieties include curly cress and mustard cress. Grows about 4 inches high. ◯ ✫	*Lepidium sativum*	Make several sowings from seed. Grows quickly in matted, compact growing pattern within 10 days.	Small leaves. Biting, peppery, crisp flavor. Use fresh only — in salads or soups, with cottage cheese, or as garnishes, on vegetables, fish or poultry. Gives bite to bland foods. Good with grains.	Cut with scissors and include 1 inch of stem.
Dill Grows about 3 feet tall. Dill bouquet is a lower-growing variety (about 2 feet tall). ◯ ✪	*Anethum graveolens*	Grow from seed in late spring. Has both delicate, feathery leaves and seed heads. Dill bouquet can be grown in pots.	Leaves are used with soups, salads, fish, poultry, potatoes, or vinegars. Seeds are used for pickles or bread.	Cut leaves, then allow some plants to form seed heads and use seeds as well.

(continued)

ALL-PURPOSE HERB CHART—*Continued*

HERB	BOTANICAL NAME	GENERAL TIPS	CULINARY USE	HARVEST AND PRESERVATION
Fennel Not to be confused with bulb fennel or Florence fennel. Has 3-foot, feathery leaves. ◻ ✹	*Foeniculum vulgare*	Plant seeds in midspring. Treat like dill.	Very aromatic. Leaves look like dill but have the distinct taste of licorice. Seeds, when soft and dried, can be used with fish, poultry, or pasta sauces.	Cut leaves, and at end of summer harvest, use soft seeds crushed. Allow seeds to dry and get brown, then keep for winter use.
Geranium, Rose-Scented Over 200 varieties with different fruit and spice aromas, e.g., coconut, lemon, apple, cinnamon, lime. We prefer the rose flavor to complement summer fruits. Grows about 2 feet across and 2 feet high. ◻ ✿ ✹	*Pelargonium graveolens*	Grow from transplant in late spring or use a stem cutting. Can grow indoors as a houseplant. Grows well in a pot.	Fresh leaves have intense rose scent and mild rose flavor. Use in puddings, cakes, cookies; with fruit, berries; custards, beverages; in jams and in finger bowls.	Harvest leaves only. Can be dried and used in winter.
Ginger Root Also called green ginger. ◻ ✹	*Zingiber officinale*	Buy the fresh root and bury it 4 to 5 inches deep. Corn-like foliage will mark where you have planted it. Can also be grown in a pot in exactly the same way.	Peel knobs and grate for soups, fish, poultry, vegetables, sauces, or desserts. Can be candied, used in pickles, sauces, and baked goods. Has a pungent, refreshing, tongue-tingling taste.	Dig up root and peel. Preserve by boiling in honey for desserts.

HERB	BOTANICAL NAME	GENERAL TIPS	CULINARY USE	HARVEST AND PRESERVATION
Lemon Balm Grows 18 inches tall. ☐ ❁ or ✩ 🐝	*Melissa officinalis*	Grow from seed or transplants. Spreads rapidly. Grows well in a container.	Fragrant, lemon-flavored, heart-shaped leaves. Use fresh only. Good with fish, poultry, pork, fruit drinks, tea, or herb butters. Can be used lavishly since flavor is mild.	Harvest by cutting several times during growing season.
Lemon Verbena Can grow as tall as 6 feet. ☐ ❁	*Aloysia triphylla*	Transplants do best. Needs protection from cold weather, and can be taken in during the winter. Grows well indoors in large containers.	Highly fragrant and truest in taste of lemon-flavored herbs, but more subtle than lemon itself. Use for fish, salad dressings, vegetables, desserts, beverages, or jellies. The long, narrow leaves can be floated in a finger bowl or in the bath.	Dries very well, but the strong flavor will intensify with drying.
Lovage Grows about 3 feet high, and sometimes as high as 6 feet. ☐ ✩	*Levisticum officinale*	Transplant in spring. Prefers cool, moist conditions. To grow from seed, plant seed in late summer for following spring crop. The plant is very tall and should be placed out of the way, where it will not interfere with lower growing herbs.	Best when used fresh. Dark green leaves look and taste like strong celery leaves. Use in soups, stuffings, or stews.	Harvest by cutting stems to ground. Use leaves in small amounts.

(continued)

ALL-PURPOSE HERB CHART—*Continued*

HERB	BOTANICAL NAME	GENERAL TIPS	CULINARY USE	HARVEST AND PRESERVATION
Marigold, Pot Not to be confused with African marigold. Also known as calendula. Grows about 2 feet tall. ◯ ✿ ✾ or ✵	*Calendula officinalis*	Start seed either in peat pots indoors or outdoors in spring.	The orange and yellow petals are used in baking for yellow color, in custards, and as a colorful addition to salads.	Will bloom all summer if you continue to pick the flowers.
Marjoram Also called sweet marjoram. Grows about 8 inches high. ▢ ✾	*Origanum majorana*	A tender perennial that does not like cold climates, it responds best when new plants are started each year. Compact and bushy and does well in a container.	Gray-green oval leaves that go well in meat dishes, vegetables, stuffings, and eggs. Stronger than oregano.	Cut leaves frequently 2 inches from ground level. Leaves dry well and can be preserved for winter use.
Mint Curly mint or Kentucky mint: Sometimes called julep mint. Peppermint: grows about 12 inches high. Spearmint: grows about 18 inches high. There are many other varieties, e.g., apple, orange, pineapple. We prefer the cleaner, uncluttered taste of the varieties we've listed. ▢ ✵ or ✴ ⚘	*Mentha crispa* *M. ×piperita* *M. spicata*	All mints have shallow roots and runners. They should be contained in a pot or the plant will take over the world! Buy or get transplants from neighbors who are overrun, cut and propagate new plants.	The varieties we've listed are cooling and sweet and very refreshing. They're not just for juleps. Use them for salad dressings, grains, peas, fish, poultry, sauces, and jellies.	Cut at base of plant. Several cuttings may be taken during the growing season. Dries well and can be used during winter.

HERB	BOTANICAL NAME	GENERAL TIPS	CULINARY USE	HARVEST AND PRESERVATION
Nasturtium There are many seed varieties, e.g., jewel mixed or dwarf double, plus a trailing variety called gleam hybrid. ○ ✿ ✪	*Tropaeolum majus*	Grow from seed. Soak overnight before planting for faster germination. Does well in pots. There are many colors and shades: bright yellow, orange, peach, red-orange, pale yellow, and crimson.	Similar in flavor to watercress. Cut and mince large, round, peppery leaves and blossoms or keep leaves whole when still tiny and young. Use fresh in salads, butters, vinegars, or cheese and pasta dishes.	Just choose the most colorful leaves.
Onions, Egyptian Grow about 24 inches high before bending over and re-seeding themselves. ☐ ✪ or ☆	*Allium cepa* var. *viviparum*	Plant bulbs in fall. New bulblets develop in clusters atop tall, hollow stems, which are also edible. Use a few bulbs to start a new crop each fall. Takes up less room in a small garden than rows of onions, and the crop can't be bought, so it's a good choice to grow.	All parts of these onions must be eaten fresh. Use bulblets when you don't have shallots. The leaves are stronger than chives and they have a strong onion flavor. Use sparingly.	Harvest bulblets when they form.
Oregano Grows about 18 inches high. ☐ ✪	There is no botanical name for the "true" oregano. However, *Origanum vulgare* is a wild marjoram that is sold under this name by seed companies.	Start transplants or dig up and divide old plants. Has a spreading, prolific growth pattern.	Fresh leaves are used for tomato-based pasta sauces, soups, salads, vegetables, bean dishes, meats, and stews.	Cut leaves only, not the stems. Dries well, although it then takes on a very intense flavor.

(continued)

ALL-PURPOSE HERB CHART—*Continued*

HERB	BOTANICAL NAME	GENERAL TIPS	CULINARY USE	HARVEST AND PRESERVATION
Pansy, Garden ■ ✿ ❀ or ✩	*Viola ✕wittrockiana*	Buy transplants. The multicolored blossoms have the look of charming little faces.	Use fresh with soups, salads, cheese, omelets, or garnishes.	Just pick the most delightful faces in the garden.
Parsley Grows about 8 inches tall. Curly-leaved parsley: Also grows about 8 inches tall. ■ ✩	*Petroselinum hortense* *P. crispum*	Grow from seed or transplants. Has a mounding topgrowth with a taproot. Both varieties can be grown in a pot.	For best flavor, always use fresh. Indispensable for all foods, and also as a garnish. Flat-leaf is more flavorsome. Use for soups, salads, fish, stews, or poultry, and always with garlic to soften the flavor. Curly type is best used for garnish.	Harvest leaves from the outside so that the plant can renew itself from the center.
Rosemary Grows about 2 feet high. Low-growing rosemary: Grows about 6 inches high. ❏ ❀ or ✩	*Rosmarinus officinalis* *R. prostratus*	Best to use transplants or cuttings. Does not winter-over well in cold climates. Does well in a container and can be moved indoors as the weather gets colder. Prefers sandy, sweet (alkaline) soil and not too much water.	Use fresh tips sparingly. The spiky, needlelike leaves have a strong, piney fragrance. Wonderful with lamb, stews, poultry, potatoes, or vinegar.	Can be dried and used during the winter months.

HERB	BOTANICAL NAME	GENERAL TIPS	CULINARY USE	HARVEST AND PRESERVATION
Sage Grows about 2 feet tall. Dwarf sage: A lower growing plant, about 8 inches high. □ ✵	*Salvia officinalis* *S. officinalis* var. *compacta*	Start with transplant or division. There are many varieties of sage, some of them only ornamental. Leaves grow on woody stems, which should be cut back in spring to encourage growth. Avoid manure as a fertilizer: It produces an undesirable flavor. Dwarf variety grows well in a pot or indoor container.	Use these silvery pebbly-surfaced leaves fresh with pork, veal, sausages, or stuffings.	Tie bunches together and hang upside down to dry. Strip and use the dried leaves.
Savory, Summer Grows 18 inches high. ◯ ✵	*Satureja hortensis*	An annual you can start from seed. It's fast growing and more delicate in flavor than winter savory. Can be grown in a container.	Use fresh for truest flavor. Use with soups, bean and grain dishes, rice, vegetables.	Strip leaves from branches. To dry leaves, cut branches and tie together, then hang them upside down. Strip off dried leaves and use.
Savory, Winter Grows about 12 inches high. □ ✵	*Satureja montana*	Start from transplant. Has small narrow leaves that grow in pairs along the stem in a shrublike growth.	Use fresh for best and truest flavor. Excellent with soups, bean dishes, and grains.	Leaves dry well for winter supply.

(continued)

HERB	BOTANICAL NAME	GENERAL TIPS	CULINARY USE	HARVEST AND PRESERVATION
Sorrel, French Grows about 18 inches high. ☐ ✿ or ✦	*Rumex scutatus*	Seed in early spring, or plant a division of an established plant. A very hardy plant. Cut the leaves when young several times during growing season. Don't let plant flower or leaves will be inferior. Grows well in a large container.	Acidic, sour, tart, light green leaves. Use sparingly and use fresh only. Excellent with soups, fish, herb butters, and mixed with other greens.	When leaves are cut at harvesttime, strip out the stems with a sharp knife and use the tender leaf parts only.
Tarragon, French Avoid the variety called Russian tarragon; although a hardier plant, it has much less flavor. Grows about 2½ feet tall. ☐ ✿ or ✦	*Artemisia dracunculus*	Does not grow well from seed. Buy transplants. Cut back early in spring to encourage new growth. Can be grown in a pot or container.	These slender, aromatic leaves have the scent of new-mown hay with a hint of licorice. Use fresh with fish, poultry, or sauces. When combining with other herbs, use sparingly or it will overpower the others.	Dries well. Tie branches and hang upside down. Strip leaves when needed. Use dried leaves very sparingly.
Thyme Also called English thyme or common thyme. Grows about 12 inches tall. Lemon thyme Wild thyme ☐ ✿ or ✦	*Thymus vulgaris* *T. ×citriodorus* *T. serpyllum*	Start from seed or transplants. Some varieties are low growing. Others form dense mats.	The tiny, fresh leaves are mild in flavor and can be used liberally. Use with chowders, meats, fish, stuffings, or jellies. Sprigs are used in bouquets garnis.	Cut sprigs from base of plant. Can be dried. Strip leaves and use.
Violets Grow about 4 inches tall. ☐ ✿ ✦ or ✳	*Viola odorata*	Start from seed or transplants. Needs rich soil and moisture.	Use fresh whole blossoms as a garnish with green salads, sweets, puddings, fruits, berries, and beverages.	Can be candied and preserved.

Garden I—A Culinary Herb Garden at the Seashore

This garden was constructed behind a sand dune, directly in the sand itself. The "soil" was built by adding peat moss, cow manure, washed seaweed, and compost. It was designed not only to supply us with culinary herbs, but also to be seen and enjoyed by Tom Ervin from the deck of his house that overlooks it. We named this garden the Norma Ervin Memorial Herb Garden.

We divided the garden into three main beds, which in turn were subdivided into small geometric shapes. Green plastic edging was used to define and separate those shapes. The beds have raised wooden rails about 1 foot high on which one can sit. We formed the beds ourselves with heavy 2×4s and then enclosed them with heavy plastic wire reaching from the base of the bed to the railings. This was covered by heavy plastic sheeting, stretched over the wire and stapled to the wooden supports. It prevents the strong ocean winds from damaging the plants and creates a warmer growing atmosphere. It also keeps the sand from drifting into the beds.

The beds are mulched with dark, washed seaweed to keep the weeds down and to prevent splashback from the sand during heavy rains. In that way we also keep the herbs from getting gritty; they are clean enough to be nibbled right in the garden as we harvest.

The garden is watered once each week and fed with a liquid fish emulsion fertilizer once every three weeks during the growing season. Each bed was designed for special growing conditions, and the herbs it contains were planted deliberately to give them the conditions they prefer.

Bed I has part sun.
Bed II gets some shade late in the day.
Bed III gets full sun all day long.
Beds IV, V, VI grow edible flowers.

All three main beds, Bed I, Bed II, and Bed III, are surrounded by an 8-foot-high chicken-wire "cage" with an entry door, for protection against foraging rabbits and especially our large deer population. Beds IV, V, and VI, which are outside the main enclosure, have separate chicken-wire boxes, which lift off to allow us to tend the flowers, yet provide protection against the animals.

Garden II—A Culinary Herb Garden Outdoors in Containers

This garden began as an effort to improve the appearance of a cesspool that had been plunked right smack in our backyard. To serve as containers for the herbs, we bought 13 chimney flue tiles at a lumberyard. After cutting them in half with a masonry saw, we sank them into the sand along the sides of the cesspool. Two were put on one end of the cesspool itself and raised slightly with pieces of 2×4 that formed a frame. We surrounded the flue tiles with washed seaweed to prevent splashback, to retain moisture, and to keep the herbs clean.

GARDEN I

A Culinary Herb Garden at the Seashore

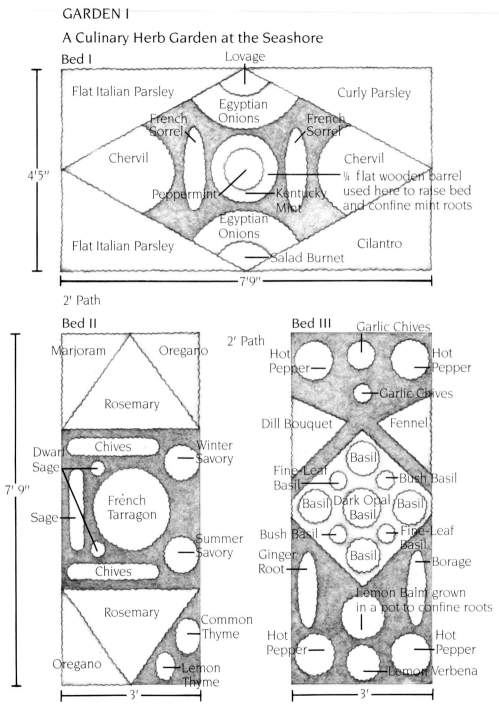

Bed I

Lovage

Flat Italian Parsley

Curly Parsley

Egyptian Onions

French Sorrel

French Sorrel

Chervil

Chervil

4'5"

Peppermint

Kentucky Mint

¼ flat wooden barrel used here to raise bed and confine mint roots

Egyptian Onions

Flat Italian Parsley

Cilantro

Salad Burnet

7'9"

2' Path

Bed II

Marjoram

Oregano

2' Path

Rosemary

Dwarf Sage

Chives

Winter Savory

French Tarragon

Sage

Summer Savory

7' 9"

Chives

Rosemary

Common Thyme

Oregano

Lemon Thyme

3'

Bed III

Garlic Chives

Hot Pepper

Hot Pepper

Garlic Chives

Dill Bouquet

Fennel

Basil

Fine-Leaf Basil

Bush Basil

Basil

Dark Opal Basil

Basil

Bush Basil

Fine-Leaf Basil

Ginger Root

Basil

Borage

Lemon Balm grown in a pot to confine roots

Hot Pepper

Hot Pepper

Lemon Verbena

3'

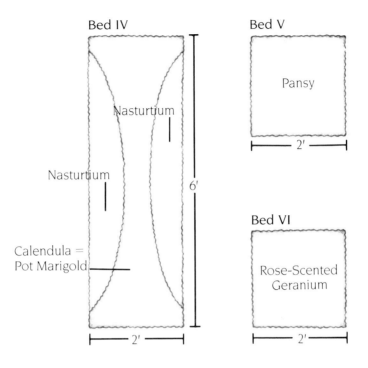

Bed IV

Nasturtium

Nasturtium

Calendula =
Pot Marigold

6'

2'

Bed V

Pansy

2'

Bed VI

Rose-Scented
Geranium

2'

We also built two brick steps on either side of the cesspool to create an interesting step-up level that gives us access to the plants from above.

Three-quarters of the herbs are in full sun and the rest are either in dappled shade or part shade during the late afternoon. When deer and rabbits are a problem (which they most certainly are on our island), long tunnellike covers of chicken wire are fitted over the tops of the contained herbs for protection.

The Norma Ervin Memorial Herb Garden

We have always tried to grow our own herbs, whether in our garden behind the Fire Island house, in pots indoors, or on the terrace outside our apartment in the city, in the worst environmental conditions where wind and soot and inadequate water were always a challenge. But, when we began this book, we realized that an adequate and continuing supply of a variety of herbs would be essential. But getting them from the

GARDEN II

A Culinary Herb Garden
Outdoors in Containers

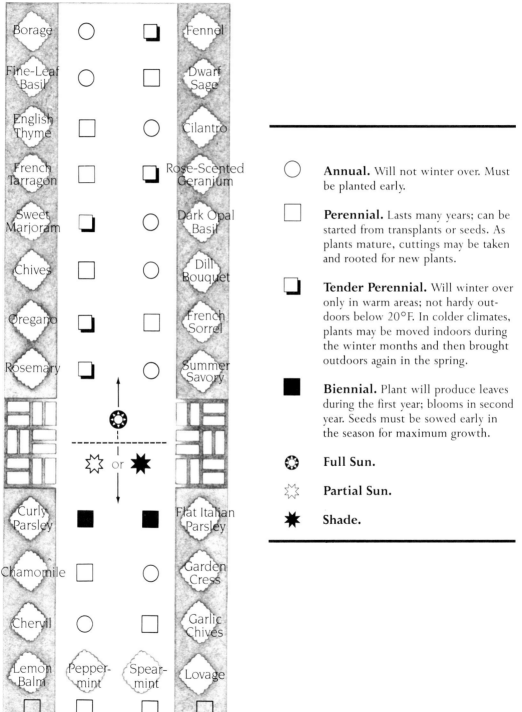

Borage	○	◨	Fennel
Fine-Leaf Basil	○	□	Dwarf Sage
English Thyme	□	○	Cilantro
French Tarragon	□	◨	Rose-Scented Geranium
Sweet Marjoram	◨	○	Dark Opal Basil
Chives	□	○	Dill Bouquet
Oregano	◨	□	French Sorrel
Rosemary	◨	○	Summer Savory

✺ Full Sun.

☆ or ✹

Curly Parsley	■	■	Flat Italian Parsley
Chamomile	□	○	Garden Cress
Chervil	○	□	Garlic Chives
Lemon Balm	Pepper-mint	Spear-mint	Lovage
□	□	□	□

○ **Annual.** Will not winter over. Must be planted early.

□ **Perennial.** Lasts many years; can be started from transplants or seeds. As plants mature, cuttings may be taken and rooted for new plants.

◨ **Tender Perennial.** Will winter over only in warm areas; not hardy outdoors below 20°F. In colder climates, plants may be moved indoors during the winter months and then brought outdoors again in the spring.

■ **Biennial.** Plant will produce leaves during the first year; blooms in second year. Seeds must be sowed early in the season for maximum growth.

✺ **Full Sun.**

☆ **Partial Sun.**

✹ **Shade.**

mainland to the island could be a problem, so it was clear that we would have to expand our growing area.

Unfortunately, large scrub pines had overgrown the small plot in back of our house and it lay in shade most of the day. Since herbs like sun, we needed a brighter growing area. Our eye fell on an abandoned garden that had formerly been lovingly tended by a friend, Norma Ervin, once the mayor of our little village. When she died, the small plots near the sea became overgrown, the beach sand drifted into them, and they lay fallow and empty. It would be the perfect place for an herb garden, we felt, so we asked Tom Ervin, Norma's husband, if we might use the land and once again bring it back to the way Norma had loved it, green and lush and giving of itself. With delight, he agreed, and we set to work to put the land in order. Within a few days it became the Norma Ervin Memorial Herb Garden, and a plaque was made to commemorate it. In a few short weeks the first green shoots began to push their way up from the sunny seaside sand.

During the months of spring and summer, it was a veritable cornucopia of plenty (the plan of the garden is on pages 36–37) with almost every imaginable herb growing and thriving under what seemed to be perfect conditions. One of our favorite plants in that garden was a small hot pepper that we grew from seeds given to us in San Antonio by Dave Thomas, a bread baker we had met on a trip down there. Dave is a retired Army general and superb gardener.

Year-round residents about to rent their homes to city folk for the summer season gave us their own pots of herbs to care for while they were gone. During all that time the herbs never failed us, and most of the recipes in this book were made with our own aromatic, carefully tended plants, flowers, and seeds.

Around the village, the memorial garden became fairly well known. As we worked there, cultivating and tilling and carefully selecting the tender herbs, visitors sometimes wandered over to chat and to examine the little identifying tags near plants that they had never known: borage or lemon verbena, and a rich, dark opal basil. When the plants were especially lush, we gave samples for our neighbors to take home and try. The garden, like all gardens, was a delight.

And then, in September, Hurricane Gloria struck, hitting with most of its fury right across Long Island and specifically on our part of Fire Island. We lost 20 large pine trees, and others were even less fortunate, suffering damage to their homes. We managed to fight our way out to the island the day after the hurricane. After making certain that our house was all right, we struggled past the fallen trees that blocked our way, up the wooden walk to the ocean to look at our little garden. During the storm, the sea had crested the dunes and washed over behind them, rolling right over the garden and destroying everything in a devastating surge of salt water. It was obvious that from then on we'd have to purchase our herbs in the city and bring them out to the island for recipe testing. But, for that time of only a few short months, the little garden had served us well.

It is winter as we write this and we can

hear the roar of the volatile ocean. The garden has been put to "bed" with a mulch of seaweed to cover it warmly against the cold, windy weather that is already upon us. But, just before spreading the seaweed, we looked closely at the dried remains of the wonderful herbs, and once again we were treated to the miracle of nature. As the result of a warming trend after the hurricane, all over the garden little specks of green were appearing, in spite of how late in the year it was! The leaves of the lemon balm and the tarragon and the oregano were actually pushing their way up between the dead branches of the earlier

plantings. Somehow, it was a promise that they would be back there again next year like welcome friends, and that the little garden would once again flourish by the sea.

There is an additional postscript to the storm. Though we were at first quite devastated by the loss of all those tall, beautiful trees, we soon realized that there was a positive side to the disaster. With the trees gone, the sun will once again shine on the *original* garden behind our house. That means that next year our growing area can be twice the size of this season's. We can hardly wait until the hibernation period is over!

Chapter 4

PRESERVING & STORING HERBS & SPICES

In terms of freshness and the ultimate flavor, it would be ideal if all cooks could buy or grow just the exact amount of fresh herbs or aromatic spices they need to use at the moment, with nothing left to store. But things in life are seldom ideal. Few of us can grow our own ginger or harvest lovage all year round — still, we want them ready and available when the recipe calls for them. Spices now come in jars that provide several years' supply of those varieties we use in such small quantities; and herbs, whether bought or homegrown, generally yield a much larger supply than the amount called for in a recipe. Moreover, if your garden is a lush, ever-yielding paradise for such herbs as basil, you will certainly want to put some away for that steaming platter of pasta with pesto next winter. You can use some simple tricks in storing herbs and spices that will help to give them the longest possible life and to minimize flavor losses.

Cleaning Fresh Herbs

The technique is simple — "swish, shake, and pat":

SWISH: Hold the tied stems and rinse them in a bowl of cool water to remove any dust or grit.

SHAKE: Shake them to remove excess water.
PAT: Lay them on paper towels and gently pat them dry.

Storing Fresh Herbs

Use a wide-based glass jar or mug, one-third filled with water. Put the stem end of the plants into the water and cover the leafy parts with a plastic bag. Keep in the refrigerator until needed. Many will keep well and stay quite crisp for more than a week if you store them this way. One extra thing that we do when storing six or seven kinds of herbs, side by side in the refrigerator with their plastic hats, is to put stick-on identification labels on the plastic. That way we can choose the right one easily.

Preserving Your Herbs

You can use several methods to preserve the herbs from your garden or those you bought in season and want to have available for winter use. Some herbs, such as basil, are much better when frozen than when dried; others, such as hot peppers, are much better air dried. This is another area in which experimentation will show you which method best suits your own needs.

Freezing Herbs

Herbs will keep from six to eight months with this method. First rinse the fresh herbs and dry them well.

&❧ For basil, oregano, sage, mint, and any other herbs with large leaves, remove the leaves from the larger stem.
&❧ For rosemary, cilantro, chervil, tarragon, dill, thyme, and marjoram, retain the thinner stems.
&❧ For chives, chop them before freezing.

Freeze the herbs by placing them on a baking sheet, spread out so that they don't freeze together. When they're thoroughly frozen, pack them in plastic bags or freezer containers so that they won't be crushed. Label and date the container or bag. When you're ready to cook with them, use them frozen. The heat of the dish you're preparing will defrost them quickly. Of course, if you're using them in a salad or other cold dish, let the herbs defrost before adding them.

Storing Herbs in Oil

Some people like to store herbs in vegetable or olive oil by alternating layers of herbs and oil, then covering the jar and refrigerating it. It is not our favorite way, since the leaves discolor. However, they will keep for a few months. One bonus from using this method is that you have available a ready-made herb-flavored oil for sauteeing or for using in some soups and stews.

Air-Drying Herbs

This is probably the most picturesque method of preserving culinary herbs and it was used by the colonists. In fact, it is a method that we use in our island kitchen since we have rafters on which to hang herbs like sage and our colorful hot red peppers from Texas. The swags of herbs are hung from nails hammered into the rafters, but you can also do very well by using a laundry drying rack or a couple of kitchen chairs. Just follow the directions below.

&❧ Harvest the plants early in the day, wash in cool water, and dry very well.
&❧ Remove any yellowed or unattractive leaves.
&❧ Bundle the stems together with rubber bands, since the stems will shrink as they dry.

In an airy room, if the weather is not too humid, the herbs will take from several days to a week to dry properly. The drying process can take place almost anywhere:

&❧ On rafters, as we have described—the most colorful and traditional way.

❧ Hook the rubber bands on a wire clothes hanger and secure them with paper clips. Then hang them upside down in your garage, toolshed, pantry, or kitchen.

❧ Using a laundry drying rack, fasten the bunches of herbs on the rack with clothespins.

❧ If space is a problem, use two chairs with rung backs, placed about 3 feet apart. Put broomsticks or dowels across the rungs to form an open platform. Then tie two bunches of herbs together with a long string and hang them over the poles. This improvised drying rack holds a surprising number of herb swags.

To keep the dust off while the herbs are drying, cover the swags with brown paper bags, punching a few holes in them for ventilation. Merely slip the bags over the swags, and then tie the tops with plastic twist ties for easy removal. When the leaves are thoroughly dried, remove them from the stems, store them in tightly closed plastic bottles, and add the stems to the compost pile.

Air-Drying Hot Peppers

Hot peppers are particularly colorful and pleasing to look at, especially if you hang them in a place where they can be seen by your guests—right from the ceiling of your kitchen, for example. You can grow your own hot peppers, even in a pot indoors. When the peppers have reached their prime

color, pull the entire plant out with the roots. Shake off the excess earth and pull off the leaves, but leave the peppers on the stems. Tie the stems, turn them upside down on a hook or nail, and just pull one off the stem when you need it for cooking. They'll last the entire season.

Oven-Drying Herbs

After washing and drying the herbs, spread them out on a baking sheet. Preset the oven to 100° to 150°F and leave the door of the oven partially open. Every few minutes, rotate the baking sheet or shake the herbs slightly so that they'll dry evenly. Remove the herbs when they are crisp, but before they are dry or burnt.

Small leaves, such as thyme, will take about 15 minutes. However, allow about 1 hour for thicker or curly leaves, such as sage. Friends tell us that a microwave oven can dry herbs in 20 to 30 *seconds,* but this is a method that we have not tried ourselves.

When the herbs are dried, immediately place them in sterile glass jars with tightly fitting lids. If any moisture mists the glass, open the jar and redry the herbs.

How to Store Dried Herbs

Herbs should be stored in opaque containers in a cool, dry place. A cool, dark closet would be best, but we realize that this is not always possible. We store our dried herbs and spices in a rather dark, distant corner of the kitchen, and it seems to be satisfactory.

Storing Spices

The same holds true for spices. For best results they should be stored in a dark, dry, airy place, since heat robs them of their flavor. Dampness, on the other hand can cake ground spices, making them difficult to measure and use. Here again, the ideal containers are opaque, not clear glass, and they should always be tightly closed.

❧ Whole spices are much better to use than powdered or ground spices, wherever you have the choice.

❧ Spices generally keep well for about six months. After that time, many spices become stale and lose their strength and specific seasoning potential. Open the jars once a month and sniff them for freshness. Also check the color. They should be bright in color, not faded, and they should give off their own individual, true scent.

❧ As soon as a spice becomes stale, replace it.

Making Life Easier

We have always been "gadget freaks," candidly admitting that some lie in the drawer unused for years until we uncover a strange-looking instrument and exclaim, "What in the world is *this* used for?" On the other hand, many have become instant favorites of ours, making themselves indispensable in our cooking and testing. In the testing of recipes for this book, several "gadgets" made the work less labor-intensive and a lot more fun. At this point, we don't know what we'd do without them.

❧ The ubiquitous and reliable food processor and the blender. Most kitchens now have one or both of these items and we're sure you agree with us about their value.

❧ A good pepper mill to grind fresh pepper. Our favorite is the "Pepper-Mate"—but whichever one you choose, make sure that it can be adjusted to grind pepper from coarse to very fine. We feel strongly that pepper must be freshly ground for true flavor.

❧ The French "Mini-Chop" made by SEB. This is a remarkable gadget and it does the finest possible mincing in *two to three seconds!* That includes garlic, nuts, dried spices, fresh herbs, and almost anything else that you want ground quickly and efficiently. It's perfect for small quantities and best of all, it is cleaned easily.

❧ A citrus zester and citrus stripper. They do the job quickly, giving you pith-free zest or strips. You can even get a left-handed stripper!

❧ A nutmeg grater.

Chapter 5

HORS D'OEUVRES

← Shrimp with Lovage and Horseradish Mustard Sauce (page 69)

Hors d'oeuvres are the spark that ignites a meal; some say "the calling card" of the chef, since they provide our first sample of the cook's abilities. However, in this era of "grazers," people who never sit still for a complete meal, but prefer to "graze" on their upwardly mobile way, hors d'oeuvres are a perfect, complete, and fulfilling meal in themselves!

Actually, hors d'oeuvres serve as a complete, light, satisfying meal for many people other than the grazers. What looks and tastes good as a pre-dinner snack with cocktails can also work well in slightly larger portions as a complete luncheon. Tapas, the Spanish version of hors d'oeuvres, are already used in just that way. Indeed, restaurants that serve *only* tapas are springing up everywhere, very much like the Chinese Dim Sum parlors that serve only their vast variety of hors d'oeuvres-type dishes.

Cheeses lend themselves well to your hors d'oeuvres repertoire; note, for example, the skim-milk ricotta in the Coeur a la Creme with Herbs, the mozzarella in the Sliced Mozzarella with Basil and Hot Pepper, or the feta cheese in the savory Feta Cheesecake with Garlic and Mixed Herbs. And we hope you'll try the other hors d'oeuvres recipes that use shrimp, mussels, sardines, flounder, pork—and a wide range of vegetables. Make plenty, for your guests will nibble away at a remarkable pace—especially the grazers. When using these recipes as pre-dinner snacks, we suggest that you try some of the beverages we provide in this chapter as perfect nonalcoholic companions.

Chevre Discs Serendipity

Makes 10 to 12 pieces

finely minced fresh chives
paprika
turmeric
finely ground pecans
freshly ground black or lemon pepper
finely minced dried herbes de Provence
tiny whole leaves of fresh lemon burnet
finely shredded orange rind
finely shredded lime rind
finely minced garlic
finely minced fresh rosemary
finely minced fresh basil
¾-pound log of chevre cheese
    (Montrachet), cut into ¾-inch slices

Spread out a sheet of waxed paper, and make separate piles of the herbs and spices. Roll the individual slices of cheese into each different pile. Arrange on a black or white plate or on fresh grape leaves in a flat basket with a flower as decoration.

Cucumber Stuffed with Chopped Egg and Peppercress

4 servings

Peppercress, preferred by the British for its distinctive flavor in tea sandwiches, can be easily grown on a windowsill. It takes only a few days to sprout on a moist sponge.

2   hard-boiled eggs, peeled
2   teaspoons finely minced fresh chives
2   teaspoons peppercress or finely
        minced watercress

¼   teaspoon dry mustard
2   teaspoons very finely minced sweet
        red peppers
2   teaspoons mayonnaise
2   teaspoons plain yogurt
        few grindings of black pepper
1   long, thin burpless cucumber

Finely chop eggs. Put into a small bowl, and mix in all ingredients except cucumber.

Cut cucumber into 1-inch pieces. Score the skin with a citrus stripper or the tines of a fork. Hollow out the centers with a small, sharp knife, removing a square-cut center plug. Fill the centers of cucumber pieces with chopped egg mixture. Sprinkle with additional peppercress.

Cheese and Tomato Parfait with Basil and Avocado

4 servings

Spicy, pink, frosty, it rests in a pale avocado bed ready to refresh you and to pique the most finicky appetite on a hot summer day.

1   tablespoon blue cheese
6   ounces cream cheese
1   teaspoon grated onions
½   teaspoon Worcestershire sauce
1   tablespoon balsamic vinegar
2   cups tomato juice
⅛   teaspoon hot pepper sauce or to
        taste
1   tablespoon finely minced fresh basil
2   tablespoons ketchup
2   egg whites, stiffly beaten
2   avocados, cut into halves and pitted

4 small wedges of lime or tomato
   (optional)

In a food processor, beat together blue cheese and cream cheese. Add all ingredients except egg whites, avocados, and lime or tomato wedges, and process until very smooth. Pour into a freezing tray (without ice cube compartments), and freeze until all but the center is firm.

Remove from tray, and place into a bowl. Break up mixture with a rotary beater, and fold immediately into beaten egg whites. Return to freezer tray, and freeze again until it has the consistency of sherbet. Do not overfreeze or it will be difficult to scoop it out of the tray. If it has frozen too much, let it come back to sherbet consistency again, and then scoop it into the hollow of each avocado half. Place a small wedge of lime or tomato on top of each serving, if desired. Serve immediately.

Cauliflower with Saffron and Coriander Seeds

4 servings

A delicate blend of golden saffron threads and aromatic coriander seeds will pique your appetite. This low-calorie hors d'oeuvre can also be served as a vegetable side dish.

1 small head of cauliflower (about
   ½ pound after trimming),
   broken into bite-size pieces
1½ tablespoons olive oil
½ cup water
¼ teaspoon coriander seeds, crushed
¼ teaspoon lemon peppercorns,
   crushed, or black pepper
½ teaspoon saffron threads

6 sprigs fresh parsley, coarsely
   chopped

Mix all ingredients together in a medium-size bowl, reserving only a bit of the parsley for garnish. Put all ingredients into a small saucepan with a cover. Bring to a boil, then lower heat, and simmer for 5 to 10 minutes. Cauliflower should be tender but crunchy. Cool. Sprinkle with reserved parsley, and refrigerate.

(This dish can be kept in the refrigerator for up to a week.) Serve at room temperature.

Hot Mulled Cider

4 servings

No autumn or winter holiday is complete without this warming, sweetly spiced hot drink.

6 cups apple cider
1 small navel orange
4 slices of lemon
3 3-inch pieces of cinnamon
3 whole cloves
¼ teaspoon ground ginger
¼ teaspoon ground nutmeg

Pour cider into a large saucepan. Peel orange with a vegetable peeler, and add rind to pot. Cut orange into 4 or 5 slices, and add to cider along with all the remaining ingredients. Bring to a boil, then lower heat, and simmer for 30 minutes. Strain, discard rinds, oranges, lemons, cinnamon, and cloves, and serve hot.

Pineapple, Lime, and Rose Geranium Punch

4 to 6 servings

 2 tablespoons honey
 4 cups water
 ¼ teaspoon ground nutmeg
 2 cups diced fresh pineapple or
  1 can (16 ounces) unsweetened crushed pineapple
 4 rose geranium leaves
 2 cups orange juice
 2 tablespoons lime juice
  bananas
  lime slices
  additional rose geranium leaves

In a 6-quart pan, boil honey and water together for 3 minutes. Add nutmeg and let cool. Add pineapple and geranium leaves. Then add orange juice and lime juice, and blend all ingredients well. Blend the mixture in 2 batches in a blender or food processor. Pour into glasses. For the garnish, cut bananas lengthwise into 4 or 6 sticks each to be used as stirrers. Add a thin slice of lime to each glass, and float a small rose geranium leaf on the lime slice.

Coeur a la Creme with Herbs

Makes 1 2-cup mold or 5 small hearts

Here are two versions of this herb-covered cheese heart mold—one a summer version with bright green fresh herbs and the other a winter version with dried herbs.

 1 quart plain yogurt
 1 cup part-skim ricotta cheese
 ¼ teaspoon finely minced garlic
 ⅛ teaspoon freshly ground black
  pepper

SUMMER VERSION

 ½ cup finely minced mixed fresh
  herbs (¼ cup parsley, ¼ cup
  combination of basil, chervil or
  salad burnet, tarragon, oregano,
  thyme, dill, fennel, chives, and
  rosemary)
  fresh basil leaves

WINTER VERSION

 ¼ cup dried herbes de Provence
 2 tablespoons toasted sesame seeds
  dried bay leaves

Line a colander with dampened cheesecloth. Spoon in yogurt, and tie the ends of the cloth with a string to form a pouch. Hang the string on the kitchen faucet with a bowl underneath to catch whey that drips from the pouch, and drain yogurt overnight. (The whey that accumulates can be used as the liquid for any bread recipe to give a most unusual flavor.

Simply store in refrigerator for future use.) The drained yogurt will have the consistency of cream cheese.

Mix yogurt in a medium-size bowl with ricotta cheese, garlic, and pepper. Line a large heart-shaped mold (or 5 small heart-shaped molds) with dampened cheesecloth, and spoon cheese into the mold(s), smoothing down the surface. Place in refrigerator, and chill for several hours (or several days, if that is more convenient).

When ready to serve, place minced herbs on a small piece of waxed paper. Then unmold heart onto a serving plate, lifting cheese out by the edges of the cheesecloth. Peel off the cloth and press herbs all over the surface. Garnish with basil leaves or bay leaves (depending upon which version you've made), and serve with thin whole grain crackers or thinly sliced pumpernickel bread.

Note: If you don't have a heart-shaped mold, oil your hands with olive oil and form large balls. Flatten each ball into a round, thick cake of cheese before pressing on the herbs, or use a small flower-pot lined with dampened cheesecloth as a mold to make a very attractive presentation.

Dolmadakia
with Avgolemono Sauce

Makes 40 pieces

This traditional Greek dish is usually stuffed with ground lamb or beef. Our version uses a vegetarian filling and is equally good.

½ cup olive oil, divided
1 cup finely chopped onions (about 2 large onions)

1 teaspoon finely minced garlic (about 1 clove)
½ teaspoon black pepper
2 cups cooked brown rice
3 tablespoons finely minced fresh dill
½ cup finely minced fresh parsley
½ cup finely chopped scallions (about 3 large scallions)
2 tablespoons pine nuts, toasted
¾ cup lemon juice (about 5 to 6 lemons), divided
3 cups chicken stock, divided
1 jar (9 ounces) grape leaves
lemon wedges
1 egg yolk

Heat 3 tablespoons of the olive oil in a 12-inch skillet. Add onions and garlic, and saute over low heat, stirring occasionally, until onions are wilted and translucent but not brown, about 10 minutes. Stir in pepper and rice, and continue to cook, stirring frequently, for 5 minutes more. Add dill, parsley, scallions, and pine nuts, and continue to cook for 5 minutes. Mix ½ cup of the lemon juice with 1 cup of the chicken stock, and pour over rice. Bring to a boil, then lower heat, cover, and simmer until all the liquid has been absorbed, about 10 minutes. There should be 3 cups of filling. Let mixture cool for 10 minutes, and transfer to a bowl. Wash and dry the skillet, and set aside. (The filling can be prepared a day ahead and refrigerated.) You will use only 2 cups of the filling. The other cup can be reserved to be mixed with ground lamb or beef for a sensational meat loaf.

(continued)

Rinse and separate grape leaves carefully under cold running water. The grape leaves may vary in size according to the brand used. If they are small, place 2 together. Place grape leaves, shiny-side down, on a flat surface, and blot with paper towels to get rid of excess water.

Place 1 teaspoon of the filling at the stem end of leaf. Fold sides in first to enclose filling. Then roll tightly toward tip of leaf, jelly-roll fashion, tucking in edges to make a neat log-shaped roll. Place seam-side down on a plate, and continue the process until all the grape leaves are used up.

To cook the grape leaves, pour remaining olive oil, lemon juice, and 1 cup of the chicken stock into the same 12-inch skillet. Arrange rolls, tightly packed in the pan, in a single layer. Place a dinner plate over rolls and weigh down the plate with a few heavy stones. Cover the skillet and simmer gently for 25 minutes. Remove the cover, tilt the plate up slightly, and carefully pour remaining stock around rolls. Cover again, and resume cooking for 15 minutes longer. Remove the stones and plate and cool slightly in the pan.

(Remember that the stones will be hot!) Carefully lift out rolls with a small spatula, and place them on a serving dish. Garnish with lemon wedges.

Pour remaining liquid through a sieve and strain. There should be about ⅔ cup. In a separate small bowl, beat egg yolk with a whisk. Slowly add hot liquid to egg yolk, beating constantly until sauce is slightly thickened. If sauce is not thick enough, warm gently, beating constantly for a few minutes. Do not boil sauce or it will curdle. Serve sauce separately to be spooned over rolls.

Endive Leaves Stuffed with Salmon, Tarragon, and Chives

Makes about 24 pieces

These make a wonderful light hors d'oeuvre or, if you'd like, two or three stuffed endive leaves can be served along with a green salad as a luncheon dish.

    1 cup poached salmon (about ½ pound) or 1 can (7½ ounces) salmon, drained

Cheese and Tomato Parfait
with Basil and Avocado
(page 50)

2 to 3 large Belgian endives,
        separated into leaves
  2 tablespoons finely minced fresh
        chives, divided
  ¼ cup finely minced celery
  2 tablespoons coarsely chopped
        fresh tarragon
  1 tablespoon lemon juice
  2 tablespoons mayonnaise
  1 teaspoon tiny capers, rinsed and
        drained
2 to 3 drops of Worcestershire sauce
  ⅛ teaspoon black pepper

Remove and discard skin and bones from salmon. Place into a bowl, and mash with a fork. Finely chop 2 endive leaves (about 2 tablespoons), and add to salmon. Reserve remaining leaves. Add 1 tablespoon of the chives and all the remaining ingredients to salmon and mix well. Fill endive leaves, leaving 1 inch near the stem end for holding. Arrange like the spokes of a wheel on a round platter, sprinkle with remaining chives, and chill until serving time.

Note: If canned salmon is used, don't be afraid to eat the bones. They are soft and contain calcium.

West Indian Ginger Pineapple Punch

8 to 10 servings

This recipe was inspired by an old Jamaican friend, Ivy Thomas. If you like ginger, you will love this refreshing summer drink.

    4 cups pineapple juice
    4 cups water, divided
    ¼ pound ginger root, unpeeled,
          scrubbed, and cut into
          ½-inch chunks
    ½ cup lime juice (about 3
          limes)
    ½ cup honey
       fresh pineapple spears

In a large bowl, mix together pineapple juice and 2 cups of the water. In a food processor, finely mince ginger. Add remaining water, and blend thoroughly. Pour through a strainer into pineapple juice, squeezing liquid from pulp with a wooden spoon. Discard pulp. Stir in lime juice. Pour honey and 1 cup of the juice mixture into the food processor, and whirl a few times to blend in honey. Pour honey mixture into pineapple juice mixture, and mix in with a wooden spoon. Pour into pitcher, cover, and chill overnight to blend flavors.

When ready to serve, pour into glasses over ice, and add a pineapple spear as a stirrer.

Flounder Seviche with Green and Red Peppers, Cilantro, and Kiwi Fruit

4 servings

    1 pound flounder or fluke fillets,
          skinned and cut into 1-inch
          squares
    ½ cup plus 3 tablespoons lime juice,
          divided
    3 tablespoons thinly sliced scallions,
          green part only
    ¼ cup diced green peppers
    ¼ cup diced sweet red peppers
    1 teaspoon finely minced seeded
          jalapeno peppers or ⅛ teaspoon
          dried red pepper flakes
    2 tablespoons finely minced fresh
          cilantro
    2 kiwi fruit, peeled and cut into
          ¼-inch slices
       alfalfa sprouts

Place fish in a medium-size nonmetallic bowl, and pour ½ cup of the lime juice over it. Cover with plastic wrap, and marinate in the refrigerator for at least 6 hours or up to 24 hours.

About 1 to 2 hours before serving, drain fish and add scallions, green peppers, red peppers, jalapeno peppers or red pepper flakes, and cilantro. Cut the slices of 1 kiwi fruit into 4 pieces each, and add to fish. Toss lightly with remaining lime juice. Serve over a bed of alfalfa sprouts on sea shells, and garnish with remaining slices of kiwi fruit.

Flounder Seviche with Green and Red Peppers, Cilantro, and Kiwi Fruit (page 56) ➡

Tomato-Buttermilk Cocktail with Tarragon

4 servings

3 cups tomato juice
1 cup buttermilk
1 teaspoon fresh tarragon leaves
2 to 3 drops of hot pepper sauce
1 teaspoon lemon juice
1 sprig of fresh tarragon

Whirl all the ingredients except tarragon sprig in a blender. Pour into a glass pitcher over ice cubes. Top with sprig of tarragon.

Fresh Salmon Tartare with Lime and Marjoram

4 servings

Much more delicate than steak tartare, this is a lovely, colorful, and sophisticated hors d'oeuvre.

¾ pound salmon fillet, skinned and boned
1 teaspoon nonpareil capers, rinsed and dried
1 tablespoon finely minced shallots
1½ tablespoons lime juice
2 teaspoons finely minced fresh marjoram leaves
1 sweet red pepper, roasted and cut into strips (page 85)
8 to 10 fresh chives, cut into 2-inch pieces
4 small wedges of lime
whole grain toast triangles
freshly ground black pepper

Run your fingers over surface of salmon, and if there are any bones left, pluck them out with tweezers or your fingernails. Chill fish in freezer for 10 minutes to firm it up for easier mincing. Then, coarsely chop with a large knife. Transfer to a medium-size bowl, and mix in capers, shallots, lime juice, and marjoram. Divide into 4 portions, and form a mound in the center of 4 salad plates. Garnish each plate with strips of red pepper, a few chives, and a wedge of lime to squeeze on fish. Serve with toast triangles and a pepper mill so that fresh pepper may be ground at the table.

Feta Cheesecake with Garlic and Mixed Herbs

12 servings

You can serve this as an hors d'oeuvre or as a light lunch accompanied by a crisp green salad. You can also serve it in small portions with fresh fruit as a dessert. This versatile, savory cheesecake is an all-purpose treat.

PASTRY

- 1 cup whole wheat flour
- 6 tablespoons butter, cut into pieces
- 1 egg

FILLING

- 1 pound feta cheese, crumbled
- 1 cup part-skim ricotta cheese
- 3 eggs
- ¼ cup lemon juice
- 2 teaspoons finely minced garlic (about 3 cloves)
- 3 tablespoons finely minced mixed fresh herbs (basil, oregano, thyme, summer savory, marjoram)
  few grindings of fresh black pepper
  sweet red pepper, cut into ½-inch triangles
  sprigs of fresh watercress

To make the pastry: Preheat oven to 350°F.

In a food processor, blend flour and butter until mealy in texture. Add egg, and process until dough forms a ball. Press dough in an even layer over the bottom and 1¾ inches up the sides of a 9 × 2-inch round springform pan. Bake 15 to 20 minutes, or until lightly browned. Set aside. If bottom puffs up, pierce all over with tip of knife to release air.

To make the filling: In a food processor, blend cheeses together. Add all the other ingredients and process. Spoon into partially baked crust, and bake at 350°F for 25 to 30 minutes. The center should quiver slightly when pan is gently shaken. Cool on a wire rack. To garnish, top with triangles of red pepper and watercress sprigs. Serve at room temperature.

You can make this cheesecake the day before. Simply cover and chill until ready to serve. Let stand at room temperature for 2 to 3 hours before serving.

Borage and Yogurt Drink

4 servings

- 3 cups plain yogurt
- 2 tablespoons fresh coarsely chopped borage leaves
- 1 teaspoon finely minced fresh chives
  club soda
- 4 blue borage blossoms

In a blender, whirl together yogurt, borage, chives, and ½ cup club soda. Pour into a glass pitcher, and add enough of the club soda to make a drink the consistency of light cream. Float borage flowers on top.

Gingered Pork and Shrimp Roll with Water Chestnuts and Cilantro

6 to 8 servings

The roll can be prepared ahead and frozen or baked as needed.

FILLING

½	pound lean ground pork
6 to 8	medium-size shrimp, cooked and coarsely chopped (about ½ cup)
8 to 10	water chestnuts, coarsely chopped
1	scallion, green part only, finely minced (about 1 tablespoon)
1	small clove garlic, peeled and finely minced
1	tablespoon finely minced fresh cilantro
2	teaspoons grated peeled ginger root
2 or 3	dashes of hot pepper sauce
2	tablespoons light soy sauce
1	egg, slightly beaten
3	tablespoons fine whole grain bread crumbs

PASTRY

½	cup whole wheat pastry flour
½	cup unbleached white flour
6	tablespoons butter, cut into pieces
2	tablespoons sour cream
	cornstarch

To make the filling: Cook pork in a dry nonstick skillet for a few minutes until it loses its color and looks white, but is not crumbly. Transfer to a medium-size bowl. Add all the remaining ingredients, and mix well. Refrigerate until you assemble the roll.

To make the pastry: Put whole wheat flour and butter in a food processor, and process until mixture is crumbly. Add sour cream, and process until mixture just holds together. Sprinkle cornstarch on aluminum foil, and wrap foil around pastry dough. Chill for 4 hours.

When ready to prepare, sprinkle additional cornstarch on 2 sheets of waxed paper. Roll pastry until quite thin between the sheets of waxed paper. (The pastry is delicate and will stick unless cornstarch is used.) Cut rolled pastry into a 9 × 14-inch rectangle. Place filling at one end of dough, leaving a 1-inch border all around. Fold over short ends first, to enclose filling, and starting from long end, roll up pastry like a jelly roll. Moisten and press end gently to seal. Place seam-side down on an ungreased baking sheet, and chill for 1 hour.

Preheat oven to 375°F. Bake roll for 45 to 50 minutes, or until lightly browned. Cool slightly before slicing into 1-inch slices.

Hot Crab Meat with Chives and Chervil Baked in Sea Shells

6 to 8 servings

When served with triangles of toast, it's an hors d'oeuvre, when baked and served over rice, it's a filling luncheon or supper dish for four people.

8 ounces cream cheese, at room
    temperature
3 tablespoons mayonnaise
2 tablespoons lemon juice
2 to 3 drops of hot pepper sauce
8 small fresh mushrooms, thinly
    sliced
2 tablespoons finely diced sweet
    red peppers
3 tablespoons finely minced fresh
    chives
6 ounces fresh or defrosted frozen
    crab meat
2 tablespoons finely minced fresh
    chervil

Preheat oven to 350°F. Butter sea shells
or a 10-inch oval baking dish.

In a medium-size bowl, beat cream cheese
with mayonnaise, lemon juice, and hot pepper sauce until well mixed. (This can also be
done in a food processor.) Stir in mushrooms,
red peppers, chives, and crab meat, and spoon
into prepared sea shells or baking dish. Bake
for 15 to 20 minutes, or until hot and bubbly.

Remove from oven, and sprinkle with
chervil. Serve hot.

Marinated Chinese Eggplants with Fresh Ginger and Chinese Five Spice Powder

4 to 6 servings

The Chinese five spice powder adds a special touch
to this attractive hors d'oeuvre. At one time, this

flavoring was difficult to find outside the larger
cities. Now it has become readily available at
Oriental markets and mail-order companies.

4 small, long eggplants
3 tablespoons corn oil
½ teaspoon finely minced garlic
1 teaspoon grated peeled ginger
    root
1 teaspoon sesame seeds
¼ teaspoon Chinese five spice
    powder
2 teaspoons Oriental sesame oil
2 tablespoons soy sauce
½ teaspoon honey
1 tablespoon rice wine vinegar
3 to 4 drops of hot pepper sauce

Trim ends of eggplants. Cut eggplants in
half lengthwise and then into ½-inch strips.
Cut strips into 2-inch lengths.

In a heavy, cast-iron skillet, heat oil until
very hot. Add eggplant strips in a single layer.
You will have to do 2 batches. Saute for 4 to 5
minutes, or until lightly browned, turning
with tongs to cook evenly. Drain on paper
towels. Mix all the remaining ingredients
together in a large bowl, and toss with hot
eggplant strips. Let stand for 2 hours to marinate at room temperature, stirring occasionally to blend the flavors. Serve with crisp
whole grain crackers.

This dish will keep in the refrigerator for
up to a week.

Sliced Mozzarella with Basil
and Hot Pepper (page 71)

Mushroom Caps Stuffed with Scallops and Garlic Chives

4 servings

The mushrooms are marinated briefly for additional flavor, and then the scallops are tucked into the mushroom hollows and the filled caps are broiled. They're very attractive and tasty.

- 8 large fresh mushrooms
- 1 tablespoon balsamic vinegar
- 1 clove garlic, peeled and crushed
- 1 teaspoon fresh rosemary leaves
- 2 tablespoons olive oil
- 2 tablespoons butter
- 1½ teaspoons minced fresh garlic chives
  few grindings of black pepper
- 1 teaspoon lemon juice
- 2 drops of Worcestershire sauce
- 3 tablespoons whole grain bread crumbs
- 8 sea scallops or ¼ pound bay scallops
- 1 teaspoon finely minced fresh parsley

Remove stems from mushrooms, and save for another use. Wipe mushroom caps with a damp paper towel, and place in a flat glass pie plate.

Mix vinegar, garlic, rosemary, and olive oil together in a medium-size bowl, and marinate mushrooms in this mixture for 1 hour, spooning some over mushrooms. (The mushrooms should absorb most of the marinade.)

Melt butter in a small skillet, and add all the remaining ingredients except scallops and parsley. Stir for a few seconds, and set aside. Place 1 large scallop or 3 to 4 small ones in each mushroom cap, and spoon a bit of the bread crumb mixture over each one. Preheat broiler, and broil mushrooms for 5 to 7 minutes. Sprinkle with parsley just before serving. Allow 2 per person.

Mussels Steamed in Orange Juice with Basil

4 servings

A colorful first course with a dipping sauce made from its own cooking broth. Pour any remaining sauce over leftover rice for an additional bonus.

 1 large navel orange
 2 tablespoons finely minced fresh basil
 2 tablespoons olive oil
 ⅛ teaspoon black pepper
16 large mussels, scrubbed and beards removed
 ⅓ cup water
 1 tablespoon finely minced shallots
    fresh basil leaves

Grate rind of orange and reserve. Cut 1 thin slice from the center of the orange, then cut this slice into tiny triangles to use as a garnish, and set aside. Squeeze juice from remaining orange. There should be about ¼ cup.

In a large, flat skillet with a tight-fitting lid, mix together minced basil, oil, pepper, mussels, water, shallots, orange juice, and half the reserved grated rind. Cover pan, bring to a boil, and steam over high heat until mussels open, 2 to 3 minutes.

Lift out mussels with a slotted spoon, and discard any that have not opened. Reserve broth. Remove the top half of the shell, and loosen mussel from the bottom half but leave it in the half shell. Finely shred 1 basil leaf, and distribute the shreds among the mussels. Arrange on a plate with whole basil leaves and tiny triangles of reserved orange. Sprinkle reserved rind on top of mussels. Pour reserved broth into a small bowl, and use as a dipping sauce.

Jamaican Nutmeg and Orange Cooler

4 servings

A creamy citrus drink that tastes best after flavors blend for two or three days in the refrigerator.

 2 cups orange juice
 1 cup evaporated milk
 1 teaspoon grated orange rind
1½ tablespoons light honey
 ¼ teaspoon ground nutmeg
    few grindings of fresh nutmeg

Mix all the ingredients except few grindings of nutmeg together in a medium-size bowl. Pour into a glass or a plastic container, cover tightly, and let flavors develop in the refrigerator for 2 to 3 days.

When ready to serve, pour into glasses filled with cracked ice, and top each with freshly grated nutmeg.

Mark Erickson
St. Andrew's Cafe
Hyde Park, New York

The chefs who run the kitchens of some of America's most famous restaurants are products of the fine training provided by The Culinary Institute of America. It is no wonder that the CIA itself has opened a restaurant of its own, one devoted to serving nutritionally balanced foods that are both wholesome and appetizing. It's called St. Andrew's Cafe, and it's located right on the grounds of the school in Hyde Park, New York. The executive chef is Mark Erickson, now 29 years old, and truly one of the new breed of chefs, dedicated to offering nutritional value as well as taste.

We don't tell our customers they're eating healthfully — we let the food speak for itself. Too many people think of "healthy food" as "health food" — tofu, sprouts, and granola bars. There is nothing wrong with these foods, but they don't, by themselves, necessarily represent good nutrition. We think our customers enjoy our food just as much as that of any well-known, well-publicized restaurant like Spago. And yet, we could say to them, "Hey, you just ate a dinner with less sodium, less fat than you'd find in a single can of processed soup!"

Mark was raised in a family that valued independence. At the age of 14, when he asked for a motorcycle, his father said, "Go out and work for it." He got a job as a dishwasher in Alexandria, Minnesota, where the chef was Ron Piscatelli, also a CIA grad.

I never saw a man who was so in love with food and his work as Ron. He saw that I was interested in food, so he moved me to the kitchen as a line chef and then suggested that I go to CIA.

The school has its own herb garden, now expanding up near the main building, and all the restaurants on the campus are partially supplied by their own crop. Like all the chefs there, Mark feels strongly about the importance of fresh herbs.

Fresh herbs have a completely different flavor; there's no real replacement for them. In using fresh herbs, especially in a restaurant like St. Andrew's Cafe, we can reduce sodium, while heightening the aromatic character of a dish. Just a simple thing like adding some basil leaves to a green salad can transform a familiar dish to one that has diners commenting on an added dimension they want to duplicate at home.

While speaking of basil, Mark told us about using it with fresh roasted corn. He peels back the husk and removes the corn silk, replacing it with a few basil leaves. The husk is returned to position and tied in place for roasting on a grill or in the oven. When done, the corn is cut from the cob and mixed with roasted sweet peppers. We like the idea of the corn-basil combination so much that we serve the roasted corn on the cob for eating as is.

"Thyme is a favorite in our kitchen. It's so easy to grow and you can use it in so many kinds of dishes." Chef Erickson uses thyme in combination with wild honey as a glaze painted on breast of duck before roasting.

For fish lovers the appeal of Mark Erickson's herbed poaching liquid is hard to resist. He flavors the stock with tarragon, saffron, fennel, and grated orange rind. Use this for poaching halibut or some other firm-fleshed fish.

Mark gave us several of his recipes, and we've chosen one that is colorful and nutritious. It also uses three fresh herbs that are easy to grow in your own garden.

Garden Terrine St. Andrew's

Makes 25 servings, 100 grams each

1 pound boneless, skinless chicken breast, ground
2 egg whites
1 cup heavy cream
1 tablespoon chopped fresh dill
1 tablespoon chopped fresh tarragon
1 tablespoon chopped fresh basil
¼ teaspoon white pepper
1 pound carrots, coarsely cut
½ pound zucchini, seeded and coarsely cut
½ pound artichoke bottoms, cut into small wedges
½ pound shiitake mushrooms, cut into batonnets (little sticks)
1 pound fresh spinach, ribs removed
1 pound sweet red peppers, cut into julienne strips

Place ground chicken in the well-chilled bowl of a food processor, along with egg whites. Process to a fine paste. Add heavy cream, dill, tarragon, basil, and pepper and turn machine on and off until ingredients are *just* incorporated. Be very careful not to overprocess. Place into a large bowl and refrigerate until vegetables are prepared.

Line several baking sheets or large trays with several layers of paper towels.

Steam carrots until tender and cooked through. Steam remaining vegetables separately until just "al dente." As vegetables are cooked, place on lined baking sheets or trays, and spread out so that vegetables will cool and towels can

Mark Erickson — Continued

absorb excess moisture. This is an important step, so be sure that vegetables are completely cooled, and if necessary, towels replaced during cooling time so that they do not become saturated with moisture.

While vegetables are cooling and drying, bring some water to a boil for the water bath.

Preheat oven to 325°F.

Coarsely chop cooled and dried spinach leaves. Fold all vegetables into chicken mousseline carefully, being sure not to overwork mixture.

Line 2 12-inch enameled loaf pans or molds with plastic wrap. Divide terrine mixture evenly between 2 molds. Cover molds with additional plastic wrap, and place into a deep baking dish or roasting pan. Place dish on middle rack of preheated oven. Add hot water so that it comes two-thirds of the way up the sides of the molds. Immediately lower oven to 275°F.

Check water bath from time to time during cooking. The water should never come to a boil and should maintain a fairly steady temperature of 170°F. (Use an instant-reading thermometer to check.) If water temperature is too high, lower oven setting slightly.

The terrine is done when an internal temperature of 140°F is reached. Remove from water bath, and remove covering of plastic wrap to aid in cooling. Allow terrine to cool to room temperature, and then refrigerate overnight before serving.

Mushrooms with Lemon Thyme

4 servings

A variation of raw mushrooms served either as an hors d'oeuvre or as a salad at luncheon or dinner. The tang of the lemon thyme is a lovely surprise.

   2 tablespoons lemon juice
   2 tablespoons olive oil
   1 tablespoon safflower oil
   ¼ teaspoon finely minced garlic
   ¼ teaspoon black pepper
   1 tablespoon fresh lemon thyme
       leaves
   ¾ pound fresh mushrooms

Mix all the ingredients together, except mushrooms, and set aside. Wipe mushrooms with a damp paper towel. Remove stems and reserve for another use. Slice mushrooms caps very thinly, and toss with dressing. Serve at once. The mushrooms should be crisp and lightly coated with dressing. If they stand too long, they will absorb the dressing.

Pickled Shrimp
in Mustard Dill Sauce

4 to 6 servings

The recipe is simple, and it's made two days before serving. As a result, it's a great dish to include in your menu when last-minute preparations will keep you busy with other things.

- 2 limes
- 2 lemons
- ½ cup olive oil
- 2 teaspoons French-style mustard
- 1 teaspoon freshly ground black pepper
  pinch of dried red pepper flakes
- ½ teaspoon finely minced garlic
- 2 tablespoons coarsely snipped fresh dill
- 1 pound medium-size raw shrimp, peeled and deveined
  cucumber slices or lettuce leaves
- 1 sprig of fresh dill
  lemon wedges

Grate rind of 1 lime and 1 lemon and reserve. Squeeze juice of both limes and both lemons into a deep glass bowl, and mix with oil, mustard, black pepper, red pepper flakes, garlic, and snipped dill. Bring a pot of water to a rolling boil, and add shrimp. They will begin to lose their transparency once they hit the water. Remove immediately, drain in a colander, and mix with pickling liquid while they are warm. Cover and refrigerate for 48 hours. Mix once after the first day. When ready to serve, lift shrimp out of liquid with a slotted spoon, and place over cucumber slices or lettuce leaves. Garnish with a sprig of dill and lemon wedges.

Sardines with Dill, Lemon, and Powdered Bay Leaves Wrapped with Lettuce

Makes 8 to 10 rolls

- 12 small lettuce leaves
- 2 cans (4⅜ ounces) sardines
- 1 teaspoon capers, rinsed and dried (optional)
- ⅛ teaspoon powdered bay leaves
  lemon juice
  hot pepper sauce
- 12 small sprigs of fresh dill
  lemon wedges

Select a soft-leaf lettuce that is not too crisp (Boston, Bibb, or homegrown leaf lettuce). Cut the bottom off so that the top will just enclose the sardine. Spread lettuce leaves on waxed paper, and lay 1 sardine on each leaf. Slightly crush capers (if used) in a small bowl. Add powdered bay leaves, a few drops of lemon juice, and hot pepper sauce. Mix well, and divide mixture among sardines. Place a sprig of dill over each sardine, and roll lettuce so that it enfolds fish and becomes a finger food. Garnish with dill and lemon wedges.

Note: Bay leaf is available in powdered form (see Mail-Order Sources). If you use *whole* bay leaf, it must be removed after flavoring the dish, since the spine of the leaf can create intestinal problems if ingested. Therefore, we think it's desirable to use the powdered form to achieve a delectable flavor, and especially at times when the whole leaf cannot be removed before serving.

Shredded Chicken and Fennel with Orange Rind and Parsley

6 servings as an hors d'oeuvre
4 servings as a luncheon dish

1 large or 2 small bulbs fennel plus
   feathery leaves (about 1½ pounds)
2 tablespoons olive oil
2 tablespoons butter
½ cup minced scallions (about 2
   scallions)
½ teaspoon finely minced garlic
¼ teaspoon black pepper
1½ teaspoons aniseeds
2 cups chicken stock
3 tablespoons lemon juice
½ pound chicken breasts, poached
   and shredded
1 tablespoon shredded orange rind
1 tablespoon finely minced fresh
   parsley

Rinse fennel bulbs. Cut away tough parts of stems, and discard. Mince and reserve 1 tablespoon of the leaves. Cut bulb in half lengthwise and then into 4 lengthwise sections. In a large, nonstick skillet, heat oil and butter together over medium heat. Add scallions and garlic, and saute, stirring, for 3 to 4 minutes. Add pepper and aniseeds, and cook for a few seconds. Stir in fennel, and saute over medium-low heat for 10 minutes, stirring occasionally. Add chicken stock, cover, and cook over low heat until tender, 10 to 12 minutes.

Remove fennel with a slotted spoon to a shallow serving dish, and set aside. Boil liquid in pan until it is reduced to ½ cup, cool slightly, and then add lemon juice to reduced sauce. Pour over fennel. Stir in shredded chicken, orange rind, parsley, and chopped fennel leaves. Refrigerate for 3 hours before serving.

Note: Chicken breasts can be poached in the chicken stock for 5 to 8 minutes and the stock reused in the recipe.

Shrimp with Lovage and Horseradish Mustard Sauce

4 servings

This dish tastes best when marinated overnight so that the tangy sauce permeates the shrimp.

10 small sprigs fresh parsley
2 tablespoons fresh lovage leaves or
   1 stalk celery with leaves
1 scallion, cut into pieces
½ teaspoon fresh tarragon leaves
1 tablespoon tarragon vinegar
2 tablespoons olive oil
1 tablespoon French-style mustard
1 heaping teaspoon horseradish
⅛ teaspoon lemon pepper or freshly
   ground black pepper
¾ pound shrimp, cooked, peeled, and
   deveined
   lettuce leaves
   cucumber slices

Combine all the ingredients in a blender except shrimp, lettuce, and cucumbers, and process until well blended. There should be about ½ cup of sauce. Toss sauce with shrimp, and put into a covered nonmetallic bowl to marinate overnight.

When ready to serve, arrange lettuce leaves and cucumber slices attractively on a serving platter, and spoon shrimp into center.

← Fresh Salmon Tartare with Lime and Marjoram (page 58)

Miglee: A Syrian Ginger Drink

4 servings

1 1-inch piece of ginger root,
    peeled and thinly sliced
2 2-inch pieces of cinnamon
2 whole cloves
1 teaspoon aniseeds
½ cup blanched whole almonds,
    ground
½ cup honey
4 cups water

Put all ingredients into a medium-size saucepan, bring to a boil, lower heat, and simmer for 30 minutes. Strain, discard spices, and serve the drink in mugs.

Swiss Chard Rolls Stuffed with Cheese and Dill

Makes about 16 rolls

These luscious green rolls can be served as an hors d'oeuvre or as a vegetable to accompany a main course of broiled chicken or fish.

16 large Swiss chard leaves with stems
¼ cup olive oil
½ cup finely chopped onions (about 1
    medium onion)
¼ teaspoon black pepper
2 tablespoons coarsely chopped fresh
    dill
½ pound feta cheese, crumbled
6 ounces pot cheese
2 eggs, slightly beaten
½ cup fine whole grain bread crumbs
⅛ teaspoon ground nutmeg
    lemon wedges

Wash and dry Swiss chard leaves. Remove stems, and finely chop them in a food processor. There should be about ¾ cup. Reserve leaves for later on by keeping them dry between layers of paper towels. Heat olive oil in a 10-inch nonstick skillet. Add onions and chopped Swiss chard stems, and saute over low heat for 10 minutes, stirring occasionally, or until moisture has evaporated. Stir in pepper and dill, and let mixture cool.

Preheat oven to 400°F. Butter both an 8 × 14-inch rectangular oven-to-table baking dish, and a large enough piece of aluminum foil to cover the dish.

In a medium-size bowl, mix both cheeses together. Then add eggs, bread crumbs, nutmeg, and reserved onion-dill mixture. Mix until smooth. There should be about 2½ cups of cheese filling. Lay Swiss chard leaves on a flat surface, stem-side up, and spoon 2 tablespoons of the cheese mixture on bottom edge of leaf. Turn bottom up, then turn sides in to enclose filling, and roll up into a bundle. Place in prepared pan in a single layer. Repeat until all of the cheese mixture is used up. Cover tightly with foil, buttered-side down, and bake for 20 minutes. Cool for 10 minutes, and serve warm with wedges of lemon to be squeezed over the rolls.

Sliced Mozzarella with Basil and Hot Pepper

4 to 6 servings

This recipe is adapted from one that was described to us by Poppa and Momma Balducci, two old friends who own one of New York's most famous markets located in West Greenwich Village.

½ pound fresh mozzarella, cut into ½-inch slices
½ teaspoon finely minced garlic
2 teaspoons finely minced fresh basil
1 teaspoon finely minced fresh parsley
1 teaspoon finely minced fresh oregano
1 teaspoon finely minced fresh thyme
⅛ teaspoon freshly ground lemon pepper or black pepper
2 tablespoons olive oil
1 teaspoon tarragon vinegar
½ teaspoon dried red pepper flakes, or more to taste
fresh basil leaves

Put cheese into a medium-size bowl. Mix all the herbs and pepper with oil and vinegar. Pour over cheese, and sprinkle with red pepper flakes. Arrange slices on a serving plate, interspersing them with basil leaves. Let stand at room temperature for 2 hours before serving.

Sweet Red Peppers Stuffed with Gorgonzola Cheese and Garlic Chives

4 to 6 servings

So easy. So colorful. So delicious.

2 medium-size sweet red peppers
6 ounces cream cheese
4 ounces Gorgonzola cheese
2 teaspoons finely minced fresh garlic chives

Slice off stem end of peppers about ½ inch down. Slice a thin section off the bottom so that pepper will stand up. Core the pepper.

In a food processor, mix together cheeses and garlic chives. Stuff peppers full with mixture, using a small spatula to push down filling. When peppers are full, refrigerate until firm, about 1 hour.

When ready to serve, lay each pepper on its side, and slice into ½-inch rounds. Serve with crackers.

Note: The Dutch red peppers have thicker walls and deeper hollows than the domestic peppers, which allows more space for the cheese filling and permits ease in slicing without crushing the peppers.

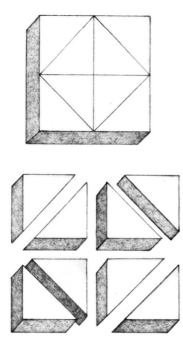

1 tablespoon finely sliced scallions
(cut on the diagonal)
⅛ teaspoon black pepper
½ teaspoon black sesame seeds

Drain tofu. Cut each piece into quarters, and then cut each quarter into triangles. You will have 16 triangles in all. Arrange them in an attractive pattern in a shallow casserole dish or bowl. Mix ginger, garlic, soy sauce, sesame oil, vinegar, water, chili pepper oil, and honey together in a small bowl. Pour sauce over tofu, scatter scallions over all, and sprinkle with pepper and sesame seeds. Let marinate in the refrigerator for 1 to 2 days. Tilt occasionally, and spoon some marinade over the top of the tofu. Serve chilled or at room temperature.

Tofu Triangles with Ginger and Black Sesame Seeds

Makes 16 pieces

1 pound tofu (2 pieces, ½ pound each)
1½ teaspoons finely minced peeled ginger root
1 teaspoon finely minced garlic
3 tablespoons light soy sauce
2 teaspoons Oriental sesame oil
2 tablespoons rice vinegar
¼ cup cold water
⅛ teaspoon hot chili pepper oil
½ teaspoon honey

Tiny Beets Stuffed with Sorrel Puree

4 servings

This is a low-calorie bite-size hors d'oeuvre that is easy to prepare.

1 pound small beets, steamed until tender
1 tablespoon butter
¼ pound fresh sorrel, stems removed and leaves shredded
few grindings of fresh black pepper

Peel beets and drain well on paper towels. Scoop out a small hole from each beet with a melon scoop, and set beets aside on a serving dish.

Melt butter in a medium-size skillet. Add sorrel and pepper, and cook just until sorrel is wilted, stirring constantly. The leaves will turn from bright green to olive green and will get very soft. Let cool slightly, and then puree. Stuff ¼ teaspoon of puree into the scooped-out part of the beets, and serve.

Young Pattypan Squash Stuffed with Sausage, Fennel, and Basil

Makes 12 pieces

12 pattypan squash about the size of a silver dollar
 1 fresh sweet Italian sausage
 2 tablespoons finely minced scallions
 2 tablespoons finely minced sweet red peppers
⅛ teaspoon black pepper
    pinch of dried red pepper flakes
¼ teaspoon fennel seeds
 1 large whole fresh basil leaf, finely shredded
    grated Parmesan cheese

Trim stem ends of squashes so that they won't fall over. Steam for 5 minutes, or until tender, then cool. Cut out a circle in the center of each squash with the tip of a knife, and then set the squash in a large baking pan.

Remove casing from sausage, crumble meat, and saute in a small skillet for 5 minutes, stirring so that it does not burn. Remove sausage with a slotted spoon, and reserve.

In the same skillet, add scallions and red peppers, and stir over medium heat until scallions are wilted. Return sausage to pan, and add all the remaining ingredients except Parmesan cheese. Spoon about ½ teaspoon of sausage mixture into each squash. Sprinkle with grated Parmesan cheese, and place under broiler (on lowest rack) for about 2 minutes to reheat. Serve warm.

Frullati di Frutta con Mentha

4 servings

We first experienced this drink on the island of Murano, not far from Venice. This recipe is a variation of that very special Italian cooler. The ripeness of the fruit is important in order to get the proper accent of mint.

 1 cup plain yogurt
 3 cups milk
 1 large ripe peach, peeled
 8 large ripe fresh strawberries
 3 tablespoons light honey
 1 teaspoon finely minced fresh peppermint
 4 fresh strawberry halves
 4 sprigs of fresh mint

Whirl all the ingredients except strawberry halves and mint sprigs in a blender until smooth. Serve in frosty glasses garnished with a strawberry half and a sprig of mint.

Chapter 6
SOUPS

← Wild and Tame Mushroom Soup with Tarragon and Nasturtium (page 90)

Most people think of soup as a nurturing food, perfect for the cold winter days, when a clear, hot broth or a rich, thick mixture of grains and vegetables can warm one's very soul. In summer, it nurtures just as well, either as a cooling preface to a luncheon or as a meal in itself. Soup can fit any mood; it is perfect for any time of the year, for any hour of the day. It has a well-deserved reputation as an ideal food, and every culture has a version of chicken soup, noted as a medicinal potion when you're feeling out of sorts.

Soups can evolve out of thriftiness, a good way to use up tidbits and scraps and the bones of yesterday's dinner; they can be lavish and expensive, an accident or an art, a whole meal or a snack. Best of all, properly made, good soups can cut down on calories and satisfy at the same time.

Carrots, onions, leeks, and celery are the most common aromatics added to the stockpot. However, fresh herbs—such as parsley, thyme, and bay leaves—are classic enhancements. If you use dried herbs, remember that their flavor is more intense, so use about a third of the amount you would use if the herbs were fresh.

Make use of the bouquet garni to ensure easy retrieval of the herbs and spices from the stock: If whole large leaves are used, fasten them with a string tied to a stalk of celery; smaller fragments such as seeds, crumbled herbs, and ground spices can be gathered in a piece of cheesecloth and anchored to a soup bone.

In the soups that we include here, the herbs and spices are the stars, of course. Try the recipes our way. Then you can vary the amounts of seasoning to suit your own taste and palate.

August Harvest Soup with Basil Broth

8 servings

This green soup, flecked with the orange of carrots and the yellow of corn, is redolent with end-of-season fresh basil. The recipe makes enough to freeze so that you can celebrate summer's bounty in midwinter.

8	cups chicken stock
2	cups coarsely chopped fresh basil
1	pound fresh spinach, coarse stems removed
6	tablespoons butter
5	large scallions, coarsely chopped
1	medium leek, coarsely chopped
2 to 3	medium-size zucchini (about 1 pound), cut into large chunks
2	large tomatoes (about ¾ pound), peeled and cubed
3	carrots (about ½ pound), cut into chunks
1	cup fresh flat Italian parsley, with 1 inch of stem
1	cup cooked corn
1	small carrot, shredded
¼	teaspoon black pepper

Place chicken stock and basil into a 6-quart pot, bring to a boil, and simmer for 30 minutes. Remove from pot, and reserve. It will have condensed a bit. Shred spinach, and set aside. (There should be 10 to 12 cups.) Wipe out pot, and melt 4 tablespoons of the butter. Add scallions and leeks, and saute for about 5 minutes, or until wilted, stirring occasionally. Add spinach and stir until wilted. Then add zucchini, tomatoes, carrots, parsley, and reserved basil stock, and bring to a boil. Lower heat, cover, and simmer for 30 to 40 minutes, or until vegetables are tender.

Puree vegetables in a blender or food processor. Return to pot, and simmer for 1 minute. Remove from heat, and stir in corn kernels, shredded carrot, pepper, and remaining butter. Serve hot.

Dioscorides, the Greek physician of the first century A.D., believed that too much basil was bad for the digestion. Centuries later the French physician Hilarius declared that a scorpion could be born in the brain of one who merely smelled basil.

Carrot and Turnip Soup with Cloves and Cardamom

4 to 6 servings

2	tablespoons corn oil
2 to 3	large shallots, peeled and thinly sliced
5 to 6	small carrots (about ¾ pound), peeled and thinly sliced
5 to 6	small turnips (about ½ pound), peeled and thinly sliced
¾	teaspoon ground cardamom
¼	teaspoon ground cloves
3	cups chicken stock

1 tablespoon long-grain brown
   rice
2 cups buttermilk
   few drops of hot pepper sauce

Heat oil in a heavy 4-quart casserole. Add shallots, and saute for 1 to 2 minutes, or until wilted, stirring constantly. Add carrots and turnips, and cook, stirring, for 5 minutes. Stir in spices, chicken stock, and rice. Bring to a boil, lower heat, cover, and simmer for 25 minutes.

Puree in batches in a blender or food processor until very smooth. Chill slightly, then add buttermilk. Chill again to blend flavors. Just before serving, add hot pepper sauce and sprinkle additional cloves and cardamom on top. Serve cold.

Cold Cabbage and Tomato Soup with Sour Cream and Dill

6 to 8 servings

This adaptation of a family recipe handed down through three generations is a thick, sweet-and-sour Middle European summer soup, and it tastes better on the second or third day.

10 cups coarsely chopped cabbage
   (about 2 pounds)
1 can (28 ounces) Italian plum
   tomatoes in tomato puree
6 cups chicken stock
4 cups coarsely chopped onions
   (about 3 large onions)

2 tablespoons butter
3 tablespoons mild honey
½ cup water
¼ teaspoon black pepper, or more to
   taste
¼ cup lemon juice (about 2 lemons)
2 eggs, slightly beaten
1 cup sour cream
1½ tablespoons finely minced fresh
   dill

Mix cabbage and tomatoes together in a heavy 6-quart Dutch oven, crushing tomatoes a bit with a wooden spoon. Add chicken stock, and bring to a boil. Lower heat, and simmer, uncovered, for 1 hour, stirring occasionally.

While the soup cooks, saute onions in a 12-inch dry skillet over medium heat for 10 minutes, stirring occasionally, until they start to turn brown. Add butter and stir until it melts. Then add honey and water, and cook for 5 minutes more, stirring occasionally, so that onions do not burn. Add onion-honey mixture to soup while it's cooking, and continue cooking until the hour is up. Then add pepper and lemon juice, and continue to simmer for 20 minutes more. Remove pot from heat, and let cool slightly.

In a small bowl, beat eggs with a whisk until foamy, and slowly add 1 cup of soup to eggs, stirring. Add egg mixture slowly to the soup, and return to the stove. Simmer for 5 minutes more, stirring so that eggs do not curdle. Chill the soup until cold. Garnish each serving with a dollop of sour cream and a sprinkling of dill. Then stir them in at the table.

The Quillec Family
Chez Daniel
Charlotte, North Carolina

I went to work on lobster boats, fishing and cooking. We were at sea for six months at a time, so I learned a great deal about sea-food, as you can imagine!

He then cooked in Paris, New York, Miami, and finally Charlotte. Daniel attributes the family love for food to his mother, who grew up on a farm and who knew and appreciated the importance of using only the freshest ingredients. She passed these values on to the sons, who still follow the tradition in running their own restaurant. Patrick began his cooking career at an even earlier age than Daniel.

This is a "cooking family." Though Patrick Quillec, 27 years old, is the executive chef, his brother Daniel is also a master chef who not only helps to design and prepare the dishes, but also "hosts" their small, charming, and very special restaurant in Charlotte. Daniel's wife, Danielle, is sous chef; Patrick's wife, Jo Ann, assists them all and serves the customers delightfully, too. For us, it was a reunion when we found them, for we knew Daniel when he owned one of our favorite restaurants in New York. Daniel, 38, has been cooking since he was 16 years old.

I started as an apprentice in a restaurant in Brittany when I was 15. Then, later on, in Miami, I worked for a few years with a very good chef from Paris. When we opened our own restaurant here, I finally had the freedom to create new dishes, and to try my own ideas.

The Quillecs use only fresh produce, of course, but they also insist on fresh herbs—some locally grown and some sent by suppliers. Patrick avoids using herbs together in a single dish.

Each herb is so distinctive, I prefer to work with only one at a time. Basil and chervil are two of my favorites. They can be used in so many ways, but they are so delicate that their beautiful flavors would be over-powered if either one were mixed with other herbs. Basil is lovely with salmon and in soups. I also shred just a little of it in salads for added zest. But I don't like basil with meats. Thyme is much nicer with lighter meats, such as lamb, veal, and rabbit. With pork, mut-ton, and game, I use rosemary; since the heartier-flavored meats can take strong-flavored herbs. The milder dishes are best suited to delicate herbs, and that's why I always use chervil with fresh shellfish. It enhances the fresh flavor of the fish without masking it.

The menu at Chez Daniel features many dishes that include such flavorings as basil and fennel and cilantro and herbes de Provence (which include flowers of lavender and thyme) Patrick's basil soup differs somewhat from our own recipe — it's a lot richer, for one thing — which only goes to show how personal the use of herbs can be.

Fresh Basil Soup

8 servings

1 pound leeks
4 medium-size potatoes
3 tablespoons butter
6 cups chicken stock
   white pepper, to taste
15 large fresh opal basil leaves
1 cup heavy cream
½ cup sour cream, at room
   temperature

Cut leeks in quarters lengthwise. Chop into small pieces. Peel potatoes, and cut into small pieces. Melt butter in a large pot. Add leeks and potatoes, and cook for 2 minutes. Then add chicken stock. Bring to a boil, and let simmer for 15 minutes. Set aside, and add pepper.

Pour half the soup into a blender set on "liquefy," and let it run for 3 minutes. Set aside. Put the other half of the soup, along with the basil, in blender and let it run for 3 more minutes. Return basil-soup mixture to large pot, and add heavy cream. Bring to a boil, and set aside at once. Pour soup into warm soup bowls, and take a teaspoonful of sour cream and draw lines on the sur-face of the soup. Then cross the lines with the point of a knife, once upward and once downward. Serve immediately.

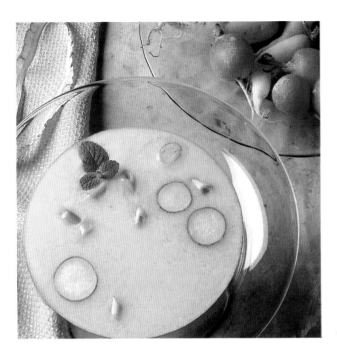

Radish and Scallion Soup
with Mint (page 86)

Cold Cream of Turnip and Potato Soup with Lemon Verbena

4 to 6 servings

Though lemon verbena, an annual herb, is not generally sold commercially, most herb gardeners are aware of its versatility. If it's not available in your area or you don't grow it yourself, you may substitute 1 teaspoon grated lemon rind and 1 teaspoon minced fresh parsley.

    2 tablespoons butter
6 to 8 medium-size turnips (about ¾
          pound), peeled and cubed
    1 cup peeled cubed potatoes
          (about ½ pound)
    2 tablespoons chopped fresh
          chives
 2½ cups chicken stock
    1 cup milk
  ½ cup heavy cream
  ⅛ teaspoon hot pepper sauce
    1 tablespoon finely minced fresh
          lemon verbena

Melt butter in a 5-quart nonstick Dutch oven. Add cubed turnips, and saute over low heat for 5 minutes. Add potatoes, stir to coat with butter, then add chives, and cook for 1 minute, stirring so that vegetables do not burn. Add chicken stock, cover, and bring to a boil. Then lower heat, and simmer, covered, for 25 minutes.

Puree vegetable mixture in a blender or food processor in several batches. Transfer to a large bowl, stir in remaining ingredients, and chill for several hours before serving.

Cream of Navy Bean Soup with Fresh Herbs and Lemon

6 servings

Normally bean soups are heavy, hearty winter fare. Not this one. It's a light soup that can be served hot or chilled with a paper-thin slice of lemon floating on the surface.

> 1 cup dried navy beans (white kidney or great northern beans may be substituted)
> 5 tablespoons butter, divided
> ½ cup sliced leeks (about 1 small leek with 1 inch of green part)
> 1 cup coarsely chopped onions (about 1 medium onion)
> 1 cup sliced celery (about 2 stalks)
> 6 cups chicken stock
> 1 dried bay leaf
> 2 large cloves garlic, peeled
> ¼ cup milk
> ¼ cup light cream
> 1 egg yolk
> 1 teaspoon grated lemon rind
> 3 tablespoons lemon juice
> coarsely minced mixed fresh herbs (2 tablespoons parsley, 2 tablespoons summer savory, 1 tablespoon basil, and 1 teaspoon tarragon)

> white pepper, to taste
> few grindings of nutmeg

Soak beans in 3 cups water overnight. Drain, and discard water. The beans will have expanded to about 3 cups. Set beans aside.

In a heavy 4-quart Dutch oven or saucepan, melt 3 tablespoons of the butter. Add leeks, onions, and celery, and saute over low heat, stirring occasionally, until vegetables are wilted, about 4 minutes. Add chicken stock, reserved beans, bay leaf, and garlic. Bring to a boil, then lower heat to a simmer, cover pot with lid slightly ajar, and cook for 1¼ hours.

Remove bay leaf, and strain into a bowl, reserving liquid. Puree beans and vegetables in a blender or food processor, along with a ladleful of stock, and blend until smooth. Return to pot with all but 1 cup of the stock.

In the same unwashed blender, add milk, cream, egg yolk, and remaining 2 tablespoons of butter, cut into small pieces. Puree with remaining cup of warm reserved stock. Return this mixture to pot with bean puree. Bring slowly to a simmer, and cook for 5 minutes, or until hot. Remove from heat, and stir in lemon rind, lemon juice, and minced herbs. Add pepper and nutmeg, and serve at once.

Dill has a long history as a folk medicine. At various times, it has been used as a cure for hiccups, insomnia, stomachaches, and indigestion.

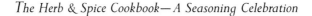

Fresh Tomato Soup with Lovage, Basil, and Dill

4 to 6 servings

8   tomatoes (about 2½ pounds), cored at stem ends and cut into large chunks
4   cups chicken stock
10 to 12 large fresh basil leaves
3   sprigs fresh lovage or celery leaves
6 to 8 sprigs fresh flat Italian parsley
2   tablespoons minced fresh dill, divided
⅛   teaspoon black pepper
4 to 6 teaspoons cold butter

Put tomatoes, chicken stock, basil, lovage or celery leaves, and parsley into a 4-quart stainless steel pot, cover, and bring to a boil. Lower heat, and simmer until tomatoes are soft, about 20 minutes.

Puree tomato mixture in a food mill and discard pulp, skins, and seeds. Return puree to pot, and heat. Add 1 tablespoon of the dill and the pepper, and simmer for 10 minutes. Serve in individual bowls, and float thin slices of cold butter on top of each serving. Sprinkle with a few strands of remaining dill.

Garlic and Beet Soup with Lemon, Bay Leaf, and Oregano

4 to 6 servings

This is a clear, light, ruby-colored version of borscht. Sweet-sour in taste, the slow simmering treats the garlic gently so that it blends with the other seasonings beautifully.

4   beef marrow bones (2-inch pieces)
1   large onion, peeled and coarsely cut
8   cups water
2   cups peeled and quartered small beets (about ¾ pound)
½   teaspoon black pepper
10 large cloves garlic, peeled and cut in half lengthwise
½   cup lemon juice (about 4 medium lemons)
1   dried bay leaf
3   tablespoons light honey
1   tablespoon white vinegar
1   tablespoon finely minced fresh oregano

Put bones, onions, and water into a heavy, 6-quart pot with a lid. Bring to a boil, lower heat, and skim any foam from surface while simmering for 30 minutes. Add beets, pepper, garlic, lemon juice, and bay leaf, and continue to simmer, covered, for 1 hour more, skimming any accumulated foam from surface of soup from time to time.

Mix honey and vinegar together in a cup, add to pot, and continue to cook for 30 minutes more. Lift out bones with slotted spoon or tongs, and remove bay leaf. Discard bones and bay leaf. Sprinkle soup with oregano and serve.

Note: We prefer to let the soup cool in the refrigerator for a few hours or overnight. Then we skim the fat off the top and reheat the soup before serving. The flavors blend during those hours.

Another variation also works well: After cooking, puree the beets and cooked garlic and return them to the soup. It will change the look somewhat—the soup will be cloudy instead of having the pure, crystal ruby color, but it will taste equally good.

Lemon Chicken Soup with Sugar Snap Peas and Chervil

4 to 5 servings

7 cups chicken stock
3 whole cloves
1 large onion, peeled
2 stalks celery, cut into 1½-inch pieces
1 large carrot, cut into 1½-inch pieces
1 dried bay leaf
1 large lemon
1 pound chicken breasts, boned and skinned
1 teaspoon soy sauce
¼ teaspoon white pepper
¼ pound sugar snap peas
3 tablespoons sliced scallions (½-inch pieces)
2 tablespoons finely minced fresh chervil

In a 6-quart pot, bring stock to a boil. Insert cloves into onion, and add to pot along with celery, carrots, and bay leaf. Lower heat, cover, and simmer for 20 minutes.

While soup is cooking, prepare lemon. Grate lemon rind from the whole lemon, and then cut lemon in half. Squeeze juice from half the lemon. Then peel white pith from the other half before cutting into paper-thin slices. Set prepared lemon aside.

Add chicken breasts to stock, and simmer for 8 to 10 minutes. Remove chicken. When cool enough, cut into ½-inch strips. Strain soup, and discard vegetables and bay leaf. Bring soup to a boil again and add soy sauce, pepper, and sugar snap peas. Cook for 1 minute, lower heat, and return chicken to pot along with reserved lemon rind, lemon juice, and scallions. Transfer to a serving tureen, float lemon slices on top, and sprinkle with chervil.

Personalized Soup

6 servings

Perfect for any special occasion, whether it is an intimate dinner or a birthday party, this chilled soup can even be used as a substitute for a place card at a large dinner party. It is actually initialed to make it special and personal.

¼ cup butter
 2 cups coarsely chopped leeks, white
       parts only (about 3 medium-size
       leeks)
 1 cup coarsely chopped onions (about
       1 large onion)
 3 large Idaho potatoes (about 1¼
       pounds), peeled and diced into
       ½-inch cubes
 5 cups chicken stock
 1 cup heavy cream
 6 drops of hot pepper sauce
 1 small bunch fresh parsley with
       stems, coarsely torn
¾ cup cold water
½ teaspoon saffron threads
     paprika

In a 5-quart Dutch oven, melt butter. Stir in leeks, onions, and potatoes, and saute over medium heat, stirring occasionally, for 8 to 10 minutes. Do not brown. Add chicken stock, and bring to a boil. Lower heat, cover, and simmer for 15 minutes. Cool slightly.

Puree vegetable-stock mixture in a blender or food processor in several batches. Stir in cream and hot pepper sauce, and chill soup for several hours. While soup is chilling, puree parsley in a blender or food processor with cold water until liquefied. Set aside. Soak saffron in 2 tablespoons of boiling water for 30 minutes.

When ready to serve, ladle chilled white soup into a flat soup bowl. Using a ¼-teaspoon measuring spoon, stir and dip into the green parsley liquid, and trickle a large initial on the surface of the soup. The green liquid will float, allowing you to make any letter of the alphabet. Using another small spoon, trace either a dotted or striped border with the yellow saffron liquid along the sides of the bowl. Use your imagination. Use small pinches of bright red paprika to make tiny red accents. Repeat for each guest.

Provencal Garlic Soup with Sage, Thyme, and Cloves

4 servings

Although this rich herb and spice soup contains a liberal amount of garlic, it is not the least bit assertive, since it is simmered gently and balanced properly.

      8 cups chicken stock
    24 small cloves garlic, peeled
           and coarsely chopped
      1 dried bay leaf
      4 whole cloves
      6 sprigs fresh thyme
10 to 12 fresh sage leaves
           pinch of saffron
      2 egg yolks
     ¼ cup olive oil
      8 slices French bread
      2 tablespoons butter, melted
 2 to 3 tablespoons Parmesan cheese
 3 to 4 drops of hot pepper sauce
      1 tablespoon lemon juice
     ⅓ cup finely minced fresh
           parsley

Heat stock in a 4- to 6-quart pot until boiling. Lower heat, add garlic, and simmer, uncovered, for 5 minutes. Put bay leaf, cloves, thyme, and sage into the center of a small piece of cheesecloth, tie with string, and add to soup along with saffron. Simmer soup, uncovered, for 30 minutes.

Meanwhile, in a small bowl, whisk egg yolks. Add olive oil, a little bit at a time, whisking constantly until fairly thick.

While soup is cooking, spread slices of bread out on a jelly-roll pan in 1 layer. Trickle with melted butter, and sprinkle with Parmesan cheese. Place in a preheated 325°F oven for 15 to 20 minutes, or until crisp and dry.

When soup is cooked, remove cheesecloth bag, and strain. Pour 1 cup of the soup and the cooked garlic into a blender or food processor, and puree. Then add this mixture to egg and oil emulsion, whisking constantly. Return to pot with remaining soup, and heat over very low heat, stirring occasionally. (Do not allow to boil.) Add hot pepper sauce and lemon juice. Ladle into soup bowls, sprinkle liberally with parsley, and float 2 slices of the Parmesan cheese toast on top.

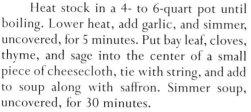

Roasted Sweet Red Pepper Soup with Gorgonzola Cheese and Garlic Chives

4 servings

This dazzling scarlet soup can be served either hot or cold.

- 5 large sweet red peppers, roasted
- 4 tablespoons olive oil
- 4 cloves garlic, peeled and minced (about 1 tablespoon)
- 5 cups chicken stock
- 2 tablespoons finely minced fresh parsley
- ¼ teaspoon black pepper
- 2 tablespoons red wine vinegar
- 2 tablespoons finely minced fresh garlic chives
- 2 tablespoons crumbled Gorgonzola cheese

Prepare red peppers (see Note that follows), and set aside.

In a heavy 6-quart pot, heat oil over medium heat. Add garlic, and saute for about 1 minute. Do not let garlic brown or it will be bitter. Add chicken stock, bring to a boil, and then reduce heat to a simmer. Stir in parsley and black pepper. Simmer for 15 to 20 minutes.

Puree red peppers in a blender or food processor, then add them to pot, and simmer for 5 to 10 minutes more. Remove from heat, and stir in vinegar. Sprinkle individual servings with garlic chives and cheese.

Note: To Prepare and Roast Sweet Red Peppers:
If you have a gas stove, turn jets to "high," and then lay a pepper on each burning jet. When the pepper's surface is charred and black, turn with tongs to char the other side. It takes only a few minutes. Place roasted peppers in a brown paper bag, close tightly, and let accumulated steam loosen skin. Allow to cool while in bag to make for easier handling. If you have an electric stove, use the broiler to do the job.

Using the point of a small, sharp knife, cut a small circle around the stem and seeds. Cut pepper in half lengthwise, and rinse off charred skin and any remaining seeds under cold water. Dry well on paper towels.

Radish and Scallion Soup with Mint

4 servings

4 cups chicken stock
2 cups sliced scallions (cut diagonally
    into ½-inch pieces with ½ cup
    green tops reserved)
¼ cup cream (sweet, sour, or creme
    fraiche)
2 teaspoons lemon juice
2 dashes of hot pepper sauce
6 radishes, sliced paper-thin
1 tablespoon finely minced fresh mint

Heat chicken stock in a 2-quart sauce-pan. When it begins to boil, add 1½ cups scallions, and cook over medium heat for 15 minutes. Remove from stove, and puree in a blender or food processor, a few batches at a time. Return to same saucepan and reheat. Add cream, lemon juice, and hot pepper sauce. Lower heat, and stir well. (Do not allow to boil.) Add reserved scallion tops and slices of radish. Ladle into individual bowls, and sprinkle each with mint.

Garlic was used as a stimulant by Roman soldiers before they went into battle. And the Egyptians who built the pyramids gained strength by eating garlic—laced with onions!

Spanish Codfish Soup with Orange, Saffron, and Parsley

4 servings

The flavor of orange is frequently used in Spain the way we use lemon. Here, with saffron and parsley, this fish soup has a subtle blend of flavors.

½ teaspoon saffron threads
1 cup boiling water
2 tablespoons olive oil
⅔ cup finely chopped onions (about 1
    medium onion)
½ cup finely chopped fennel bulb
    (about ½ small bulb)
1 tablespoon finely minced garlic
1 pound codfish steaks
¼ teaspoon black pepper
1 teaspoon fresh thyme leaves
⅛ teaspoon powdered bay leaves or 1
    whole dried bay leaf (remove
    before serving)
1 can (14 ounces) Italian plum
    tomatoes with liquid
1 cup water
1 heaping teaspoon grated orange rind
¼ cup plus 2 tablespoons coarsely
    chopped fresh parsley
½ cup orange juice

Soak saffron in boiling water for 30 minutes.

In a 5-quart Dutch oven, heat oil. When oil is hot, add onions, fennel, and garlic, and cook over medium heat, while stirring, for 3 to 4 minutes. Add fish, and cook for 1 minute on each side. Sprinkle with pepper, thyme, and powdered bay leaves or whole dried bay leaf. Add saffron water, tomatoes and liquid, water, and orange rind, and bring to a boil. Stir in ¼ cup of the parsley, cover, lower heat, and simmer for 5 to 8 minutes, or until fish flakes when tested with the point of a knife. Remove fish with a slotted spoon, set aside to cool, and continue to simmer soup for 20 minutes more. While soup is simmering, remove skin and bones from fish. At the end of the 20-minute simmering period, return chunks of fish to soup along with orange juice. Simmer for 5 minutes longer, and just before serving, sprinkle with remaining parsley.

Sorrel Soup with Poached Herbed Egg White Puffs (Potage Germiny a la Neige)

4 to 6 servings

Chive-flecked poached egg whites float on this pale green, tartly refreshing hot or cold soup.

SOUP

- ½ pound fresh sorrel
- 1 tablespoon butter
- 1 cup coarsely chopped leeks
- 1 medium-size potato, diced
- 4 cups chicken stock
- 1 egg yolk, beaten
- ¼ teaspoon hot pepper sauce
  leftover milk from poached egg white puffs

PUFFS

- 2 egg whites
- ¼ teaspoon cream of tartar
- ¼ teaspoon cornstarch
  dash of cayenne pepper
- 2 tablespoons finely minced fresh chives
- 1½ cups simmering milk

To make the soup: Fold sorrel leaves in half, and with a sharp knife, cut out and discard entire leaf stem. Shred the tender leafy parts, and set aside. There should be about 4 cups.

Melt butter in a 4-quart saucepan. (A nonstick or enamel-lined pot should be used. Do not use aluminum.) Add leeks and potatoes, stir, and cook over medium heat for 1 minute. Add sorrel, and stir with a wooden spoon until wilted. Add stock, and bring to a boil. Lower heat, and simmer for 20 minutes. Cool slightly.

Puree soup in a blender or food processor, a few batches at a time. Return to pot, and stir in egg yolk and hot pepper sauce, but do not reheat yet.

To make the puffs: Beat egg whites in a medium-size bowl with a hand beater until foamy. Add cream of tartar, cornstarch, and cayenne, and continue to beat until stiff. Add chives, and beat again for a few turns of the egg beater.

The milk should be simmering in a wide-bottom skillet. Skim away any skin that forms on surface of milk. Using a soup spoon, scoop up heaping spoonfuls of egg whites, and carefully place them into milk, using a rubber spatula to slide puffs from the spoon into milk. Do not let them touch while cooking. Poach puffs slowly for 4 to 5 minutes on each side, turning carefully with 2 spoons when one side is poached.

While puffs are poaching, reheat soup slowly. Remove puffs with a slotted spoon, and place them on a flat dish. Strain milk (there should be about ⅔ cup), and stir into soup. Serve each bowl topped with 2 puffs.

When sorrel is in season, you can freeze it for future use. Just strip the sorrel of its center stem, puree the leaves, and freeze. Use it for a sorrel soup or as a sauce for fish.

Spanish Almond and Grape Soup with Tarragon

4 servings

Refreshing as a breeze on a hot day, this icy white soup is subtle and tantalizing.

    1   cup blanched almonds, toasted
    2   large cloves garlic, peeled
    1   large roll or 3 thick slices bread
    2½ cups ice water, divided
    ⅓   cup olive oil
    3   tablespoons tarragon vinegar
    ⅛   teaspoon white pepper
    1½ tablespoons fresh tarragon, coarsely
          chopped
    2   tablespoons thinly sliced almonds,
          toasted
    ¾   cup seedless green grapes

Place almonds and garlic into a blender or food processor, and blend until finely ground.

Soak bread in water, then squeeze out well, tear into pieces, and add to blender or food processor along with 1 cup of ice water. With machine on, slowly add olive oil and then vinegar and pepper. Transfer mixture to a bowl, and stir in remaining 1½ cups of ice water. Chill until very cold.

Chill soup bowls. When ready to serve, stir in tarragon, reserving a few pinches for garnish. Sprinkle each bowl of soup with sliced almonds, a few grapes, and tarragon.

Springtime Soup

6 servings

The color of this soup is the same as the first new growth of spring. The fresh herbs add warmth and nuance to the sweetness of the peas.

    3   tablespoons butter
    2 to 3 scallions, coarsely chopped
            (about 1 cup)
    1   head of leaf lettuce, chopped
            (about 2 cups)
    ¼   teaspoon black pepper
    2   cups fresh or frozen peas
    5   cups chicken stock
    2   tablespoons finely minced
            fresh mint
    1   teaspoon finely minced fresh
            chervil
    1   teaspoon finely minced fresh
            basil
    ½   teaspoon finely minced fresh
            marjoram
    ½   teaspoon fresh thyme leaves
    1   teaspoon grated lemon rind
    3   tablespoons light cream
    2 or 3 drops of hot pepper sauce
    3 or 4 leaves of fresh spinach, shredded

Melt butter in a 4-quart pot. Add scallions, lettuce, and pepper, and cook, stirring constantly, for 1 to 2 minutes, or until wilted. Stir in peas, then add stock, and bring to a boil. Lower heat, and simmer for 5 minutes. Add all the fresh herbs, and cook for 30 seconds more. Puree in a blender or food processor, a few batches at a time, then return to pot, and heat slowly. Stir in lemon rind, cream, and hot pepper sauce. Serve with shredded spinach as a garnish.

Tomato and Cucumber Soup with Basil, Mint, and Yogurt

4 servings

This soup depends upon ripe, fresh tomatoes for its flavor. It is subtly flavored with basil, enhanced by the additional sparkle of mint, and served very cold. A delight for lunch on a hot day, it can also be served as a first course for dinner.

1 tablespoon olive oil
1 cup coarsely chopped onions
3 large ripe tomatoes (about 2 pounds), peeled and cubed
1 medium carrot, sliced
1 cup chicken stock
1 cup cubed cucumber
1 tablespoon tomato paste
1 teaspoon paprika
 small pinch of cayenne pepper
6 large fresh basil leaves, torn into pieces
1 cup plain yogurt
1 tablespoon finely chopped fresh mint

Heat oil in a 4-quart pot. Add onions, and saute over medium heat, stirring for 5 minutes, or until wilted but not brown. Add tomatoes, carrots, and chicken stock, and bring to a boil. Lower heat, add cucumbers, tomato paste, paprika, cayenne, and basil, and simmer for 15 minutes. Cool slightly, and puree in a blender or food processor, adding yogurt to the blender as well. Chill and serve ice cold, sprinkled with mint.

Note: If the tomatoes are too acidic for your taste, add a bit of mild honey to counterbalance the tartness.

Wild and Tame Mushroom Soup with Tarragon and Nasturtium

4 to 6 servings

This soup is excellent when served ice cold. If you prefer your soup hot, heat over low heat so that the sour cream does not curdle.

4 to 5 dried mushrooms (porcini, cepes, or chanterelle)
¾ cup boiling water
1 medium potato, peeled, cubed, and cooked until tender
½ pound fresh mushrooms
1 tablespoon butter
½ cup chopped leeks, white part only
4 cups chicken stock
1 teaspoon finely minced fresh tarragon
¾ cup sour cream
 paprika
4 to 6 nasturtium blossoms, whole or torn into pieces
4 to 6 small sprigs of fresh tarragon (optional)

Place dried mushrooms into a measuring cup, and pour boiling water over them. Let stand for 20 minutes. Strain into another cup using a fine mesh strainer. Rinse mushrooms well under cold water to remove any grit, and return to cup with reserved mushroom liquid. Puree mushrooms and liquid, potato, and fresh mushrooms in a blender or food processor until fine, and set aside.

Melt butter in a 5-quart saucepan. Add leeks, and saute, stirring until wilted. Add chicken stock and reserved mushroom-potato puree, bring to a boil, lower heat, and simmer for 5 minutes. Remove from heat, add tarragon, and let cool to lukewarm. Whisk in sour cream, and chill until serving time. Just before serving, sprinkle surface with paprika. Garnish with nasturtium blossoms and tarragon sprigs, if desired.

Sour Eggplant Soup with Chick-peas, Lentils, and Mint

6 servings

A lemony, chunky soup that is cooled with mint.

- 3 tablespoons olive oil
- 2 small leeks with 1 inch of green part (about 1 cup), chopped coarsely
- 1 tablespoon finely minced garlic
- 1 large eggplant (about 1 pound), peeled and cut into 1-inch pieces
- 1 can (28 ounces) Italian plum tomatoes
- 3 cups chicken stock
- ½ cup dried lentils
- 1 can (15½ ounces) chick-peas, drained and rinsed
- ½ teaspoon black pepper
- ½ teaspoon dried thyme
- ¼ cup lemon juice (1 to 2 lemons)
- 3 tablespoons coarsely chopped fresh mint

Heat oil in a heavy 6-quart pot. Add leeks and garlic, and saute over medium heat, stirring, until wilted but not brown, about 5 minutes. Add all remaining ingredients, except lemon juice and mint, and bring to a boil. Lower heat, cover, and simmer for 45 minutes. When ready to serve, stir in lemon juice and mint.

Three-Bean Soup with Pasta and Basil

8 servings

- ¾ cup dried pea beans
- 12 cups water
- 3 tablespoons Barth's Nutra Instant Chicken Soup
- 2 potatoes (about 1 pound), cut into 1-inch cubes
- 4 to 5 medium-size ripe tomatoes, peeled and cubed
- 1 pound mixed yellow squash and zucchini, cut into 1-inch pieces
- 1½ pounds lima beans, or 1 package (10 ounces) frozen lima beans
- ½ pound string beans, cut in half diagonally
- 3 cloves garlic, peeled
- 14 to 16 large fresh basil leaves
- 3 tablespoons olive oil
- 2 ounces thin capellini or vermicelli pasta
- ¼ teaspoon black pepper

Put beans and water into a 6-quart pot. Bring to a boil, cover, and simmer for 40 minutes. Add Nutra Soup and potatoes, and simmer, covered, for 30 minutes more. Add tomatoes, squash, zucchini, lima beans, and string beans, and simmer for 45 additional minutes.

During the last 15 minutes that the soup is simmering, chop garlic in a food processor. Add basil to the food processor, and then slowly add olive oil to make a slightly thick sauce. Set aside.

When ready to serve, add pasta, and simmer for 2 to 3 minutes. Add basil sauce and pepper. Serve hot.

SALADS & DRESSINGS

← Fresh ingredients for Tofu, Avocado, Calendula Petals, and Chive Salad with Ginger-Lime Dressing (page 111)

For a great many years, the main point of discussion concerning a salad was whether to serve it *before* the main course (as they do in California), *after* the main course (as in Europe), or even *with* the main course, which some of us most prefer. Salads were all pretty much the same anyway — lettuce and tomatoes. Rather dull. But today, the often-ignored salad has acquired a new importance.

One reason for this is the proliferation of salad bars in restaurants across the country, where we can choose the ingredients we like best or try new ones that look interesting. Salad bars can also be found at many local produce markets, where busy young people stop after work to select what will be their easy-to-prepare nutritious dinner.

The salad — when it includes additional ingredients, such as vegetables, meat, fish, and certainly flowers and herbs — can also serve as a main course at lunch or dinner. Match it to the proper dressing, perhaps one infused with garlic or tinged with tarragon or sharpened with mustard, and it makes a satisfying meal.

Try for interesting color contrasts and flavor combinations when composing a salad. If you're using beets and radishes, for example, choose yellow tomatoes instead of red ones and *green* peppers to provide relief from red. The crunch of kale is a nice foil for mild, tender garden lettuce; use spicy green garden cress to enhance mild-flavored reddish beet greens. Calendula petals, nasturtium blossoms, or violets also add variety in color and flavor.

When you make the dressing for a salad, add herbs or spices to the vinegar before adding the oil; the acid helps to release the flavor and aroma. If you are using dried herbs, crush them between your fingers to awaken the fragrance, then soak them in the vinegar for about 30 minutes before adding the oil. Mayonnaise and cooked dressings also benefit from the addition of herbs and spices. Three tablespoons of freshly chopped herbs, or 1 tablespoon of crushed dried herbs, to 1 cup of dressing works well.

Don't overdress the salad. Generally, 3 or 4 tablespoons of dressing are ample for 1 quart of prepared greens.

Belgian Endive, Frilled Chicory, and Mustard Greens with Orange and Mint

4 servings

SALAD

3 cups frilled chicory, torn into bite-size pieces
1 cup mustard greens, leaves only (We use a variety called "Mizuna" from our garden, but any young mustard leaves will do)
1 cup Belgian endive, torn into bite-size pieces
1 tablespoon finely minced fresh mint
2 navel oranges
a few black olives
1 sprig of fresh mint

DRESSING

2 teaspoons red wine vinegar
¼ cup reserved orange juice
¼ cup safflower or olive oil
¼ teaspoon paprika

To make the salad: In a large bowl, mix all the greens and mint together. Cut 1 orange in half and squeeze juice from one half for dressing. There should be about ¼ cup. Set aside.

Peel remaining 1½ oranges, and remove white pith. Then thinly slice the whole orange, and set aside. Cut up remaining half orange into tiny pieces, add to greens, and toss.

Pour 3 tablespoons orange dressing over greens mixture. Then top greens with a ring of the orange slices. Place black olives in the center, and garnish with sprig of mint.

To make the dressing: In a small bowl, mix all the ingredients together with a wire whisk. It should make ½ cup of dressing.

Bibb Lettuce with Chervil Lemon-Cream Dressing

4 servings

The tart lemony dressing is prepared one hour before and then spooned over tiny individual heads of lettuce that look like large flowers on the plates.

DRESSING

2 tablespoons heavy cream
1 tablespoon mayonnaise
1 tablespoon lemon juice
½ teaspoon light honey
1 tablespoon finely minced fresh chervil
pinch of celery seeds

SALAD

4 small heads of Bibb lettuce

To make the dressing: Mix all ingredients together in a small bowl, and let stand at room temperature for 1 hour to allow the flavors to blend.

To make the salad: Wash lettuce well under cold running water. Dry upside down on paper towels. Place on a fresh paper towel after cutting a tiny slice off core. Refrigerate until chilled. The lettuce will fall open into a flowerlike pattern. Help it along by opening the outer leaves. Serve on individual chilled plates, and spoon 1 tablespoon dressing over each head.

Italian Sweet Pepper Salad
with Basil and Mint (page 99)

Bread, Red Onion, Tomato, Cucumber, and Mint Salad

4 to 6 servings

DRESSING

- 1 to 2 cloves garlic, peeled and finely minced
- ¼ cup lemon juice
- ½ cup plain yogurt
- ⅛ teaspoon black pepper
- 3 tablespoons olive oil
- ¼ cup finely minced fresh mint
- ¼ cup finely minced fresh parsley

SALAD

- 1 large burpless cucumber, cut into ¾-inch pieces
- 2 large ripe tomatoes, cut into ¾-inch pieces
- 1 cup bite-size pieces whole wheat pita bread or any whole wheat bread
- 1 bunch watercress, tough stems removed
- ¼ cup thinly sliced red onions (scallions may be substituted)

To make the dressing: Mix all the ingredients together in a small bowl, and refrigerate for at least 1 hour or overnight to let the flavors mellow.

To make the salad: Toss all ingredients together in a large bowl. Just before serving, pour dressing over salad, and toss again.

Add a slice of lemon, a clove of crushed garlic, a hot dried pepper pod—or all three—to an aromatic herb oil.

Celery Root Salad Remoulade with Paprika and Shrimp

6 to 8 servings

You can serve this dish as a salad or as an hors d'oeuvre. Celery root, sometimes called celeriac, is a favorite of ours—served alone or tossed with small shrimp.

SALAD

- 2 cups water
- ½ cup white vinegar
- 1 pound celery root
- 1 tablespoon tarragon vinegar
- 2 tablespoons olive oil
- ¼ teaspoon white pepper
- ¼ teaspoon dry mustard

REMOULADE

- ¾ cup mayonnaise
- 1 tablespoon French-style mustard
- 1 teaspoon capers, rinsed and dried (optional)
- 1 teaspoon finely minced fresh chives pinch of crushed dried tarragon
- 1 tablespoon finely minced fresh parsley or watercress
- ¼ teaspoon dry mustard
- ⅛ teaspoon paprika
- ⅛ teaspoon freshly ground black pepper

- ¼ pound tiny shrimp, cooked, peeled, and deveined (optional)

To make the salad: In a 3-quart saucepan, boil water and white vinegar together. Peel celery root, and cut into matchsticks (julienne strips). Add all at once to boiling vinegar-water mixture. Cook for 30 seconds, drain, and place into a medium-size bowl. In a cup, mix tarragon vinegar, oil, pepper, and dry mustard together. Pour over warm celery root, and toss. Refrigerate overnight or for several hours.

To make the remoulade: Mix all the ingredients except shrimp (if used) together in a medium-size bowl and chill. Then, add to celery root along with shrimp (if used), toss, and return to refrigerator to chill for 1 to 2 hours to blend flavors. Serve on lettuce leaves if you wish, with an additional sprinkle of paprika and parsley for color.

Chick-pea Salad with Chervil, Tarragon, and Oregano

4 servings

- 2 cups cooked chick-peas, drained or 1 can (16 ounces) chick-peas, rinsed and drained
- 1 tablespoon finely minced fresh parsley
- 1 tablespoon finely minced fresh chervil
- ½ teaspoon finely minced fresh tarragon
- ½ teaspoon finely minced fresh oregano
- ¾ cup coarsely chopped scallions
- ½ teaspoon finely minced garlic
- 1 tablespoon nonpareil capers, rinsed, dried, and coarsely chopped (optional)

¼ teaspoon black pepper, or more to
　taste
¼ cup tarragon vinegar
1 teaspoon French-style mustard
3 tablespoons olive oil
　lettuce leaves

Mix together chick-peas, herbs, scallions, garlic, capers (if used), and pepper in a medium-size bowl. In a measuring cup, mix vinegar with mustard until mustard is dissolved. Mix in olive oil. Pour dressing over seasoned chick-peas, and stir well. Do not chill. Let stand at room temperature for 2 hours before serving on a bed of lettuce leaves.

Pliny recommended drinking the vinegar in which chervil seeds are soaked as a cure for hiccups.

Chinese Shredded Chicken Salad with Cucumber and Ginger Root

4 servings

This salad can be prepared several hours ahead and kept chilled in the refrigerator. For optimum flavor, bring it to room temperature before serving.

SALAD

½ pound cooked boneless chicken
　breasts, cut into long thin
　strips
1 carrot, sliced into thin shreds
　with a vegetable peeler
3 scallions, cut diagonally into
　1-inch pieces

1 to 2 cucumbers (about ½ pound),
　cut into quarters lengthwise,
　seeded, and sliced into thin
　crescent shapes
5 to 6 leaves of young mustard greens
　or Chinese cabbage
2 teaspoons sesame seeds, toasted
1 tablespoon slivered almonds,
　toasted
1 tablespoon whole fresh cilantro
　leaves

DRESSING

1½ tablespoons light soy sauce
1½ tablespoons rice vinegar
1½ tablespoons corn or peanut oil
1 teaspoon Oriental sesame oil
1 teaspoon hot chili oil
½ teaspoon mild honey
¼ teaspoon fennel seeds
1 scant tablespoon finely minced
　peeled ginger root

To make the salad: Arrange chicken, carrots, scallions, cucumbers, and mustard greens or cabbage in stripes on a large serving platter. Sprinkle sesame seeds over cucumbers and almonds over chicken. Scatter cilantro leaves over all, and chill while preparing dressing.

To make the dressing: Mix all the ingredients together in a cup, and spoon evenly over salad.

Ginger, saffron, and garlic were all widely used during the Middle Ages as weapons in the battle against the Black Death. Another remedy tried against the Plague was to cloud patients' rooms with the smoke of burning sage.

Cucumber and Feta Cheese Salad with Dill

4 servings

The cheese is pureed with the dressing for this salad and then brightened with lemon juice.

½ pound feta cheese
¼ cup lemon juice (about 1½ lemons)
3 tablespoons olive oil
2 tablespoons water
⅓ cup thinly sliced scallions, green part only
⅓ cup finely diced green peppers
4 cups cucumbers, cut into ½-inch slices, then into quarters
2 tablespoons minced fresh dill
⅛ teaspoon black pepper
1 tomato, cut into quarters

In a blender or food processor, puree cheese, lemon juice, oil, and water. Remove to a medium-size bowl. Add scallions, green peppers, and cucumbers, and toss. Sprinkle with dill and black pepper. Garnish with tomato quarters.

Endive and Watercress Salad with Walnuts and Pansies

4 servings

A touch of exotica lifts this salad above the ordinary. The pansies give it a burst of color and a delicate flavor.

DRESSING

1 tablespoon red wine vinegar
3 tablespoons walnut oil
few grains of cayenne pepper
⅛ teaspoon black pepper

SALAD

½ bunch watercress, tough stems removed
2 large heads of Belgian endive, cut into ½-inch strips about 2 inches long
1 tablespoon finely minced fresh chives
¼ cup coarsely broken walnuts, toasted
12 pansies, stems removed

To make the dressing: In a small bowl, mix all the ingredients together with a wire whisk, and set aside.

To make the salad: Toss watercress, endive, and chives together in a glass serving bowl. Sprinkle with walnuts, arrange pansies on the surface, and chill. When ready to serve, pour dressing on salad at the table, and toss lightly.

Green and Yellow Bean Salad with Saffron, Basil, and Pine Nuts

4 servings

A summery salad to make when young green beans and basil are at their peak.

¾ pound green beans
¾ pound yellow wax beans
3 tablespoons lemon juice
¼ cup olive oil

⅛ teaspoon black pepper
2 threads of saffron, crushed
3 tablespoons finely shredded fresh
    basil leaves
2 tablespoons pine nuts, toasted

Cut beans diagonally into 2-inch pieces. Steam for 4 minutes, or until crisp/tender. Mix lemon juice, oil, pepper, and saffron together in a small bowl. Place beans into a medium-size bowl, and mix with dressing. Add basil and pine nuts, and toss. Refrigerate for several hours, and then bring to room temperature before serving.

Coarsely cut onion slices. Steam beans until crisp/tender, 3 to 5 minutes. While still hot, place in a medium-size bowl, and add all ingredients except cheese. Let stand at room temperature for 1 hour or longer, mixing occasionally. When ready to serve, transfer to a serving dish, and sprinkle with cheese.

Green Bean Salad with Gruyere Cheese and Summer Savory

4 servings

This dish can be prepared well in advance and served at room temperature.

¼ cup thinly sliced red onions
1 pound green beans, cut into
    2-inch pieces
⅓ cup olive oil
1½ tablespoons red wine vinegar
1 teaspoon finely minced fresh
    marjoram
¼ teaspoon black pepper
1 tablespoon finely minced fresh
    summer savory
½ cup shredded Gruyere cheese

Italian Sweet Pepper Salad with Basil and Mint

4 servings

3 large sweet peppers (1 green, 1 red,
    1 yellow), roasted (page 85)
1 medium clove garlic, peeled
1 large ripe tomato, peeled and cubed
3 tablespoons olive oil
¼ teaspoon lemon pepper
1 tablespoon minced fresh basil
1 tablespoon minced fresh mint,
    divided
1 tablespoon capers, rinsed and dried
    (optional)

Cut peppers into ½-inch strips. Chop garlic in a food processor. Add tomatoes, oil, and lemon pepper, and puree. Place peppers in a medium-size glass bowl, and pour puree over them. Add basil and half of the mint, mix well, and let stand at room temperature for 1 hour. Sprinkle with remaining mint and capers (if used), and serve with crusty bread.

Mesclun au Provence

4 servings

Mesclun is traditionally served in the south of France. It's a combination of 11 different varieties of greens—some sweet, some peppery—and can be grown in any garden in cool weather. You can order the seed from Le Jardin du Gourmet, West Danville, VT 05873.

DRESSING

 2 tablespoons red wine vinegar
 2 teaspoons dijon mustard
 3 tablespoons olive oil
 2 tablespoons walnut oil
 ¼ teaspoon black pepper

SALAD

 5 cups mesclun, torn into bite-size pieces
 2 tablespoons finely minced fresh chervil
   or if you don't have a garden, substitute this combination:
 ½ cup arugula leaves
 ½ cup watercress leaves
 1½ cups Bibb, romaine, or frilled green-leaf lettuce
 2 cups chicory, dandelion, and endive
 ½ cup corn salad

To make the dressing: In a small bowl, beat ingredients with a wire whisk until slightly thickened. Let stand for 10 minutes to develop flavor.

To make the salad: In a large bowl, toss greens with 3 tablespoons dressing. Reserve the rest of the dressing for another salad.

Moroccan Radish and Orange Salad with Mint

4 servings

A refreshing, soothing, simple salad to accompany and cool any spicy main dish.

 2 large navel oranges
   juice of 1 large lemon (about ¼ cup)
 2 teaspoons light honey
 2 bunches red radishes (¾ to 1 pound)
 12 soft lettuce leaves (Bibb or Boston)
 1 tablespoon finely minced fresh mint or 1 teaspoon dried mint

Peel oranges carefully so that none of the white bitter pith remains. Divide into sections, cut each section into 2 or 3 small pieces, and set aside. Mix lemon juice and honey together in a cup, and set aside. Coarsely shred radishes. (This can be done in a few seconds using a food processor with the shredding blade.) In a medium-size bowl, mix radishes and orange sections with lemon-honey dressing, and mound on salad plates lined with lettuce. Distribute mint evenly over each portion. *Serve at once.* If salad is allowed to stand, liquid will accumulate at the bottom of the plate.

Oriental Shrimp Salad with Sugar Snap Peas and Ginger Root

4 servings

This light, refreshing luncheon salad or first course leaves your taste buds with a hint of the Far East.

And, for those with gardens, the bounty of sugar snap peas makes this a perfect dish for family or guests. If sugar snap peas are not available to you, substitute snow peas.

DRESSING

    2 tablespoons lemon juice
    1 tablespoon safflower oil
    ½ teaspoon soy sauce
    1 teaspoon finely minced peeled
          ginger root

SALAD

    2 cups water
    1 teaspoon pickling spice
    ½ pound medium-size raw shrimp
    5 cups torn leaf lettuce (bite-size
          pieces)
    1 cup bean sprouts
  1½ cups blanched sugar snap peas
    ½ bunch watercress, tough stems
          removed

To make the dressing: Mix all ingredients together in a cup, and let stand while preparing salad.

To make the salad: In a large saucepan, bring water and spices to a boil. Add shrimp, and cook for 1 minute. Drain, cool, peel and devein shrimp, and cut them in half. Set aside to chill.

Arrange torn leaf lettuce on the outer edge of a large, flat serving dish. Working toward the center of the dish, scatter a ring of bean sprouts, then sugar snap peas, then watercress, ending with chilled shrimp in the center. At the table, spoon dressing over all, and toss.

Plum Tomatoes Stuffed with Spinach, Yogurt, and Mint

4 servings

Mint and yogurt add a refreshing note to this colorful combination.

4 or 5 small plum tomatoes
    1 pound fresh spinach, stems
          removed
    1 tablespoon olive oil
    2 tablespoons pine nuts
    2 tablespoons finely minced
          shallots
    1 small clove garlic, peeled and
          finely minced
    1 tablespoon finely minced fresh
          mint
    ⅛ teaspoon ground nutmeg
    ¼ teaspoon black pepper
    ½ cup plain yogurt
          additional plain yogurt
4 or 5 sprigs of fresh mint

Cut tomatoes crosswise in saw-toothed fashion, scoop out pulp, and set aside. Shred spinach, and set aside.

Heat oil in a large skillet over moderate heat. Add pine nuts, and cook, stirring, for 1 to 2 minutes, or until tan. Remove with a slotted spoon, and set aside. To the same skillet, add shallots and garlic, and saute, stirring, for 1 to 2 minutes. Add spinach to skillet, lower heat, and stir until wilted. Stir in mint, nutmeg, pepper, and reserved pine nuts. Cool for a few minutes, then drain in a sieve, pressing out excess liquid. Stir in yogurt. Stuff tomatoes with spinach mixture. Top each with a bit of additional yogurt and a sprig of mint. Serve at room temperature.

Gary Waldron of Glie Farms

An Herb Garden in the South Bronx, New York

The *Wall Street Journal* headlined their story on Glie Farms, "Urban Herbs: Why Rosemary and Basil Ride on the Subway." They have been featured in The *New York Daily News,* in *People* magazine, and on network television. Daily their messengers deliver over 30 varieties of fresh herbs to over 200 of New York's prime eating establishments including La Cirque, The Quilted Giraffe, Lutece, Tavern on the Green, and La Grenouille. Several large supermarket chains are also on the list in order to make the herb harvest readily available to consumers all over New York. And this agrarian success story originated in, of all places, an area of the South Bronx that has been called, among other things, Fort Apache.

The resident genius at Glie (pronounced *glee*) is Gary Waldron, still in his early forties, a former executive at IBM. He took a leave of absence from the corporation for one year to help get the project started. The aim was to organize a business on a $100,000 grant intended to provide work opportunity for the young people of the neighborhood, with its rock-strewn empty lots and burned-out shells of buildings. After a year, Waldron decided to leave IBM and to devote all his time and energy to making Glie turn a profit and expand into a growing endeavor.

Potato Salad with Nasturtium Leaves

4 to 6 servings

This is a lovely and interesting variation of the ubiquitous luncheon potato salad.

1½ pounds small unpeeled new
   potatoes
½ cup finely chopped scallions
⅓ cup finely diced celery
1 carrot, shredded (about ½ cup)
¼ cup finely minced fresh parsley
5 nasturtium leaves, finely minced
⅓ cup apple cider vinegar
⅓ cup mayonnaise
2 heaping tablespoons sour cream
   freshly ground black pepper, to
   taste
   leaf lettuce

Has it worked? We've gotten lots of support from outside capital. We've built a new greenhouse that takes up most of a city block, and all our herbs are hydroponically grown.

Professor Harry Janes of Rutgers University calls it the most advanced system in the country for growing herbs. The plants, imbedded in lava rock and stacked on A-frame racks, are fed by a computer-controlled system that determines the right amount of water and nutrients as well as the correct temperature for the optimum growth of the herbs.

We now have 53 employees here in the Bronx, mostly black and Hispanic people who live right here in the neighborhood. We also employ 20 people in Puerto Rico where we're developing a 200-acre farm so that we can grow herbs outdoors all year round.

Glie now grows about 80,000 pounds of herbs a year, and in a typical day they ship over 200 pounds of basil and 100 pounds of tarragon.

Actually, it was a matter of recognizing the market. We saw the potential as more and more restaurants, more menus, more cooking articles were calling for the use of fresh herbs. That's also why we're now in supermarkets and in the mail-order business. We've become the largest year-round nursery in the state of New York.

Glie, incidentally, stands for *Group Live-in Experience,* the name of a non-profit community organization that deals with abused and runaway children, on whose board Waldron sat. We must add, finally, that we have a special affinity for Glie since Mel was born right in that South Bronx neighborhood (on Charlotte Street). We also have another reason for feeling close to the Fort Apache nursery since they supplied many of the herbs for the testing of our recipes at the Rodale Test Kitchen in Emmaus, Pennsylvania.

1 hard-boiled egg, peeled and
 quartered
2 tablespoons finely minced fresh
 chives

Place potatoes into a medium-size saucepan and add enough water to cover. Bring water to a boil, lower heat, and simmer until tender, about 15 minutes. Drain, and cool just enough so that you can peel and quarter them. While potatoes are still warm, combine with scallions, celery, carrots, parsley, and nasturtium leaves in a large bowl. Toss with vinegar while still warm, and let stand at room temperature for 20 minutes.

In a cup, mix mayonnaise, sour cream, and pepper together, and toss with potato mixture. Chill in refrigerator for 2 to 3 hours before serving. Line a serving bowl with leaf lettuce, spoon salad into the center, garnish with egg quarters, and sprinkle with chives.

Ripe Tomatoes 8 Easy Ways

8 servings

Choose your most beautifully globe-shaped and succulent tomatoes. Cut them into imaginative shapes, and fill them with a variety of different fillings or several of the same kind. You can make one of each for your buffet table, or make several of the same kind. They look gorgeous any way you choose to prepare them.

NUMBER ONE

  1 medium-size ripe tomato
  7 thin slices of cucumber, unpeeled
  1 tablespoon sour cream
  ½ teaspoon finely minced fresh chives
  1 small sprig of fresh dill

Cut out stem of tomato, leaving a 1½-inch opening on top. Cut 7 slits with a very sharp knife, slicing from stem end almost to bottom but not all the way through to the center all around the tomato. Insert 1 slice of cucumber into each slit so that half of it protrudes. Mix sour cream with chives in a cup, and then spoon into opening. Place a sprig of dill on top.

NUMBER TWO

  1 medium-size ripe tomato
  ½ teaspoon oil
  ½ teaspoon vinegar
3 to 4 small sprigs of fresh watercress
3 to 4 small cherry tomatoes

Cut tomato crosswise one-quarter of the way down. Scoop out the center of the large bottom part, leaving a deep cup shape. Chop pulp, and mix with oil and vinegar in a small bowl. Line tomato cup with watercress sprigs, spoon tomato pulp back into cup, and top with cherry tomatoes.

NUMBER THREE

  1 medium-size ripe tomato
  1 tablespoon diced avocado
  ½ teaspoon finely minced fresh cilantro
    few drops of lime juice
    few drops of hot pepper sauce

Cut out stem end of tomato, making a 4-leaf-clover shape as you do so. Make a tiny hole in the top of the cut-off end, and insert a sliver of avocado peel to give the appearance of a stem. Set cap aside. Scoop out a small amount of tomato pulp, chop it, and mix in a small bowl with all the remaining ingredients. Stuff tomato with this mixture, and place the clover-shaped cap on top.

NUMBER FOUR

  1 medium-size ripe tomato
  1 tablespoon cream cheese
  ½ teaspoon finely minced red onions
  1 teaspoon mayonnaise
  1 tablespoon finely minced fresh parsley

Cut off stem end and core out tomato. Starting at stem end, peel paper-thin skin from tomato two-thirds of the way down. Don't cut into the fleshy part of the tomato. In a cup, combine cream cheese, red onions, and mayonnaise. Hold tomato in the palm of your hand, and with a small spatula, spread cheese mixture on top and over peeled portion of tomato (like an ice cream cone). (The cheese will adhere to the fleshy part of the tomato but will slip off the skin.) Scatter minced parsley over the cheese mixture.

NUMBER FIVE

    1 medium-size ripe tomato
    1 tablespoon cottage cheese
    ½ teaspoon finely minced fresh
        basil
    1 sprig of fresh basil

Cut off stem end and core out tomato. Then turn tomato upside down and, halfway down, cut tomato crosswise in a saw-tooth fashion, making about 5 or 6 "teeth." Put stem half on a plate, and scoop out pulp. Chop and drain pulp, and add to cheese. Mix in basil. Fill tomato. Make a tiny hole in the center of other half of tomato, and insert a sprig of basil into it. Cap filled half of tomato with this top.

NUMBER SIX

    1 medium-size tomato
        leftover or freshly made cole
        slaw, tuna, chicken, or cold
        fish salad
    1 teaspoon fresh thyme leaves
    1 sprig of fresh thyme

Cut off stem end of tomato. Starting at the center of the other end, cut tomato into 8 pieces, but do not cut quite to the bottom. Scoop out pulp with a spoon, chop, and add to any of the fillings you have chosen. Blend in thyme leaves. Fill tomato, and gently press

wedges back to enclose filling. Garnish with a sprig of fresh thyme.

NUMBER SEVEN

    1 medium-size ripe tomato
    1 tablespoon cream cheese
    2 tablespoons blue cheese
    1 teaspoon finely minced fresh
        chives
    3 to 4 fresh chives, cut into 3-inch
        lengths

Cut out stem of tomato, and slice tomato crosswise into 4 slices. In a cup, mix both cheeses and minced chives together. Starting with the bottom tomato slice, spread on some of the cheese mixture, then top with next slice, repeating until tomato is reassembled. Bend cut chives in middle and tuck into cored-out top.

NUMBER EIGHT

    1 medium-size ripe tomato
        egg salad flavored with 2
        leaves of fresh tarragon or
        filling of your choice
    1 sprig of fresh tarragon

Cut stem end from tomato. Starting at opposite end, cut a spiral shape around tomato three-quarters of the way down. Pull spiral gently aside. Scoop out some pulp from center of tomato, and fill it with egg salad or filling of your choice. Replace spiral top, and tuck sprig of tarragon into top filling.

Romaine with Watercress Dressing

4 servings

A thick pureed dressing with the bite of watercress enlivens this salad.

DRESSING

2 cups watercress leaves, finely chopped
1 tablespoon lemon juice
1 teaspoon tarragon vinegar
¼ teaspoon dijon mustard
½ teaspoon light honey
¼ cup olive oil

SALAD

1 medium-size head of romaine lettuce, torn into bite-size pieces
3 to 4 radishes, sliced paper-thin
1 tablespoon minced fresh chives

To make the dressing: Chop watercress in a food processor. Add remaining ingredients, and puree.

To make the salad: Toss lettuce, radishes, and chives together in a large bowl. Use 3 to 4 tablespoons of dressing, spooning on 1 tablespoon at a time and tossing after each spoonful so that greens are well coated.

Sprout and Flower Salad with Lemon and Mint Dressing

4 servings

This is a gardener's serendipity salad, since you cannot buy herb flowers. The flowers are more pungent than the herbs themselves, and they surprise your palate with tiny bursts of unexpected flavors.

SALAD

5 cups shredded romaine lettuce
½ cup bean sprouts
1 cup alfalfa sprouts

mixed seasonal edible flowers of herbs, vegetables, or ornamentals, such as:
Herb Flowers: borage, marjoram, dill head, thyme, oregano, chive, basil
Vegetable Flowers: arugula, mustard, squash
Edible Ornamental Flowers: pansies, violets, violas, calendula, nasturtium, rose petals

DRESSING

2 tablespoons lemon juice
3 tablespoons safflower oil
⅛ teaspoon black pepper
1 teaspoon finely minced fresh mint

To make the salad: Place shredded lettuce on a large flat platter. Scatter sprouts over the top. Use 1 or 2 blossoms of the wide variety listed above, or any combination that suits your fancy. Scatter the most colorful blossoms on top of the salad.

To make the dressing: Mix all the ingredients together in a small bowl. Pour dressing over salad at the table, toss, and serve.

To add color and surprise as well as flavor to your green salads, snip lavender chive blossoms, white garlic chive blossoms, blue borage blossoms, multihued nasturtium blossoms, orange day lilies, yellow zucchini blossoms, or purple violets, and add just before tossing.

← Bread, Red Onion, Tomato, Cucumber, and Mint Salad (page 95)

Spinach, Mushroom, and Chive Blossom Salad

4 servings

This salad is simple, colorful, and very elegant. The chive blossoms give a delicate onion taste that does not overpower the spinach and mushrooms.

¾ pound fresh spinach, stems removed and torn into bite-size pieces
½ pound fresh mushrooms, sliced paper-thin
3 tablespoons red wine vinegar
¼ cup olive oil
¼ teaspoon black pepper
10 to 12 chive blossoms

Place spinach into a large salad serving bowl. Add mushrooms. In a small bowl, mix vinegar, oil, and pepper together with a fork or small wire whisk. Pour over salad, and toss lightly.

The chive blossoms are composed of tiny lavender flowers, which form a cluster. Separate these tiny flowers from each chive blossom, and scatter them over salad before serving.

Note: If you can find fresh enoki mushrooms, use ¼ pound of them, along with ¼ pound of the regular mushrooms.

Spring Vegetable and New Potato Salad with Cottage Cheese, Dill, and Sorrel

4 servings

1 cup low-fat cottage cheese
1 cup plain yogurt

½ teaspoon finely minced garlic
¼ teaspoon black pepper
1 tablespoon coarsely chopped fresh dill
¼ cup thinly sliced scallions
1½ cups finely shredded fresh sorrel leaves, spines of leaves removed
2 pounds small new potatoes, cooked, peeled, and cut into quarters
1 cup thinly sliced radishes
1 cup julienne cucumbers

In a food processor, mix cheese, yogurt, garlic, and pepper together. Remove to a bowl, and stir in dill, scallions, and sorrel. Mix well and add potatoes. Mix again, cover bowl, and refrigerate for several hours or overnight. Before serving salad, toss with radishes and cucumbers. Garnish with a few additional scallions if you wish.

Tomato Sherbet with Cloves, Bay Leaf, and Thyme

4 to 6 servings

A scoop of frosty, tangy tomato sherbet makes an attractive centerpiece for any salad — fish, chicken, or cottage cheese.

3¼ cups tomato juice, divided
¼ cup sliced scallions (about 1 medium-size scallion)
2 tablespoons tomato paste
⅛ teaspoon hot pepper sauce
¼ cup tarragon vinegar
⅛ teaspoon black pepper
½ teaspoon Worcestershire sauce
¼ teaspoon light honey

Spinach, Mushroom, and
Chive Blossom Salad
(page 108)

1   dried bay leaf
3   sprigs fresh thyme
3   whole cloves
2   teaspoons unflavored gelatin
¼   cup cold water
1   tablespoon lemon juice
2   egg whites

Mix together 1 cup of the tomato juice, scallions, and tomato paste in a blender or food processor until scallions are liquefied. Stir mixture into remaining tomato juice, and pour into a medium-size nonstick saucepan. Add hot pepper sauce, vinegar, pepper, Worcestershire sauce, and honey to tomato juice mixture. Combine bay leaf, thyme, and cloves in a square of cheesecloth, tie, and add to tomato juice mixture. Bring to a boil, then lower heat, and simmer for 10 minutes. Remove herb and spice bag, and discard. Mix gelatin with water, stir until dissolved, and then add to tomato juice mixture. Stir in lemon juice, and pour entire mixture into a 8¼ × 8¼ × 2-inch Pyrex (not metal) baking dish. Cool at room temperature for 10 minutes, and then freeze for 1½ hours.

Beat egg whites in a large bowl until stiff. Then remove tomato mixture from freezer, and break up with a spoon. Whirl in a blender on low speed until mixture is slushy. Fold into beaten egg whites, and spoon into a container to freeze again for at least 2 hours. When ready to serve, soften at room temperature and spoon out portions with an ice cream scoop or a deep spoon. This sherbet keeps well for 3 to 4 weeks in the freezer.

Three Variations on Tomato, Cheese, and Herb Salad

I. Tomato, Feta Cheese, and Dill Salad

4 servings

Prepare and keep at room temperature at least one hour before serving time to blend flavors. Really succulent, ripe tomatoes are best when they're not chilled.

> 2 large ripe tomatoes (about 1 pound)
> 2 ounces crumbled feta cheese
> 1 tablespoon thinly sliced scallions (sliced diagonally)
> freshly ground black pepper, to taste
> 1 tablespoon red wine vinegar
> 2 tablespoons extra-virgin olive oil
> 1½ tablespoons coarsely minced fresh dill
> 4 Greek black olives, pitted and sliced (optional)

Core stem ends of tomatoes. Slice tomatoes, and arrange on a platter so that they overlap, in a single layer. Sprinkle with cheese, and scatter scallions on top. Sprinkle with pepper. Drizzle vinegar and then oil over tomatoes. Sprinkle with dill. If you use the olives, scatter them over the top.

II. Tomato, Mozzarella, Chives, and Parsley Salad

4 servings

> 2 large tomatoes, cored at stem end and thinly sliced
> ½ pound mozzarella cheese, thinly sliced
> freshly ground black pepper, to taste
> 1 tablespoon red wine vinegar or balsamic vinegar
> 3 tablespoons extra-virgin olive oil
> 2 tablespoons finely minced fresh chives
> 2 tablespoons coarsely minced fresh flat Italian parsley

Arrange sliced tomatoes in a row on a serving platter. Alternate slices of mozzarella between the tomato slices. Sprinkle with pepper. In a small bowl, whisk together vinegar and oil, and pour over tomatoes and cheese. Sprinkle with chives and parsley.

III. Tomato, Chevre, and Basil Salad

4 servings

> 4 medium-size tomatoes (about 1 pound)
> 4 ounces Montrachet chevre cheese
> 24 or more whole fresh basil leaves
> freshly ground black pepper, to taste
> 1 tablespoon red wine vinegar
> 3 tablespoons extra-virgin olive oil

Slice tomatoes, and arrange in overlapping slices in a circle, on 4 individual salad plates. Cut cheese into ½-inch slices. Tuck cheese slices and basil leaves between slices of tomato. Sprinkle with pepper. Mix vinegar and oil together in a small bowl, using a wire whisk. Spoon about 1 teaspoon of dressing over each salad.

Tofu, Avocado, Calendula Petals, and Chive Salad with Ginger-Lime Dressing

4 servings

DRESSING

¼	cup light soy sauce
1	tablespoon water
1	teaspoon rice wine vinegar
½	teaspoon finely grated peeled ginger root
½	teaspoon finely minced garlic
½	teaspoon shredded lime rind
2 or 3	drops of hot pepper sauce
½	teaspoon Oriental sesame oil

SALAD

½	pound tofu, cut into cubes
1	medium avocado, cut into cubes
⅓	cup coarsely chopped scallions
⅔	coarsely chopped celery
8	red-leaf lettuce leaves
	alfalfa sprouts
	petals of 1 orange calendula
1	tablespoon sunflower seeds, toasted
1	tablespoon finely minced fresh chives

To make the dressing: Mix all ingredients together in a small bowl, and set aside.

To make the salad: In a medium-size bowl, combine tofu, avocado, scallions, and celery. Pour dressing over all, let marinate at room temperature for 2 hours, and then chill.

When ready to serve salad, place 2 lettuce leaves on each of 4 chilled plates. Spoon out 4 portions of tofu-avocado mixture onto center of each plate. Ring with alfalfa sprouts. Top with a scattering of calendula petals, sunflower seeds, and chives.

Winter Vegetable Salad with Lovage and Winter Savory

4 servings

SALAD

4	small new red potatoes
½	pound brussels sprouts (about 2 cups)
2	thin carrots, cut into 2-inch pieces, and then quartered

DRESSING

2	tablespoons beaten egg
2	tablespoons apple cider vinegar
1	tablespoon French-style mustard
2	tablespoon olive oil
2	tablespoons safflower oil
2	tablespoons coarsely chopped fresh lovage or celery leaves
1	teaspoon whole fresh winter savory leaves
¼	cup thinly sliced scallions
⅛	teaspoon black pepper

To make the salad: Steam all the vegetables in the same steamer. First steam potatoes for 5 minutes, then add brussels sprouts. After 5 minutes more, add carrots, and cook another 5 minutes, or until all the vegetables are tender. The total cooking time should be between 15 and 20 minutes. Drain vegetables. Cut potatoes into quarters.

To make the dressing: Whisk egg in a small bowl. Add vinegar and mustard, and whisk until smooth. Slowly add oils, while whisking. Then stir in lovage or celery, savory, scallions, and pepper. Pour over hot vegetables. Serve salad at room temperature.

Whole Hominy Salad with Roasted Hot and Sweet Peppers, and Cumin Vinaigrette

4 to 6 servings

This salad has a South American accent and yet, Native Americans have always eaten hominy, particularly in the Southwest. It can be prepared the day before and kept for a day or two in the refrigerator before serving.

VINAIGRETTE

  2 teaspoons finely minced shallots
  ½ teaspoon finely minced garlic
  3 tablespoons finely minced fresh cilantro leaves
  3 tablespoons red wine vinegar
  ¼ cup safflower oil
  ⅛ teaspoon black pepper
  ¼ teaspoon ground cumin

SALAD

  2 cans (16 ounces each) whole hominy, rinsed and drained
  ⅓ cup thinly sliced celery
  ¾ cup thinly sliced red onions
  ½ cup diced green peppers
  1 medium sweet red pepper, roasted and diced (page 85)
  1 tablespoon finely minced roasted and seeded jalapeno peppers
  1 large ripe tomato, cut into ¾-inch pieces
     lettuce leaves

To make the vinaigrette: Mix all ingredients together in a small bowl, and let stand for 1 hour or more to develop flavor.

To make the salad: Mix all ingredients together in a large bowl except lettuce. Toss gently with vinaigrette, and serve on lettuce leaves at room temperature.

Note: Wear rubber gloves when handling hot peppers. The capsicum oil in the seeds and the inside of the pepper can act as a skin irritant.

The people of the Middle Ages used cumin to keep lovers loyal and to prevent poultry from straying. The customary parting gift to soldiers from their sweethearts was a cumin bread, partly for nutrition, and perhaps partly to keep the young man from straying.

Chapter 8

MAIN COURSES

← Steamed Seafood with Individual Fresh Herb Bouquets (page 179)

Somewhere among these pages of recipes that feature pork, lamb, beef, poultry, and fish, you may find the star of tonight's dinner menu or a special dish for tomorrow's luncheon, its flavor enhanced with herbs and spices.

Herbs and spices turn everyday fare into pleasant new taste experiences. For example, lemon balm imparts a subtle but unmistakable flavor to chicken. We use up this fast-growing herb by filling an entire chicken cavity with several cups of it. And scarlet roasted peppers, pureed with fresh thyme and spooned over the pristine white of a chicken breast become part of an edible still life when placed alongside the green jade of sugar snap peas.

Pearls of barley enriched with the licorice taste of fennel seed, or the piney flavor of rosemary, combine very well with lamb. Tiny bay scallops mingle beautifully with the purple bits of opal basil, thyme, and the almost-cucumber flavor of borage in a seafood and vegetable medley. Fresh raw salmon is celebrated in a Mexican dish by adding hot chili peppers and cilantro.

With skilled use of herbs and spices the variations are unlimited: *chicken* with sesame seed or lemon balm or fines herbes or basil and walnuts; *pork* with thyme or cloves and ginger or coriander and chives; *lamb* with turmeric, coriander seeds, and cumin; *beef* with sage or thyme, allspice, and cloves; *seafood* with a range of herbs and spices; and *veal* with basil, lemon thyme, or nutmeg. And, since we eat *eggs* less frequently than we did before, we try to give them more importance by preparing them with special herb and spice combinations when we use them as a main course.

If ever there was a place for herbs and spices to shine, it is here with the main courses for luncheon or dinner.

115

POULTRY

Baked Chicken with Potatoes, Mushrooms, Rosemary, and Parsley

4 servings

    whole wheat flour, for dredging
1 3- to 3½-pound chicken, cut into quarters
¼ teaspoon black pepper
3 tablespoons olive oil
3 cups cubed unpeeled Russet or Idaho potatoes (about 2 medium-size potatoes)
1½ cups fresh mushrooms (about ¼ pound), cut into quarters, if large, and cut into halves, if medium size
3 cloves garlic, peeled
1 tablespoon coarsely chopped fresh rosemary
½ cup chicken stock
2 tablespoons lemon juice (about ½ lemon)
2 tablespoons finely minced fresh parsley

Put flour into a paper bag. Add pieces of chicken, and shake to coat evenly. Sprinkle chicken with pepper. Heat olive oil in a large cast-iron skillet. Add chicken, skin-side down first, and brown for 5 minutes on each side. You may need to do 2 batches. While chicken is browning, steam potatoes for 15 minutes, and set aside.

Preheat oven to 400°F. Transfer chicken, skin-side up, to a large shallow oven-to-table casserole. Scatter potatoes, mushrooms, garlic, and rosemary over all. Add chicken stock and lemon juice, and bake for 30 minutes, basting every 10 minutes. Remove garlic and discard. Sprinkle with parsley before serving.

Baked Lemon-Lime Chicken with Dill, Tarragon, Parsley, and Ginger

4 servings

A generous amount of fresh herbs, ginger, and citrus permeates the chicken while it bakes.

¼ cup butter, melted, divided
1 3-pound chicken, cut into quarters
1 lemon
1 lime
¼ teaspoon black pepper
1 teaspoon finely minced garlic
1 tablespoon grated peeled ginger root
1 tablespoon finely minced fresh tarragon
3 tablespoons coarsely chopped fresh dill
3 tablespoons finely minced fresh parsley
¼ teaspoon paprika

Preheat oven to 375°F. Line a medium-size roasting pan with aluminum foil.

Spoon 1 tablespoon of the melted butter over foil, and place chicken, skin-side up, on foil. Grate rind of lemon and lime, and set aside. Cut lemon and lime in half, and squeeze juice from half of each. Slice remaining halves horizontally into thin slices, and set aside for garnish. Pour citrus juices over chicken, and sprinkle with all the remaining ingredients as well as the grated rind. Spoon remaining melted butter over chicken, cover loosely with foil, and bake for 30 minutes. Then remove foil, and bake for 25 to 30 minutes more. Transfer to a warm serving platter, spoon any pan juices over chicken, and garnish with slices of reserved lemon and lime.

Broiled Chicken Breast Rolls Stuffed with Mushrooms and Fines Herbes

4 servings

 1 tablespoon finely minced fresh parsley
 1 tablespoon finely minced fresh chervil
 1 tablespoon finely minced fresh chives
 1 teaspoon finely minced fresh tarragon
 ½ teaspoon finely minced fresh oregano
 1 tablespoon finely minced shallots
 3 ounces fresh mushrooms, finely chopped
 2 tablespoons lemon juice
 ¼ cup olive oil
 1 teaspoon grated lemon rind
 ¼ teaspoon black pepper
 2 whole chicken breasts (about ½ pound each), boneless, skinless (Do not use chicken cutlets, but both sides of breasts, attached, in 1 piece)

Combine all the ingredients except chicken breasts in a medium-size oven-to-table casserole. Place chicken over herb-mushroom mixture, and let marinate for 1 hour or more, turning 2 to 3 times to coat.

Preheat broiler.

Scrape marinade mixture from outside of breasts, and spread on inner surface of chicken only. Roll up breasts to enclose filling, and secure with a toothpick. Broil for 15 minutes, turning once, and baste with any juices that accumulate. Remove toothpicks when breasts are cooked, and cut each one in half across the width of the roll to make 4 servings.

Broiled Chicken Breasts Stuffed with Pesto

4 servings

Pesto, made with basil, nuts, garlic, and olive oil, is tucked under the skin of the chicken so that it doesn't burn while broiling.

 4 chicken breast halves
 ⅛ teaspoon black pepper
 ¼ cup Pesto Genovese (page 261), divided
 ¼ cup lemon juice
 3 tablespoons Parmesan cheese

Preheat broiler.

Sprinkle chicken with pepper. Run fingers under skin of chicken, being careful not to tear it. Slip 1 tablespoon of pesto under skin of each breast. Place chicken in a medium-size oven-to-table baking dish, skin-side down. Pour lemon juice over chicken, and broil for 10 minutes, basting once. Turn chicken skin-side up, baste, and broil for about 10 minutes more, basting occasionally. Sprinkle with cheese before serving.

Broiled Chicken Breasts with Mustard and Parsleyed Shallot Butter

4 servings

This dish takes less than 10 minutes to prepare, yet it's elegant enough for company.

SAUCE

> 2 tablespoons finely minced shallots
> 1 tablespoon red wine vinegar
> ¼ cup butter, cut into 4 pieces
> 2 tablespoons finely minced fresh
>   parsley
> ⅛ teaspoon black pepper

CHICKEN

> 4 boneless, skinless chicken breast
>   halves (about 1 pound)
> 1 tablespoon olive oil
> ⅛ teaspoon black pepper
> 2 tablespoons French-style mustard

To make the sauce: Put shallots, vinegar, and 1 tablespoon of the butter into a small saucepan, and heat until mixture starts to simmer. Remove saucepan from stove, and add the remaining butter and parsley, stirring with a small wire whisk. Add pepper, and reserve sauce until chicken is cooked.

To make the chicken: Preheat broiler.

Trim any fat from chicken, and pound between 2 sheets of waxed paper if breasts are more than ½ inch thick. Pour oil into a medium-size oven-to-table shallow baking dish large enough to accommodate chicken breasts in a single layer, and turn chicken in oil to coat both sides. Sprinkle with pepper, and spread mustard on the top side only. Place in broiler about 4 inches from heat, and broil

mustard-side up for about 4 minutes, or until brown. Then turn chicken breasts mustard-side down, and broil for 1 minute more. Spoon sauce over chicken, and serve at once.

Broiled Chicken Breasts with Mustard, Thyme, and Bread Crumbs

4 servings

> 3 tablespoons melted butter
> 4 chicken breast halves, boned,
>   skinned, and pounded
> 3 tablespoons French-style mustard
> ¼ cup dry white wine, divided
> ⅛ teaspoon cayenne pepper
> ¼ teaspoon Worcestershire sauce
> 1 teaspoon finely minced shallots
> ½ cup fine whole grain bread crumbs
> 1 teaspoon fresh thyme leaves

Preheat broiler.

In a medium-size oven-to-table baking dish, melt butter on top of stove. Add chicken and toss, turning to coat on both sides. Arrange chicken in a single layer, and set aside.

In a small measuring cup, mix mustard with 2 tablespoons of the wine, cayenne pepper, Worcestershire sauce, and shallots, and spoon half of this mixture evenly over chicken. Mix bread crumbs with thyme, and spoon half over mustard mixture, pressing slightly so that bread crumbs adhere. Broil for 5 minutes on lowest rack of broiler so that crumbs won't burn. Turn chicken, repeat mustard and bread crumb coating, and broil for 5 to 6 minutes more, or until cooked through. Add remaining 2 tablespoons of wine to pan. The wine will bubble up and form a bit of a sauce to spoon over breasts before serving.

The British frequently use fried parsley as a garnish. Strip the leaves from the parsley stems, and wash and dry them very thoroughly to prevent spattering. Place small clumps of the leaves in very hot oil for 30 seconds, and remove with a slotted spoon. Drain on paper towels.

Chicken in the Pot with Herb Dumplings

4 servings

A favorite with the French, this "pot au feu" is a hearty and satisfying one-dish dinner.

CHICKEN

- 1 3-pound chicken
- 6 cups chicken stock
- 1 dried bay leaf
- 2 whole cloves
- 8 peppercorns
- 3 ribs celery, split lengthwise and cut into 2-inch pieces
- 3 carrots, cut into 2-inch pieces
- 1 large leek, cut into 2-inch pieces
- ½ pound small turnips, peeled and cut in half

DUMPLINGS *(Makes about 18 dumplings)*

- ½ cup whole wheat pastry flour
- ½ cup unbleached white flour
- 1 teaspoon baking powder
- ¼ teaspoon white pepper
- 1 tablespoon finely minced fresh chives
- 1½ tablespoons finely minced fresh parsley
- 1 teaspoon fresh thyme leaves
- ½ teaspoon finely minced fresh marjoram
- 2 egg yolks
- ¼ cup plus 1 tablespoon milk melted butter

To make the chicken: Rinse chicken thoroughly. Truss chicken, and place in a narrow, deep stock pot so that chicken fits snugly. Cover with water, bring to a boil, remove chicken, and then drain off water. Return chicken to pot, add stock, bring to a boil again, and then lower heat. Put bay leaf, cloves, and peppercorns into a square of cheesecloth, tie with string, and add to pot along with all the remaining ingredients. Cover, and simmer for 40 to 45 minutes, or until chicken is tender. Remove and discard cheesecloth bag. While chicken is cooking, prepare and cook dumplings.

To make the dumplings: Sift whole wheat pastry flour, unbleached white flour, and baking powder together into a medium-size bowl. Add pepper and herbs, and toss well. Beat egg yolks and milk together, and stir only until smooth. Batter will be thick.

To cook dumplings, use a 10-inch skillet with a tight-fitting lid. Fill skillet with water, and bring to a boil. Wet a teaspoon and your hands, and drop batter by teaspoonfuls into boiling water. Dumpling will sink to the bottom and then rise to the surface. Cover, and cook over medium heat without removing lid for 10 to 15 minutes. Lift out dumplings with a slotted spoon, and drain well. Place dumplings into a warm dish that contains a bit of melted butter to prevent them from sticking together. When ready to serve, cut chicken into serving pieces, and serve in large soup bowls along with broth, vegetables, and dumplings.

Chicken Breasts with Red Pepper Sauce, Thyme, and Sugar Snap Peas

4 servings

The smokey taste of roasted sweet red peppers and the sweet flavor and crispness of sugar snap peas make an attractive presentation and a delicious light dish.

SAUCE

2   large sweet red peppers, roasted (page 85)
1   tablespoon butter
1½ tablespoons shallots
2   tablespoons creme fraiche
1   tablespoon fresh thyme leaves
⅛   teaspoon black pepper
½   cup chicken stock

PEAS

½   pound sugar snap peas

CHICKEN

1   pound boneless, skinless chicken breasts
1   tablespoon butter, melted
1   teaspoon grated lemon rind
    few small sprigs of fresh thyme

To make the sauce: Puree roasted peppers in a blender. Set aside. In a small skillet, melt butter. Add shallots, and saute, stirring constantly, until wilted. Add pepper puree, creme fraiche, thyme, black pepper, and chicken stock, and heat, while stirring, for 1 minute. Keep warm while preparing peas and chicken.

To make the peas: Blanch peas for 30 seconds, and set aside.

To make the chicken: Preheat broiler.

Place chicken in a medium-size buttered baking pan. Pour melted butter over chicken. Broil 2 to 3 minutes on each side. Place chicken on a warm serving dish, and scatter lemon rind over it. Pour any pan juices into red pepper sauce. Spoon sauce around chicken, but not over it. Place the sugar snap peas on top of sauce in a decorative manner, and garnish with sprigs of thyme.

Chicken Fricassee with Tiny Meatballs and Paprika

4 servings

An old-fashioned favorite that uses chicken wings.

3   tablespoons butter, divided
2   cups thinly sliced onions (about 3 medium-size onions)
1   teaspoon finely minced garlic
2   teaspoons sweet paprika, divided
1½ pounds chicken wings
½   pound chicken gizzards, cut in half whole wheat flour, for dredging
¼   teaspoon plus ⅛ teaspoon black pepper, divided
1½ cups chicken stock
½   pound lean ground beef
1   tablespoon finely minced mixed fresh herbs (2 teaspoons parsley, ½ teaspoon marjoram, ½ teaspoon thyme leaves)
3   tablespoons fine whole grain bread crumbs

In a heavy 5-quart pot, melt 1 tablespoon butter. Add onions, and saute over medium-high heat until onions start to color.

Add garlic and ½ teaspoon of the paprika, and continue to saute until brown. Remove with a slotted spoon, and reserve. Melt remaining 2 tablespoons of butter in the same pot. Dredge wings and gizzards in flour and ¼ teaspoon of the pepper, and brown a few at a time. If there is any flour left from dredging, sprinkle it over reserved onions. When wings and gizzards are brown, return onions to the pot, add chicken stock and remaining 1½ teaspoons of the paprika, cover, and bring to a boil. Then lower heat, and simmer for 1 hour.

While wings and gizzards cook, mix ground beef with herbs, bread crumbs, and remaining black pepper. With wet hands, form into marble-size meatballs, tuck into pot, and continue cooking for 30 minutes more, or until gizzards are tender and chicken practically falls off the bone. Serve with rice or fine pasta.

Chicken Pate
with Cucumber, Watercress,
and Nutmeg

4 to 6 servings

Delicate, yet tinged with the peppery bite of watercress, this dish can be served as a main course or as an hors d'oeuvre.

  1 large bunch watercress, tough stems removed
  ½ cup finely minced onions (about 1 medium onion)
  ¼ cup finely minced sweet red pepper
  1 small cucumber, peeled, or 1 unpeeled "burpless" cucumber
  1 pound boneless, skinless chicken breasts
  ¾ cup fine whole grain bread crumbs
  1 egg yolk, slightly beaten
  ½ cup heavy cream
  ⅛ teaspoon ground nutmeg
  ¼ teaspoon black pepper
    sprig of watercress

Preheat oven to 400°F.

Butter an 8½ × 4½-inch loaf pan. Boil a kettle of water. Chop watercress in a food processor. There should be ¾ to 1 cup. Scrape out into a medium-size bowl, and set aside. In the same processor bowl, process onions and red peppers until very fine. Scrape out, and add to watercress. Switch blade to shredding blade, and process cucumber. There should be about ½ cup. Scrape out cucumber, squeeze out liquid between palms of hands, and add to bowl with other ingredients. Reserve.

Cut chicken breasts into chunks, and process until fine. Add reserved vegetables to chicken in the food processor, and process until combined. Add all the remaining ingredients except sprig of watercress, and process again until combined. Spoon into buttered loaf pan, and smooth the surface. Butter a sheet of aluminum foil, press it lightly against chicken, and then press the rest of the foil on top and around the pan to cover and enclose it. Place loaf in a larger roasting pan, pour boiling water three-quarters of the way up the sides of the loaf pan, and bake for 1 hour and 15 minutes. Let stand on a rack to cool slightly. Juices will form and then will be almost entirely reabsorbed into the pate. Whatever liquid remains can be spooned over the sliced pate at serving time.

When ready to serve, run a knife around the loaf, and unmold onto a serving dish. Garnish with sprig of watercress, and serve at room temperature.

Sy Cohen
Guest Chef

I was confined to a hospital over Christmas back in 1969 and there was nothing to do. I was watching television and Julia Childs was on. And—I fell in love!

We first met Sy when he was executive chef at Cafe Domel in New York. While shopping at our local greengrocer, we noticed Sy selecting fresh herbs and we began to comment on his confidence in choosing just the right ones. That night we ate at the restaurant and sampled his cooking. Right then and there we decided that he must have a place in this book. Before Cafe Domel, he worked at the well-known and popular Greenwich Village restaurant, Vanessa, where he covered every station in the kitchen except for salads.

Working as a chef taught me a lot, but I learned most of what I know through books. My upbringing didn't help much. It was a long time before I discovered that vegetables were green and red and not gray. In my house, carrots came out the same color as peas, and my mother would boil canned vegetables to kill any microorganisms!

His grandmother, on the other hand, was a wonderful cook, who used to make candy out of radishes.

I never could find out how she did it. The whole neighborhood smelled from the cooking radishes, but the candy was wonderful!

On the subject of herbs, he—like all good chefs—prefers to use them fresh:

Herbs are the joy of the kitchen! When you work with fresh herbs, fresh rosemary or thyme or tarragon, the aroma takes you where you're going. Herbs fill my head with wonder! I am excited by all the possibilities they offer. Several years ago, I started to add chopped fresh rosemary to pizza dough as I mixed it before baking. Imagine the flavor and aroma that adds! You can do the same with fresh thyme when you prepare the dough for savory meat pies. Don't sell thyme short, by the way. It's a workhorse among herbs; thyme seems to improve the flavor of virtually everything from stocks to pates to potted beef dishes.

If you are looking for interesting new ways to use herbs, try mixing a pinch of dry tarragon in with the ground coffee before brewing. It adds a marvelous and distinctive flavor to the drink. Or try using a hint of rosemary to flavor apple sorbet, as a chef friend of mine used to do. His customers loved it, though I must admit I never tried it myself.

As a word of advice, Sy, who believes in using herbs as freely as you wish ("I love to use copious quantities of coarsely chopped parsley with perfectly cooked carrots — colorful and tasty."), says to be careful about overseasoning with spices. The recipe he's given us uses fresh parsley, fresh tarragon, and sesame seeds, as well as one of the tastiest of vegetables, porcini mushrooms.

Chicken Breasts with Porcini Mushrooms, Lemon, Tarragon, and Parsley

6 servings

3 ounces dried porcini mushrooms
3 whole chicken breasts, boned and halved (6 portions)
  juice of 1 large lemon
  white pepper, to taste
6 ounces fresh white mushrooms
12 ounces unsalted butter (3 sticks), divided
  grated rind of 1 large lemon
3 tablespoons chopped fresh parsley
2 tablespoons peanut oil
1 tablespoon plus ¼ teaspoon ground sesame seeds, divided
  water chestnut flour or wheat flour, for dredging
3 tablespoons chopped shallots
⅓ cup dry vermouth
⅓ cup unsalted chicken stock
1 tablespoon chopped fresh tarragon

Place dried porcini into a small bowl of warm water to soak for 1 to 1½ hours. Clean chicken breasts of excess fat and cartilage. Remove tendons from fillets. Squeeze lemon juice over chicken, and sprinkle each breast with white pepper. Set chicken aside to marinate for 1 hour at room temperature. (Chicken can be marinated longer if refrigerated.)

Clean and finely chop fresh mushrooms. Wrap them in a kitchen towel, then squeeze them over a small bowl to catch their liquid. Reserve. Scoop porcini from soaking water, and rinse thoroughly to remove grit. Pour remaining soaking liquid through a sieve lined with a damp kitchen towel. Reserve ¼ cup, and add to liquid squeezed from fresh mushrooms. Save the rest for another use, or discard. Finely chop porcini.

Melt 4 ounces (1 stick) of the butter in a skillet large enough to accommodate the chopped mushrooms. Saute fresh mushrooms until they give off all of their remaining liquid and release the butter they will have absorbed in the process. Add porcini and white pepper. Saute 4 to 5 minutes more over low heat, and remove from pan. Mix in lemon rind and parsley.

Using your fingers, make a pocket under the skin of each breast half (slit open from the wider end). Spoon 1 heaping tablespoon of the mushroom mixture into pocket of each breast. Pat mixture into place, and chill breasts until ready to saute them, or proceed at once with the preparation.

Heat 2 tablespoons of the butter, and the oil in a large skillet. Mix together 1 tablespoon of the ground sesame seeds and water chestnut flour or wheat flour. Dredge chicken in flour mixture, shake off the excess, and saute, skin-side first, until golden on both sides (8 to 10 minutes in all). Remove sauteed chicken to a warm oven. Then, in the same pan,

adding a little butter, saute shallots briefly. Add vermouth, and scrape loose all of the browned bits of chicken that have adhered to the pan. Reduce vermouth by half, then add mushroom liquid and chicken stock to pan and give it several turns of the pepper mill. Reduce vermouth-stock mixture by half again. Add tarragon, and reduce for 1 minute more. Swirl in remaining butter and ¼ teaspoon ground sesame seeds. Taste for seasoning. Remove chicken to a warm platter, and nap with sauce. Serve at once.

Note: Water chestnut flour is now available at most Chinese food stores or by mail order. It is excellent for people who are allergic to gluten. In addition, water chestnut flour puts a lovely crisp crust on chicken.

Chicken Pot Pie with Cilantro and Jalapeno Pepper-Cheddar Cheese Crust

6 servings

An old-fashioned Pennsylvania Dutch staple with a Tex-Mex twist. Prepare ahead and refrigerate until ready to cook, then fix the corn biscuit topping and bake.

CHICKEN

  1   3- to 3½-pound chicken
  3   cups water

  1   tablespoon Barth's Nutra Instant Chicken Soup
  ½   teaspoon black pepper, divided
  2   medium turnips, peeled and cut into ½-inch pieces (about 1 cup)
  2   slim carrots, cut into ¼-inch pieces (about 1 cup)
  2   long stalks celery, sliced into ¼-inch pieces (about 1 cup)
18   small whole pearl onions, peeled

1 package (10 ounces) frozen green peas
1 teaspoon grated lemon rind
¼ cup butter
¼ cup whole wheat flour
1½ tablespoons finely minced fresh cilantro

CRUST

½ cup buttermilk
½ cup stone-ground yellow cornmeal
½ cup whole wheat flour
½ cup unbleached white flour
1 tablespoon baking powder
3 tablespoons butter
1 tablespoon finely minced seeded jalapeno peppers (about 1 pepper)
½ cup grated cheddar cheese
few sprigs of fresh cilantro (optional)

To make the chicken: Rinse chicken, and dry thoroughly. Put chicken, water, instant soup, and ¼ teaspoon of the pepper into a 5-quart pot, laying chicken on its side. Bring to a boil, then lower heat, and simmer, covered, for 20 minutes. Turn chicken, and continue to simmer, covered, for 20 minutes more.

Lift chicken out of pot with a slotted spoon, reserving stock, and place on a plate. When cool enough, discard skin and bones, cut chicken into bite-size chunks, and set aside. Strain reserved chicken stock, and return to the same pot. Add turnips, carrots, celery, and onions, and simmer for 5 to 8 minutes, or until tender but still firm. During the last 3 minutes, add peas. Strain vegetables, and reserve stock. Add vegetables to chicken, and mix gently with lemon rind. Set aside.

Melt butter in a medium-size nonstick saucepan, then add flour, and stir over low heat for 1 to 2 minutes. Measure 2 cups of reserved stock, and slowly add to the butter-flour mixture, stirring with a whisk to keep it smooth. Simmer over low heat for 10 minutes, or until sauce is thick, stirring occasionally with a whisk. Add cilantro and remaining pepper, and pour sauce over chicken-vegetable mixture. Butter a 9 × 2-inch round casserole, and spoon chicken-vegetable mixture into it. At this point, you may refrigerate the casserole and finish it at another time.

To prepare the crust: When ready to serve, preheat oven to 425°F, and prepare the top crust. Warm buttermilk in a small nonstick saucepan over low heat until bubbles begin to form on the edges of the milk. Do not heat to boiling or milk will curdle. Remove from heat. In a medium-size bowl, mix together cornmeal, whole wheat flour, unbleached white flour and baking powder. Cut butter into flour with a pastry blender or 2 knives until texture is crumbly. Add jalapeno peppers and cheese. Stir in warm buttermilk, and mix well with a wooden spoon. Gather dough, turn out onto a lightly floured surface, and knead 5 times to make it smooth. Pat into a circle 2 inches smaller than the diameter of the casserole (about a 7-inch round) and 1½ inches thick. Cut into 6 pie-shaped wedges and carefully lay them over the top of chicken-vegetable mixture. Bake for about 20 minutes, or until top is light tan in color and sauce is bubbling around the edges of the casserole. Garnish with cilantro, if desired, and serve at once.

Chicken with Balsamic Vinegar Sauce and Chives

4 servings

Balsamic vinegar gives this chicken dish a mild, deep flavor and a lovely mahogany color.

  2 tablespoons butter
  1 3-pound chicken, cut into quarters
  2 medium-size cloves garlic, peeled and finely minced
  ½ teaspoon black pepper, divided
  ½ cup balsamic vinegar or red wine vinegar
  ⅓ cup chicken stock
  1 tablespoon tomato paste
  2 tablespoons minced fresh chives

Melt butter over high heat in a large skillet with deep sides to accommodate pieces of chicken without crowding. Place chicken skin-side down, and sprinkle with garlic and half the pepper. Lower heat, and brown for 6 to 8 minutes; turn pieces to the other side, sprinkle with remaining pepper, and saute for 5 minutes more.

Lift pieces of chicken out of skillet, and set aside. Pour off any accumulated fat, return skillet to stove, and add vinegar, scraping up any pan drippings with a wooden spoon. In a cup, mix chicken stock with tomato paste, add to vinegar, and bring to a boil. Return chicken to skillet, skin-side down, and lower heat. Tilt the pan, spoon some sauce over chicken, and continue to cook over low heat for an additional 30 to 45 minutes, turning pieces once and basting with sauce again.

Transfer chicken to a warm serving platter, and spoon some sauce over it. (Most of the sauce will have condensed into a glaze.) Sprinkle with chives, and serve at once.

Chicken with Bulgur, Basil, and Walnuts

4 servings

A crisp salad of cucumber, yogurt, and dill completes this meal.

  1 2½- to 3-pound chicken, cut into quarters
  2 tablespoons lemon juice
  ¼ teaspoon black pepper
  2 tablespoons butter
  1 tablespoon corn oil
  ⅔ cup chopped onions
  1 cup chicken stock
  ⅛ teaspoon ground allspice
  1 cup coarse bulgur
  ½ cup coarsely chopped walnuts, toasted
  3 tablespoons fresh bush basil or 4 tablespoons minced fresh sweet basil, divided

Lay pieces of chicken in a flat dish or casserole. Sprinkle with lemon juice and pepper, and let stand for 20 minutes.

In a large skillet, heat butter and oil. When hot, add onions, and saute until wilted, stirring occasionally. Add chicken stock, and bring to a boil. Lower heat, add chicken along with lemon juice marinade, cover, and simmer for 20 minutes.

Preheat oven to 425°F.

Lift pieces of chicken out of skillet with a slotted spoon, place them in a large oven-to-table baking dish, and sprinkle with allspice. Bake chicken for 30 to 35 minutes while preparing bulgur. Heat stock-onion mixture remaining in skillet to boiling, and stir in bulgur. Cover, and lower heat to simmer for 10 minutes. Then remove from heat, and let stand undisturbed to absorb remaining liquid while chicken bakes. When ready to serve, add walnuts and three-quarters of the basil to bulgur, and fluff with a fork. Place chicken pieces on a plate, and spoon bulgur into the same baking dish in which the chicken was cooked. Lay pieces of chicken on top, place in oven to warm for about 5 minutes, and sprinkle with remaining basil just before serving.

Note: The tiny leaves of bush basil can be used whole and are more pungent than the more common larger leaf sweet basil.

Chicken with Paprika and Sour Cream

4 servings

This Hungarian dish goes well with thin egg noodles.

- 1 3-pound chicken, cut into quarters
- ½ teaspoon black pepper or lemon pepper
  whole wheat flour, for dredging
- 2 tablespoons butter
- 1 tablespoon finely minced garlic
- 1 cup thinly sliced onions
- 1 tablespoon sweet paprika
- ½ cup chicken stock
- ¾ cup sour cream
  sprig of fresh parsley

Sprinkle chicken with pepper, and dredge in flour. Heat butter in a heavy skillet large enough to accommodate chicken in a single layer. Add chicken, skin-side down, and brown over medium-high heat for 5 minutes. Turn, and continue to cook until second side is brown, about 5 minutes more. Sprinkle garlic

and onions around chicken, and then sprinkle paprika over all. Add chicken stock, cover, and simmer for 25 minutes. Turn chicken, and cook for 5 minutes more. Transfer chicken to a warm serving platter. Add sour cream to skillet. Stir and cook over low heat for 2 minutes. Pour sauce over chicken, and garnish with sprig of parsley.

Crunchy Baked Chili Chicken

4 servings

- 1 2½- to 3-pound chicken, cut into serving pieces
- 2½ teaspoons chili powder, divided
- ⅛ teaspoon black pepper
  whole wheat flour, for dredging
- 1 egg, beaten
- 2 tablespoons milk
- 5 cups unsalted potato chips, crushed in a food processor (about 1¼ cups crumbs)

Sprinkle chicken with 1 teaspoon of the chili powder and pepper, then dredge lightly in flour. In a cup, mix together egg and milk, and pour mixture into a flat pie pan. Place crushed chips on piece of waxed paper, and mix with remaining 1½ teaspoons of chili powder. Line a large shallow baking pan (a jelly-roll pan is fine) with aluminum foil.
Preheat oven to 375°F.
Dip floured chicken pieces in egg mixture, and then roll in crushed chili-chips mixture, pressing so that chips adhere. Place pieces of chicken in the pan in a single layer, and bake, turning once, for 50 to 60 minutes, or until outside is brown and crunchy and chicken is done.

Easy Roasted Sesame Chicken with Cilantro and Garlic

4 servings

2 tablespoons butter, softened
1½ tablespoons finely minced fresh cilantro
1 teaspoon finely minced garlic
⅛ teaspoon dried red pepper flakes
1 teaspoon grated lemon rind
1 3- to 3½-pound chicken
2 tablespoons Oriental sesame oil
2 tablespoons light soy sauce

Preheat oven to 500°F.

In a cup, mix together butter, cilantro, garlic, red pepper flakes, and lemon rind, and coat inside cavity of chicken with this mixture. Then sew and/or skewer both the neck opening and the bottom cavity, making certain that they are completely closed and that hot mixture cannot leak during roasting.

Rub 2 pieces of aluminum foil with a bit of the sesame oil. Line a large baking pan with 1 piece of aluminum foil, and place chicken on it. In a cup, mix remaining sesame oil with soy sauce, and pour it on top of chicken. Roast chicken, uncovered, in hot oven for 15 minutes. Then baste, cover lightly with the other piece of aluminum foil, making a tent-shaped hood, lower heat to 350°F, and roast for 30 minutes more. Remove foil, raise heat to 500°F again, and roast for 10 more minutes. Tilt pan and baste every 3 minutes during final cooking time. Remove chicken from oven, cover again loosely with foil to keep warm, and let rest before cutting into serving pieces at the table. As the bird is cut, the herbed butter will spill out to form a sauce that can be spooned over chicken.

Orange-Ginger Chicken with Sugar Snap Peas

4 servings

Once the preparation for this dish is done, the cooking time is only five minutes!

2 navel oranges
2 tablespoons butter
½ teaspoon finely minced garlic
½ teaspoon grated peeled ginger root
¼ teaspoon ground cinnamon
1 pound boneless, skinless chicken breasts, sliced into ⅛-inch-thick pieces
½ sweet red pepper, slivered
½ pound sugar snap peas
1 teaspoon minced fresh cilantro pinch of black pepper
2 tablespoons chili sauce
¼ cup broken walnuts, toasted few sprigs of fresh cilantro

Grate 1½ tablespoons of rind from oranges, and reserve. Section 1 orange, and reserve. Squeeze juice from remaining orange (about 4 tablespoons), and reserve.

Heat butter in a large skillet. Add garlic, 1 tablespoon of the orange rind, ginger, and cinnamon, and stir fry for a few seconds. Add chicken and red pepper, and stir fry for 2 to 3 minutes. Stir in sugar snap peas and minced cilantro, and cook for 1 minute. Sprinkle with black pepper, add chili sauce and orange juice, and cook 1 minute longer. Turn into a warm serving dish, add orange sections, and sprinkle with nuts and remaining orange rind. Garnish with cilantro sprigs. Serve over cooked rice.

Crunchy Baked Chili Chicken (page 127) ➜

Honey-Glazed Citrus Chicken with Lemon Thyme

4 servings

The chicken marinates for at least 2 hours in a citrus-honey-lemon thyme marinade, which is later reduced to a glaze that gives the chicken a mahogany color and a special crispness.

 1 tablespoon grated orange rind
 1 teaspoon grated lemon rind
 ½ cup orange juice
 ¼ cup lemon juice
 2 tablespoons light soy sauce
 1 tablespoon corn oil
 ¼ cup light honey
 ¼ teaspoon black pepper
 1 tablespoon lemon thyme leaves
 1 teaspoon dry mustard
 1 3- to 3½-pound chicken, cut into
     quarters

In a medium-size bowl, mix all the ingredients together, except for chicken, and pour over chicken pieces. Let marinate for at least 2 hours and up to 6 hours in the refrigerator.

Preheat oven to 375°F.

Lift chicken from marinade with a slotted spoon, place in a single layer in a foil-lined medium-size baking pan, skin-side down, and pour marinade into a medium-size saucepan. Bake chicken for 20 minutes while preparing basting sauce. Boil marinade, uncovered, until it is reduced to ⅓ cup.

After 20 minutes, spoon some of the marinade over chicken, and bake for 10 minutes more. Then turn chicken pieces skin-side up, spoon remaining sauce over chicken, and bake for 25 minutes more, basting occa-sionally. At the end of the baking time, place chicken under broiler for 1 to 2 minutes to char slightly. Watch it carefully. Remove pieces to a warm serving dish, and spoon any remaining sauce over chicken.

Roasted Stuffed Chicken with Sausage and Mixed Herbs

4 servings

This dish is festive enough for a small dinner party, and once it's in the oven, you can spend that extra hour with your guests. No basting, no fuss.

 2 fresh sweet Italian sausages, removed
     from casings and crumbled
 ¼ cup finely chopped onions
 ¼ teaspoon finely minced garlic
 2 chicken livers, finely minced
 ¾ cup whole grain bread crumbs
 ¼ cup milk
 1 teaspoon grated lemon rind
 1 egg yolk
 ¼ cup finely minced mixed fresh herbs
     (parsley, oregano, thyme,
     rosemary, and basil)
 ¼ teaspoon black pepper
 1 2½- to 3-pound chicken
     juice of 1 lemon

In a large skillet, cook sausage briefly, and then add onions and garlic. When meat loses its color, add chicken livers, and cook, stirring, for about 1 minute. Remove from heat, add remaining ingredients except for chicken and lemon juice, and stir well. Let cool for 10 minutes.

Preheat oven to 400°F.

Stuff chicken, truss it, and place on a wire rack in a large roasting pan. Pour lemon juice over chicken. Bake for 1 hour without basting. Do not open oven door while baking. Remove chicken, and place under an aluminum-foil tent to rest for 10 minutes. Cut into 4 serving pieces, keeping stuffing under each piece of chicken as a tasty surprise.

Roast Duck with Fennel Seeds, Ginger, and Pumpkin Pie Spice

4 servings

The duck is marinated in an Oriental sauce overnight and then is roasted to a crispy brown outside while remaining moist inside.

 1 5-pound duck
 2 tablespoons soy sauce
 1 tablespoon light honey
 1 tablespoon pumpkin pie spice
 1 teaspoon fennel seeds, crushed
 1 teaspoon finely minced peeled
     ginger root
 1 teaspoon finely minced garlic
 ⅛ teaspoon black pepper
 1 cup boiling chicken stock
 8 large romaine lettuce leaves,
     shredded

Rinse inside and outside of duck with cold water. Pull off and discard any fat. Pat dry with paper towels. In a cup, mix soy sauce, honey, pumpkin pie spice, fennel seeds, ginger root, garlic, and pepper together. Brush or spoon mixture inside and outside of duck. Place duck in a nonaluminum pan, cover lightly with waxed paper, and refrigerate overnight or longer if you wish.

Preheat oven to 450°F.

Mix whatever marinade is left in pan with boiling chicken stock. Close neck opening flap of duck with skewers. Tilt duck, bottom-side up, and pour liquid into body cavity. Skewer bottom opening closed, place duck, breast-side up, on a wire rack in a medium-size roasting pan, and roast for 20 minutes without basting. Lower heat to 325°F. Remove duck from oven, and remove all fat from pan with a baster. Return duck to oven, and continue roasting for 1 hour or more, occasionally spooning off any accumulated fat from pan. Turn duck over, breast-side down, increase heat to 450°F, and roast for 10 minutes more.

Place shredded lettuce on a heated platter, remove skewers from duck, and set bird on bed of lettuce. Cut into quarters with poultry shears, letting cavity juices spill over onto lettuce, wilting it. Serve duck with wilted lettuce.

Note: If you wish to make an additional sauce, pour ¾ cup boiling water into roasting pan, heat, and scrape up brown bits from bottom of pan. Strain sauce, return to saucepan, add 1 thin slice of butter, bring to a simmer, and serve.

A bunch of herbs tucked into the cavity of any fowl before roasting will permeate it with flavor.

Sesame Seed Baked Chicken

4 servings

Crisp and nutty on the outside, succulent and juicy within, this baked chicken has an Oriental accent achieved by marinating it for two hours before baking.

1	3-pound chicken, cut into quarters
1/3	cup light soy sauce
1	teaspoon finely minced garlic
2	teaspoons finely grated peeled ginger root
2 to 3	drops of hot pepper sauce
2	tablespoons lime juice
1	egg, slightly beaten
2/3	cup whole wheat flour
1/3	cup sesame seeds
1/4	cup butter, melted

Place chicken into a bowl or flat pan with sides. Mix soy sauce, garlic, ginger, hot pepper sauce, and lime juice together in a small measuring cup, and pour over chicken. Marinate in refrigerator for 2 hours, turning pieces occasionally and spooning marinade over them.

Preheat oven to 375°F.

In a cup, mix beaten egg with 2 tablespoons of the marinade, and pour into a pie plate. Discard remaining marinade. In another pie plate, mix flour and sesame seeds together. Dip chicken first into egg mixture and then into flour-sesame seed mixture, coating evenly. Place skin-side down in a medium-size oven-to-table baking dish in a single layer. Spoon half the melted butter over the surface, and bake for 30 minutes. Turn chicken pieces to other side, skin-side up, spoon remaining butter over them, and bake for 20 to 25 minutes more.

Skewered Chicken with Pineapple, Green Peppers, Chinese Five Spice Powder, and Ginger

4 to 6 servings

The chicken marinates for several hours. Broiling time takes only eight minutes.

3	whole chicken breasts (about 1½ pounds), boned, skinned, and cut into 1½-inch cubes
4	thin slices ginger root, peeled and cut into slivers
1	clove garlic, peeled and cut into slivers
1/4	teaspoon Chinese five spice powder
1/8	teaspoon black pepper
1	tablespoon soy sauce
1/4	cup pineapple juice
2	tablespoons corn oil
1	tablespoon honey
1	can (8 ounces) unsweetened pineapple chunks, drained, or 1 cup fresh pineapple, cut into 1½-inch pieces
2	green peppers, cut into 1½-inch squares, and parboiled for 2 minutes
14	medium-size fresh mushrooms

Place chicken in a large nonmetallic bowl. In a small bowl, mix all the remaining ingredients together, except the pineapple chunks, green peppers, and mushrooms. Pour over chicken. Marinate in refrigerator for at least 4 hours, or longer if you wish.

When ready to cook, drain chicken, and reserve marinade. Thread chicken pieces, pineapple chunks, green peppers, and mushrooms alternately on skewers. Pour marinade into a small saucepan, and bring to a boil. Place skewers in a pan to catch any drippings, spoon marinade over skewers, and broil for 8 minutes, or until chicken and vegetables are cooked. Do not overcook. Baste with sauce, and turn skewers after 5 minutes.

Stuffed Chicken Breasts with Honey-Sesame Seed Glaze and Sugar Snap Peas

4 servings

STUFFING

- 2 thin slices whole grain bread, crusts removed
- ¼ cup milk
- ½ pound lean ground pork
- 2 scallions, thinly sliced
- 6 water chestnuts, finely chopped
- 2 teaspoons finely minced peeled ginger root
- ¼ teaspoon black pepper
- 2 teaspoons soy sauce

CHICKEN

- 4 whole chicken breasts with skin, boned (about ½ pound each)
- 2 tablespoons light honey
- 2 tablespoons sesame seeds
- ½ pound sugar snap peas, blanched for 1 minute

To make the stuffing: Tear bread into pieces. In a small bowl, mix bread and milk together, and let stand for 5 minutes. Add all the remaining ingredients, and mix well. Refrigerate.

To make the chicken: Preheat oven to 425°F. Oil a 9 × 13 × 2-inch baking dish.

Place chicken breasts skin-side down between 2 pieces of waxed paper, and pound

to flatten slightly. Place ⅓ to ½ cup of stuffing on each breast. Fold side ends over, and roll to enclose stuffing. Place seam-side down in center of baking dish, and bake for 20 minutes. Trickle honey over breasts, sprinkle with sesame seeds, and bake for 10 minutes more, basting with any pan juices. (If chicken is too dry, you may add ¼ cup water.) Arrange sugar snap peas around the sides of the baking dish, and serve immediately.

Sauteed Chicken Breasts with Lemon and Mint

4 servings

The elegant coolness of mint, the tartness of lemon, and the delicacy of chicken all combine to make this an easy, tasty, very light main course.

- 4 boneless, skinless chicken breast halves, pounded flat
  whole wheat flour, for dredging
- ¼ teaspoon black pepper
- 3 tablespoons butter
- ¼ cup lemon juice
- 1 tablespoon finely minced lemon rind
- 2 tablespoons finely minced fresh mint

Dredge chicken in flour and pepper. Melt butter in a 10-inch skillet until foamy. Saute breasts quickly on both sides over medium-high heat for about 2 minutes on each side. Add lemon juice to pan. Tilt pan, and baste chicken with lemon-butter mixture, continuing to cook until cooked through but not overcooked, about 2 to 3 minutes more, depending upon how thick breasts are. Transfer to a warm serving dish or platter, sprinkle with lemon rind and mint, and serve.

Baked Veal Shank with Oranges, Mixed Herbs, and Fennel

4 servings

The meat marinates for six to eight hours in a citrus, herb, spice, and onion marinade, which is then made into a marvelous and tasty sauce after the veal is baked. It's an elegant dish that can be served over fine pasta such as capellini.

3 pounds meaty veal shank, cut into 2 large pieces (have butcher saw end bone tips off so that only center cut is used)

¾ teaspoon freshly ground black pepper

2 lemons

3 oranges

2 cups finely chopped onions (about 1 pound)

2 tablespoons coarsely chopped fresh basil

1 dried bay leaf

1 tablespoon fresh thyme leaves

1 small bulb fennel, bulb coarsely chopped and feathery leaves minced

½ teaspoon ground cloves whole wheat flour, for dredging

2 tablespoons butter

1 tablespoon olive oil

1 tablespoon vinegar (preferably balsamic)

1 teaspoon light honey

¼ cup chicken stock

Place meat into a large, nonmetallic bowl, and sprinkle generously with pepper. Squeeze juice of lemons into a small cup. Grate rind of 2 oranges, and reserve. (There should be about 2 tablespoons.) Squeeze juice of the 2 oranges, and add to lemon juice. Peel skin and white membrane from third orange, divide into sections, and reserve. Add lemon-orange juice, onions, basil, bay leaf, thyme, fennel bulb, and cloves to meat. Cover, and marinate for 6 to 8 hours, turning occasionally. When ready to cook, lift meat out of bowl, and reserve marinade. Dry meat well on paper towels, and dredge in flour.

Preheat oven to 350°F.

On top of the stove, in a large heavy Dutch oven with a lid, heat butter and oil until very hot. Add meat and brown on all sides. Add marinade, cover, and bake for 1½ hours, turning meat once during baking time.

When ready to serve, remove meat to a warm serving platter, and keep warm. Remove bay leaf, and discard. Pour sauce into a blender, let cool slightly, and liquefy. In the same Dutch oven on top of the stove, add vinegar, honey, and chicken stock. Stir over medium heat, scraping any bits from the bottom and sides of the pot. Cook for 1 minute. Add liquefied sauce and 1 tablespoon of the orange rind to vinegar-honey mixture, and simmer slowly for about 2 minutes. Add reserved orange sections. When orange sections are heated through, spoon some of the sauce and oranges around the bottom of the serving platter. Sprinkle meat with remaining orange rind and the fennel leaves. Serve remaining sauce at the table to be spooned over cooked rice or fine noodles.

The Puritans customarily chewed fennel seed when they went to religious services, so it became known as "the meetin' seed."

◄ Veal Chops with Mushrooms and Lemon Thyme Cream (page 148)

Braised Endives Stuffed with Veal, Pork, and Fennel Seeds

4 servings

An elegant luncheon dish for four. Or serve it as an appetizer to feed eight guests.

½ pound fresh sweet Italian sausage, casing removed
1 medium onion
½ pound lean ground veal
2 tablespoons light cream
⅓ cup milk
2 tablespoons grated Parmesan cheese
¼ cup fine whole grain bread crumbs
1 egg, beaten
1 teaspoon dried fennel seeds
⅛ teaspoon black pepper
2 tablespoons finely chopped fresh parsley
1 teaspoon grated lemon rind
8 large Belgian endives
¼ cup butter, divided

Crumble sausage into a small saucepan, and saute for a few minutes, stirring constantly, until color is lost. Chop onion in a food processor, and then add sausage, veal, cream, milk, cheese, bread crumbs, egg, fennel seeds, pepper, parsley, and lemon rind. Process for a few seconds until well mixed. There will be about 3 cups of meat mixture. Spoon into a medium-size bowl, and set aside while preparing endives.

Cut endives in half lengthwise. Carefully cut out the center part, leaving boat-shaped shells. (The center parts can be cut up and used for a salad.) Stuff each half with meat mixture, and place 2 halves together. Wrap and tie them with thin white string. Melt 2

tablespoons of the butter in a heavy 12-inch skillet (it should accommodate the endives in a single layer). Dot endives with remaining butter, and cover tightly. Braise over low heat for 30 minutes.

Remove endives to a warm serving platter, and cut the strings. Meanwhile, continue to heat liquid remaining in skillet. If there seems to be too much, reduce over high heat for 4 to 5 minutes, and then pour over endives.

Osso Bucco Milanese: Braised Veal Shanks with Mixed Herbs

4 to 5 servings

A condiment called Gremolata—grated citrus rind, garlic, and parsley—is sprinkled over the meat when it's ready to serve. It's great with rice, orzo, or crusty bread.

8 2-inch pieces meaty shin of veal, with bone and marrow (about 6 pounds)
 whole wheat flour, for dredging
½ teaspoon black pepper
2 tablespoons butter
3 tablespoons olive oil
1 tablespoon finely chopped fresh sage
½ teaspoon powdered bay leaves (optional)
1 tablespoon fresh thyme leaves
1 teaspoon coarsely chopped fresh rosemary
1½ cups finely chopped onions
1 cup finely chopped carrots
½ cup finely chopped celery

1 tablespoon plus 1 teaspoon finely
    minced garlic, divided
1 cup dry white wine
1¼ cups chicken stock
3 tablespoons tomato paste
1 teaspoon grated lemon rind
2 teaspoons grated orange rind
¼ cup finely minced fresh parsley

Dredge meat all over in flour mixed with pepper. In a large heavy skillet, heat butter and oil together until foamy. Brown meat on all sides, a few pieces at a time. Remove to a large Dutch oven, and arrange pieces on their sides so that marrow will not fall out. Sprinkle meat with herbs, onions, carrots, celery, and 1 tablespoon of the garlic. Cover pot tightly, and braise for 10 minutes over medium heat. In a large measuring cup, mix wine, stock, and tomato paste together, and pour over meat. Cover, lower heat to a simmer, and cook for about 2 hours, or until meat is very tender.

Mix the Gremolata by stirring citrus rinds, remaining garlic, and parsley together. Transfer meat to a large warm serving platter, and sprinkle half the Gremolata over meat. Pass the remainder in a small dish at the table.

Roast Veal
with Mustard-Tarragon Sauce

4 to 5 servings

Pale, delicate, and luxurious, this is a roast for all seasons and all occasions.

1¼ pounds top sirloin of veal or
    boneless veal shoulder
2 tablespoons softened butter
¼ teaspoon black pepper

⅓ cup finely chopped carrots
⅓ cup finely chopped celery
¾ cup finely chopped onions
1 teaspoon finely minced garlic
1 tablespoon whole fresh tarragon
    leaves
⅓ cup chicken stock
¾ cup heavy cream
2 teaspoons French-style mustard
1 teaspoon finely chopped fresh
    tarragon leaves

Preheat oven to 400°F.

Rub veal with butter, and sprinkle with pepper. Place in a medium-size shallow roasting pan, and roast for 30 minutes.

Mix together carrots, celery, onions, garlic, and whole tarragon leaves in a medium-size bowl, and scatter mixture around meat. Pour in stock, cover loosely with aluminum foil, and continue to roast for 20 minutes more, basting with pan juices. Lift roast out of pan, and cover with foil to keep warm while preparing sauce.

Pour off all the liquid and the vegetables from the roasting pan into a small nonstick saucepan, and cook over high heat for 8 to 10 minutes. Then strain sauce through a fine sieve, pressing solids against the sides of the sieve to extract as much of the liquid as possible. You should have about ¼ cup of liquid. Discard solids. Return sauce to small saucepan along with any juices that have accumulated around roast, and add cream. Heat sauce until hot, then stir in mustard and simmer for 5 minutes. Add chopped tarragon. Thinly slice veal, and place on a warm platter, spooning a bit of the sauce down the center of the slices. Pass remaining sauce at the table in a sauceboat.

The Greeks braided rosemary into their hair before school examinations to fortify the brain and refresh the memory.

Rosy Veal Scallops with Paprika, Rosemary, and Thyme

4 servings

You might try this colorful entree accompanied by an equally colorful vegetable such as Sweet and Sour Lettuce with Dill (page 237). They go well together.

- 2 tablespoons olive oil
- 1 teaspoon paprika
- ¾ pound thin veal scallops, pounded to a ⅛-inch thickness
- 1 tablespoon butter
- 3 tablespoons finely minced shallots
- ¼ cup dry white wine
- 1 large tomato, peeled and cubed
- 1 tablespoon tomato paste
- 2 teaspoons minced fresh rosemary
- 1 teaspoon fresh thyme leaves
- ⅛ teaspoon black pepper
- ½ cup plain yogurt

In a large skillet, heat oil until very hot. Add paprika. Saute scallops quickly for about 1 minute on each side. Remove to a serving dish, and keep warm. In the same skillet, melt butter. Add shallots, and saute, while stirring, until wilted but not brown, about 2 minutes. Add wine and tomatoes, and cook, stirring occasionally, over medium heat until sauce is reduced, about 5 minutes. Stir in tomato paste, herbs, and pepper, and cook for 1 to 2 minutes more. Remove from heat, and quickly stir in yogurt. Spoon sauce around scallops, and serve immediately.

Veal Braised with Sage

4 servings

Serve this simple and elegant dish over small pasta (orzo or tubettini) or rice.

- 2 tablespoons butter
- 2 tablespoons olive oil
- 1 tablespoon finely minced shallots (about 3 large shallots)
- 1½ pounds boneless veal shoulder, cut into 2-inch pieces
- ¼ cup whole wheat flour, for dredging
- ¼ teaspoon black pepper
- ⅔ cup dry white wine
- 20 whole fresh sage leaves
- 2 fresh sage leaves, coarsely chopped

Heat butter and oil in a heavy 12-inch skillet. Add shallots, and slowly saute until tender over low heat, stirring occasionally so that they don't burn. Lift out shallots with a slotted spoon, and set aside. Dredge meat lightly in flour. Turn heat up under skillet until butter and oil are foamy, add meat, and saute until brown, lowering heat a bit if necessary and turning meat with tongs to brown evenly on all sides. Sprinkle with pepper, then add wine and whole sage leaves, and bring to a boil. Lower heat to a simmer, cover skillet tightly, and cook slowly for 45 to 60 minutes, stirring occasionally. During the last 15 minutes of cooking, check to see whether liquid has been reduced too much. If so, add ⅓ cup water, return shallots to skillet, and continue simmering. Serve sprinkled with chopped sage leaves.

Shrimp and Sea Scallops in Green Sauce (page 177) ➜

Veal Scallops with Mozzarella and Basil

4 servings

8 thin veal scallops
  freshly ground black pepper
2 hot Italian sausages, casings
    removed and meat crumbled
4 slices mozzarella cheese, minced
8 fresh basil leaves, finely minced
¼ cup grated Parmesan cheese
  whole wheat flour, for dredging
¼ cup butter, divided
1 tablespoon olive oil
⅓ cup chicken stock
⅓ cup dry white wine
1 tablespoon finely minced fresh
    parsley

Pound veal scallops between 2 pieces of waxed paper so that they lie flat. Sprinkle with pepper, and reserve. Place crumbled sausage into a small skillet and saute, stirring occasionally, for about 5 minutes. Transfer cooked sausage to a small bowl, and add mozzarella, basil, and Parmesan cheese. Mix well, and then squeeze and roll this mixture into 8 balls, small enough for scallops to enclose them. Place a ball of filling on each scallop, fold in sides of veal first, then roll up to enclose filling. Fasten with a toothpick, and dredge each roll lightly in flour, coating all sides evenly.

Use a skillet large enough to accommodate the veal rolls in a single layer. Heat 3 tablespoons of the butter and the olive oil until hot and bubbly. Add veal and brown quickly on all sides, turning carefully. Cook 3 to 4 minutes on each side. Transfer to a warmed serving platter, remove toothpicks, and keep warm in the oven.

In a cup, mix chicken stock and wine together, add to skillet, and bring to a boil stirring to scrape up any brown bits. Cook, stirring constantly, until sauce is reduced by half and is syrupy in consistency. Swirl in remaining butter, and pour sauce over meat. Sprinkle each roll with a bit of parsley before serving.

Veal Chops with Mushrooms and Lemon Thyme Cream

4 servings

4 rib veal chops (1½ to 2 pounds)
¼ teaspoon black pepper
  whole wheat flour, for dredging
2 tablespoons olive oil
2 tablespoons butter
2 tablespoons finely minced shallots
¼ pound fresh mushrooms, sliced
1 teaspoon lemon juice
¾ cup beef stock
2 tablespoons creme fraiche
1 teaspoon fresh lemon thyme leaves

Season chops with black pepper, and dredge lightly in flour. In a large skillet, heat oil until very hot. Add chops, and saute over high heat for 3 to 4 minutes on each side, or until brown. Remove chops to a hot serving platter, and keep warm.

Wipe out skillet with paper towels, and melt butter. Add shallots, stir for a few seconds, then add mushrooms, and cook, stirring constantly, for 2 to 3 minutes more. Add lemon juice and stock. Cook over medium-high heat for 5 minutes. Stir in creme fraiche, and cook for 2 to 3 minutes more, or until sauce has thickened slightly and has been reduced. Add lemon thyme to sauce, and pour over chops.

Veal Loaf with Mushroom and Marjoram Sauce

6 servings

Yet another way to get away from the ubiquitous meat loaf made with beef. It's a new and tasty variation of an old favorite.

VEAL LOAF

      2 teaspoons butter
      ¼ cup finely chopped scallions
          (about 2 thin scallions)
      ½ teaspoon finely minced garlic
          (about 1 clove)
      1 teaspoon finely minced fresh
          rosemary leaves
      ¼ pound fresh mushrooms, finely
          chopped (about 1 cup)
    1¼ pounds lean ground veal
      ¼ teaspoon black pepper
      ⅛ teaspoon powdered bay leaves
      ⅔ cup whole grain bread crumbs
      3 tablespoons milk
      1 egg, slightly beaten
      2 tablespoons finely minced fresh
          parsley

SAUCE

      3 tablespoons butter, divided
      2 tablespoons whole wheat flour
      ¾ cup chicken stock

      ⅛ teaspoon black pepper
      1 tablespoon finely minced shallots
      ¼ pound mushrooms, thinly sliced
      ¾ cup milk
      1 tablespoon finely minced fresh
          marjoram

To make the loaf: Preheat oven to 350°F. Butter a 4½ × 8½ × 2¾-inch loaf pan.

In a medium-size skillet, melt butter. Add scallions and garlic, and saute for 1 minute, stirring constantly. Add rosemary and mushrooms, and cook until mushrooms give up their liquid. Cool for 5 minutes.

In a large bowl, mix all the remaining ingredients together, mixing well. Blend in mushroom mixture, then pack smoothly into prepared loaf pan, and bake for 55 minutes. Cool for 15 minutes before slicing.

To make the sauce: Melt 2 tablespoons of the butter in a medium-size nonstick saucepan. Whisk in flour, mixing until smooth over medium-low heat. Add chicken stock, a bit at a time, whisking constantly until sauce is smooth. Add pepper, and lower heat to a simmer. Whisk occasionally for 10 minutes, or until sauce is cooked. Set aside. This is a veloute base.

In a medium-size skillet, melt remaining butter. Add shallots, stir for 1 minute, and then add mushrooms. Cook over medium-high heat until mushrooms give up their liquid, stirring occasionally. Add mushroom mixture to veloute base. Add milk, and whisk over low heat until sauce is smooth. Cook to just before the boiling point. Stir in marjoram, and if there is any accumulated juice from the meat, whisk it into the sauce as well. This last step can be done right before serving. Serve sauce separately to be spooned over slices of veal loaf.

Veal Marengo with White Pearl Onions, Mushrooms, Tomatoes, and Mixed Herbs

4 to 6 servings

This tasty veal dish goes well with fine green noodles.

¼ cup olive oil
1½ pounds eye round veal, cubed
3 tablespoons butter, divided
¾ cup peeled tiny white pearl onions (25 to 30 onions)
1 cup whole fresh button mushrooms or sliced larger fresh mushrooms
1½ tablespoons whole wheat flour
1 tablespoon finely minced garlic
1 cup dry white wine
3 medium-size tomatoes, peeled and chopped
1½ teaspoons fresh thyme leaves
¾ teaspoons fresh marjoram leaves
¼ teaspoon black pepper
3 tablespoons finely minced fresh parsley, divided
1 cup chicken stock

Heat olive oil in a 10-inch skillet until very hot. Make sure meat is dry. Add meat cubes to skillet without crowding, and brown on all sides. You may need to do 2 batches. Remove meat to a plate with a slotted spoon, and set aside.

Add 1 tablespoon of the butter to the same skillet. Add onions, and cook over medium-high heat for 1 to 2 minutes. Remove to a bowl with a slotted spoon, and set aside. Add mushrooms to the same skillet, stir, and cook for a few seconds. Remove to the same bowl as the onions. To the same skillet, add remaining butter, melt it slowly, and add flour. Cook and stir over low heat until butter-flour mixture is tan in color, 3 to 4 minutes. Then add garlic, and cook for a few seconds, stirring constantly. Add wine, and cook until it boils. Stir in tomatoes, thyme, marjoram, pepper, and 1 tablespoon of the parsley. Add chicken stock, and bring to a boil. Lower heat, add meat, onions, and mushrooms, and bring to a boil again. Lower heat, cover, and simmer for 45 minutes.

Lift out meat and vegetables with a slotted spoon, place in a warm serving dish, and keep warm. Reduce sauce by cooking over high heat for about 10 minutes, or until reduced by half. Stir occasionally as it cooks. Spoon sauce over meat, and sprinkle with remaining parsley. Serve with fine green noodles.

Veal Rollatine with Basil and Thyme

4 servings

Whenever we cook any kind of rollatine, someone at the table always comments, "Rollatine is one of my favorite dishes!" Whether it's the surprise of the filling or the taste, this dish never fails to please.

4 thin, long veal scallops, about ¼ pound each, pounded lightly
½ cup whole grain bread crumbs
½ teaspoon finely minced garlic
3 tablespoons Parmesan cheese
2½ tablespoons finely minced fresh parsley
¼ teaspoon black pepper

Chicken Pot Pie with Cilantro
and Jalapeno Pepper-Cheddar
Cheese Crust (page 124)

1 teaspoon grated lemon rind
1 tablespoon finely minced fresh
   oregano
2 tablespoons finely minced fresh
   basil
2 tablespoons light cream
4 tablespoons butter, melted, divided
   whole wheat flour, for dredging
½ cup chicken stock
1 teaspoon lemon juice
1 cup cubed peeled ripe tomatoes
1 teaspoon minced fresh parsley

Lay veal scallops on a sheet of waxed
paper, and set aside. In a small bowl, mix
bread crumbs, garlic, cheese, parsley, pepper,
lemon rind, herbs, cream, and 2 tablespoons
of the butter. Spread about 1½ tablespoons of
this mixture evenly on each scallop. Roll up,
and secure with a toothpick. Dredge each roll
lightly in flour, and set aside.

In a large skillet, melt remaining butter
over medium-high heat. When hot, add veal
rolls, and brown quickly on all sides, turning
with tongs. Remove to a warm serving dish,
and set aside. Pour chicken stock into skillet,
scraping up any brown bits with a wooden
spoon. Add lemon juice and tomatoes, and
bring to a boil. Lower heat, and crush tomatoes a bit while stirring. Return veal rolls to
skillet, spoon some sauce over them, and
simmer for 5 minutes on each side. Transfer
to a serving dish, and sprinkle with parsley.

Veal Scallops Piccate with Lemon and Tarragon

4 servings

- 8 very thin veal scallops (about 1 pound), pounded lightly
- ⅛ teaspoon black pepper
  whole wheat flour, for dredging
- 3 tablespoons butter, divided
- 1 tablespoon olive oil
- 8 very thin slices of lemon
- ¾ cup chicken stock
- 2 tablespoons lemon juice
- 1 teaspoon coarsely chopped fresh tarragon
- 1 teaspoon capers, rinsed and dried (optional)

Sprinkle veal scallops with pepper, and dredge in flour. Heat 2 tablespoons of the butter and the oil in a large heavy skillet. When it foams up, add veal scallops, and cook for 1 minute on each side. Remove veal from skillet with a slotted spoon, and place on a warmed serving platter. Place 1 slice of lemon on each scallop. Keep warm.

Return the same skillet to the top of the stove. Add chicken stock, stirring to scrape up any brown bits. Then add lemon juice, stir, and cook until sauce begins to boil. Lower heat, add remaining butter, tarragon, and capers (if used), and heat for a few seconds. Spoon sauce over veal, and serve immediately.

PORK

Boneless Loin of Pork with Ground Coriander Seeds and Cloves, Baked with Pineapple

6 servings

- 2 pounds boneless loin of pork, rolled and tied
- ⅛ teaspoon ground cloves
- ¼ teaspoon ground coriander
- ¼ teaspoon dry mustard
- ¼ teaspoon black pepper
- 2 cloves garlic, peeled and finely minced (about 1 teaspoon)
- ¼ cup white wine vinegar
- ¼ cup light soy sauce
- ¼ cup olive oil
- 2 tablespoons frozen pineapple juice concentrate
- ¼ cup light honey
- 1 small pineapple
- 1 to 2 pears, peeled, cored, and sliced
  red grapes
  sprigs of watercress

Place pork into a medium-size shallow roasting pan. In a small saucepan, mix together all the remaining ingredients except pineapple, pears, grapes, and watercress, and bring to a boil. Simmer for 30 minutes, uncovered, and then cool.

Preheat oven to 350°F.

Cut off both ends of pineapple, and cut in half lengthwise. Scoop out the flesh, cut it into cubes, and reserve. Reserve one half of pineapple shell, discarding other half. Brush meat generously with sauce, cover it with reserved pineapple shell, and bake for 50 to 60 minutes. Remove pineapple shell, raise heat to 400°F, baste pork, and continue to bake for 10 minutes more, basting once or twice. Let rest for 10 minutes. Remove string, and slice meat into thick slices. Place in the center of a warm platter with slices overlapping. Artfully arrange the cubes of pineapple, sliced pears, and grapes in clusters around pork with watercress sprigs.

Brochettes of Pork with Fennel Seeds, Pearl Onions, and Cilantro

This festive dish has an Indonesian flavor.

- ¼ cup light soy sauce
- ½ cup water
- ¼ cup honey
- 2 tablespoons red wine vinegar
- 1 tablespoon finely minced garlic
- 1 tablespoon finely minced peeled ginger root
- 2 or 3 drops of hot pepper sauce
- 1 teaspoon paprika
- 1 tablespoon fennel seeds, crushed with a mortar and pestle
- 1½ pounds boneless loin of pork, cut into 1½-inch cubes
- 2 tablespoons butter
- 16 white pearl onions, peeled
- 1 tablespoon lemon juice
- 1 tablespoon finely minced fresh cilantro

Soak 8 wooden skewers in boiling water for 15 minutes. This will keep them from igniting under the broiler. (Metal skewers may also be used.) Mix together in a small bowl, soy sauce, water, honey, wine vinegar, garlic, ginger, hot pepper sauce, paprika, and fennel seeds. Marinate pork cubes in this mixture for at least 15 minutes. Strain marinade into a cup, and reserve spices. Heat ⅓ cup of the strained marinade in a small saucepan. Add reserved spices, and bring to a boil. Add butter, and simmer for 10 minutes.

Preheat broiler.

Skewer meat and onions, alternately, on the skewers, place on a rack in a broiler pan, and broil for about 10 minutes on each side. Meanwhile, remove marinade from heat, strain again, and discard solids. Add lemon juice and cilantro to strained sauce. Pour into a sauceboat, and spoon over brochettes when they're done.

Braised Pork Chops with Green Peppercorns and Mustard Sauce

2 to 4 servings

A colorful confettilike sauce with the bite of green peppercorns and mustard gives everyday pork chops a gourmet treatment.

    4   thinly sliced center-cut lean pork
          chops (about 1 pound)
   ⅛   teaspoon black pepper
   ¼   cup whole wheat flour
   ½   teaspoon paprika
    1   tablespoon corn oil
   ⅓   cup finely chopped onions (about
          1 small onion)
   ⅓   cup finely chopped carrots (about
          1 small carrot)
    1   teaspoon finely minced garlic
   ½   dried bay leaf
    1   teaspoon fresh thyme leaves
   ½   cup water
   ½   cup chicken stock
    2   tablespoons French-style mustard
    1   teaspoon water-packed green
          peppercorns, rinsed and crushed
    1   tablespoon finely minced fresh
          parsley

Sprinkle chops with pepper. Mix flour and paprika together in a cup, and dredge chops. Heat oil in a medium-size heavy skillet over medium heat. Add chops, and brown on both sides, about 3 minutes to each side. Pour off any accumulated fat, and sprinkle chops with onions, carrots, and garlic. Add bay leaf, thyme, water, and chicken stock. Cover, and cook over low heat for 15 to 20 minutes. Remove chops to a warm platter.

Discard bay leaf, add mustard to pan drippings, and heat but do not boil. Stir in peppercorns and parsley. Spoon sauce over chops, and serve immediately.

Honey-Glazed Loin of Pork with Cloves and Ginger

4 to 6 servings

    1   large clove garlic, peeled
   ½   teaspoon black pepper
    3   pounds center-cut loin of pork
          (about 7 chops in 1 piece with
          bone cut part way through for
          easy carving at the table)
    1   cup orange juice
   ⅓   cup light honey
    1   tablespoon ground ginger
   ¼   teaspoon ground cloves

Preheat oven to 350°F.

On a sheet of aluminum foil, mash garlic and pepper together by using the heel of a flat-bottomed knife until a paste forms. Spread over top of pork. Place pork on a rack in a medium-size roasting pan, and roast for 30 minutes, uncovered.

Meanwhile, in a small nonstick saucepan, mix orange juice with honey, ginger, and cloves, and simmer for 30 minutes. Brush this glaze over roast 2 or 3 times during the last hour of roasting time. Total time for roasting should be about 1½ hours. Then remove from oven, and cover with a foil tent. Allow pork to rest for 10 minutes. When ready to serve, transfer to a warm platter and carve chops with a strong knife.

Tie a bunch of fresh herbs together and use them as a "paint brush" to apply basting liquids or butter sauce while grilling meats, fish, or vegetables.

---

for 15 minutes. Reduce heat, turn ribs top-side up, and bake for 35 to 40 minutes more. If ribs seem dry toward the end of the baking time, add some water, and baste to keep them moist. Place under broiler for the last 1 or 2 minutes to char slightly. Cut into serving portions, allowing about 3 ribs per person.

Marinated Pork Spareribs with Citrus and Rosemary

4 servings

We find that pork tastes best when it's marinated, letting the flavors permeate the meat before we cook it. In this recipe we use a marinade of citrus, garlic, and fresh herbs.

¼ cup lemon juice
¼ cup orange juice
2 tablespoons olive oil
1 tablespoon French-style mustard
¼ teaspoon black pepper
1 teaspoon finely minced garlic
2 tablespoons coarsely chopped fresh rosemary leaves
2½ pounds lean pork spareribs in 1 piece

In a food processor, mix all the ingredients together, except ribs. Coat ribs on both sides with marinade, cover with aluminum foil, and refrigerate for at least 8 hours. The ribs can be kept in the refrigerator overnight and right up until dinnertime the next day if you'd like. Spoon some of the marinade over ribs several times during that period.

Preheat oven to 375°F.

Bake ribs, uncovered, bottom-side up,

Pork Loaf with Basil, Parsley, and Pine Nuts

6 to 8 servings

This is a plain and simple meat loaf that's economical and easy to prepare. Slice and serve it as a main course, or try it cold on whole grain bread as an hors d'oeuvre.

1 pound lean ground pork
¼ teaspoon black pepper
1 tablespoon olive oil
1 tablespoon finely minced garlic
¾ cup fine whole grain bread crumbs
⅓ cup pine nuts, toasted
½ cup finely minced fresh basil
⅓ finely minced fresh parsley
⅓ cup grated Parmesan cheese
1 egg, slightly beaten

Preheat oven to 400°F. Oil an 8½ × 4½-inch loaf pan.

Put pork into a medium-size bowl, and add pepper. Heat oil in a small skillet. Add garlic, and saute until wilted. Add to pork along with all the remaining ingredients. Mix well, and pack mixture into loaf pan. Bake for 1 hour, and then let stand for 15 minutes, covered loosely with aluminum foil. Loosen edges with a knife, and invert onto a serving plate.

Pork Chops
with Prune-Nutmeg Sauce

4 servings

A traditional French way of serving pork chops. We still remember our first taste in a small restaurant overlooking the Loire.

- 4 center-cut lean loin pork chops (about ¼ pound each), pounded until thin
  whole wheat flour, for dredging
- ⅛ teaspoon black pepper
- 15 pitted prunes
- ⅛ teaspoon ground nutmeg
- 2 tablespoons red wine vinegar
- ⅔ cup water
- 2 tablespoons corn oil
- ½ cup finely chopped onions
- ¾ cup chicken stock
- 1 tablespoon butter
  sprig of fresh parsley

Dredge chops lightly in flour, and sprinkle with pepper. Put prunes into a medium-size saucepan, add nutmeg, wine vinegar, and water, and bring to a boil. Lower heat, and simmer, uncovered, for about 10 minutes, or until almost all the liquid is evaporated.

While prunes are cooking, heat oil in a medium-size heavy skillet. Brown pork chops for 4 to 5 minutes on each side, and transfer to a warm serving dish. Pour off any remaining fat from skillet. Add onions, lower heat, and cook while stirring, until wilted and slightly browned. Add chicken stock, and stir to dissolve any brown bits that may cling to pan. Add prune mixture to skillet, and heat for 2 to 3 minutes. Swirl in butter, pour sauce over pork chops, garnish with sprig of parsley, and serve warm.

Portuguese Pork with Clams,
Bay Leaves, and Cayenne Pepper

4 servings

We first tasted this dish on the coast of Portugal where we were producing a film on the building of the new bridge across the Tagus River outside Lisbon. The pork and clams make a lovely combination, besides bringing back memories.

- 1 pound boneless lean pork, cut into ¾-inch cubes
- ⅓ cup white wine
- 2 tablespoons red wine vinegar
- 2 dried bay leaves or ¼ teaspoon powdered bay leaves
- 2 cloves garlic, peeled and crushed
- 1 teaspoon sweet paprika
- ⅛ teaspoon cayenne pepper
- 3 tablespoons olive oil, divided
- 2 cups thinly sliced onions (about 1 large onion)
- 1 teaspoon finely minced garlic
- 1 cup thin sweet red pepper strips
- 1 cup peeled and cubed tomatoes
- ⅛ teaspoon black pepper
- 2 dozen small littleneck clams in shells, well scrubbed
- ¼ cup coarsely minced fresh parsley
- 4 lemon wedges

In a medium-size nonmetallic bowl, mix pork cubes with wine, vinegar, bay leaves, crushed garlic, paprika, and cayenne pepper, and let marinate at room temperature for 1½ to 2 hours. Then, lift out pork with a slotted spoon, and drain well on paper towels. Reserve marinade, and discard dried bay leaves if used. Heat 2 tablespoons of the olive oil in a deep 10-inch skillet with a tight-fitting lid. Add onions, minced garlic, and red peppers, and saute over medium-high heat until soft, but not brown, stirring occasionally. Lift out with a slotted spoon, and reserve.

In the same skillet, heat remaining olive oil. Add pork, and saute over high heat, turning cubes so that they brown on all sides. Add marinade, stirring to scrape up any brown bits from the bottom of the skillet. Stir in tomatoes, and cook for 1 minute. Return onion-red pepper mixture to skillet along with black pepper, and simmer, covered, for 5 minutes. Add clams, hinged-sides down, cover tightly, raise heat to medium-high, and cook for 5 to 8 minutes, or until shells open. Transfer to a serving dish, sprinkle with parsley, and garnish with lemon wedges to be squeezed over all at the table. Serve with crusty bread to soak up the sauce.

Note: Some clams are stubborn. If a few of them don't open during the first cooking, let them remain in the skillet while you transfer the others to the serving dish and cook them, covered, for an extra few minutes over high heat. If they still don't open, discard them.

whole wheat flour, for dredging
⅛ teaspoon black pepper
2 tablespoons butter, divided
1 tablespoon olive oil
8 sprigs of fresh thyme
1 tart green apple, unpeeled, cored, and cut into ¼-inch slices
pinch of ground cinnamon

Dredge chops lightly in flour and pepper. Heat 1 tablespoon of the butter and the oil in a large cast-iron skillet. Add chops, and saute for 5 minutes on each side over medium-high heat. While they are cooking, place 2 sprigs of thyme under each chop so that they stick to the meat. Remove chops to a serving dish, and keep warm. Using the same skillet, melt remaining tablespoon of butter. Add apples, and saute for 4 to 5 minutes, or until soft but not mushy. Spoon apple slices around pork, and sprinkle apples with cinnamon. Serve hot.

Sauteed Pork Chops with Thyme and Sliced Apples

4 servings

Pork is a rich meat, usually eaten in the winter when heartier foods are appropriate but fresh thyme may be hard to come by. Therefore, you can use 1 tablespoon of dried thyme, sprinkled on both sides of the pork chops.

4 lean loin pork chops, ½ inch thick (about 1¼ pounds), pounded lightly

Basil has made something of a reputation as a literary hiding place for decapitated heads:

❧ *Salome hid the head of John the Baptist in a pot of basil.*

❧ *Boccaccio's Lisabetta buried the head of her lover in a pot of basil.*

❧ *Keats's Isabella also buried the head of her lover, Lorenzo — guess where — and watered the plant with her tears.*

Stuffed Pork Chops
with Mushrooms and Marjoram

4 servings

¼ pound fresh sweet Italian sausage
    with fennel (about 2 links)
¼ cup finely minced onions
½ teaspoon finely minced garlic
    (1 small clove)
⅔ cup finely chopped fresh
    mushrooms
1 tablespoon finely minced fresh
    marjoram
¼ teaspoon black pepper
    dash of cayenne pepper
¼ cup whole grain bread crumbs
    (preferably corn bread)
1 egg, beaten
4 center-cut lean pork chops, 1 inch
    thick
    whole wheat flour, for dredging
2 tablespoons butter
1 cup chicken stock

Remove sausage from casing, and crumble into a 10-inch skillet. Cook and stir over low heat until meat loses its pink color. Then add onions and garlic, and cook, while stirring for 3 to 4 minutes, making sure that the onions do not burn. Add mushrooms, marjoram, black pepper, and cayenne, and cook, stirring constantly, for 2 minutes more. Then add bread crumbs, remove from heat, and cool slightly. Stir in egg. There should be about 1 cup of stuffing. Cool stuffing while preparing pork chops.

Slit the meaty part of each chop in half crosswise, and lay it open like a book. The bone should form the "spine"; do not separate the meat from the bone. Pound each flap gently with a meat pounder or a heavy cleaver. Spoon 2 to 3 tablespoons of stuffing into the center of each chop, close flaps, and then tie with string or secure with toothpicks to enclose filling. Dredge in flour, and set aside.

In a large heavy skillet big enough to hold all the chops, heat butter. Add chops and brown over medium heat for 3 to 4 minutes on each side. Then add chicken stock, cover, and lower heat to a simmer. Cook slowly for 15 minutes. Remove cover, turn chops, and cook, uncovered, for 10 to 12 minutes more, or until most of the liquid evaporates. Transfer chops to a warm serving platter, remove strings or toothpicks, and spoon any remaining sauce over each to glaze slightly.

LAMB

Baked Lamb Ribs,
Tibetan Style, with Turmeric,
Coriander Seeds, and Cumin Seeds

4 servings

This dish is first marinated for four hours and then basted with a soothing yogurt sauce spiked with fresh ginger root, spices, and hot pepper.

4 pounds breast of lamb
½ cup plain yogurt
½ teaspoon minced garlic
¼ teaspoon black pepper
⅛ teaspoon cayenne pepper
2 tablespoons ketchup
1 teaspoon cumin seeds, ground in a
    spice grinder
1 teaspoon coriander seeds, ground in
    a spice grinder
½ teaspoon turmeric

1　teaspoon grated peeled ginger root
½　cup water
3　tablespoons finely chopped
　　fresh mint

Trim any excess fat from lamb. Cut into small pieces of 1 rib each, but leave them connected to one another at the base of the rack. Place lamb ribs into a large, shallow nonmetallic baking dish. In a small bowl, combine the rest of the ingredients, except mint, and spoon over lamb, turning to coat the other side as well. Refrigerate for a minimum of 4 hours (or overnight).

When ready to bake, preheat oven to 350°F.

Place ribs on a rack in a large, shallow aluminum-foil-lined baking pan. Baste lamb with accumulated liquid. Bake for 1 hour. Turn ribs to the other side, add water to pan, and continue to bake and baste with sauce until ribs are tender, crisp, and brown, about 30 minutes more. Transfer to a warm serving dish, and sprinkle with mint.

Baked Lamb Shanks with Mixed Fresh Herbs and New Potatoes

4 servings

1　medium onion, peeled and
　　coarsely chopped
1　large carrot, coarsely chopped
2　stalks celery, coarsely chopped
1　dried bay leaf
1　teaspoon fresh rosemary leaves
　　or ½ teaspoon dried
　　rosemary
1　tablespoon fresh oregano or
　　1½ teaspoons dried oregano

3　sprigs of fresh thyme or
　　1 teaspoon dried thyme
4　lamb shanks, trimmed of fat
　　whole wheat flour, for
　　dredging
½　teaspoon black pepper
3　tablespoons olive oil
2　cloves garlic, peeled and finely
　　minced
¾　cup dry white wine or ¾ cup
　　water mixed with juice of
　　1 lemon
¾　cup tomato sauce
8 to 10　small unpeeled new potatoes
1　tablespoon finely minced fresh
　　parsley

Preheat oven to 375°F.

In a large heavy pot or casserole with a lid, place vegetables, sprinkle herbs over them, and set aside.

Use a large enough skillet to accommodate all the shanks in a single layer. Dredge lamb in flour, and sprinkle each shank with pepper. Heat oil in skillet, and then brown shanks over high heat, turning to brown evenly. On the last turn, add garlic. Remove shanks, and place them on top of the vegetable-herb bed. Add wine or lemon water to skillet, and deglaze pan over medium heat for about 1 minute, scraping any brown bits from the sides. Add tomato sauce, then pour mixture over lamb and vegetables, cover, and bake for 1 hour.

Add potatoes to casserole, cover, and bake for 20 minutes more, or until potatoes are tender. Then raise the temperature of the oven to 400°F, uncover, turn shanks and potatoes over, and bake for another 20 minutes. Remove bay leaf, and sprinkle with parsley before serving.

Brochettes of Pork with Fennel Seeds, Pearl Onions, and Cilantro (page 153)

Ground Lamb Kabobs with Dried Spices and Mint

4 servings

A Middle Eastern specialty. Try it with a simple brown rice and bulgur pilaf.

1½   pounds ground lean shoulder or leg of lamb
1   large onion, peeled and grated in a food processor
¼   teaspoon cayenne pepper
⅓   cup coarsely chopped fresh mint
¼   teaspoon finely chopped garlic
¼   cup finely chopped fresh parsley
½   teaspoon dried marjoram
⅛   teaspoon ground coriander
⅛   teaspoon ground cumin
¼   teaspoon dried oregano
½   teaspoon grated lemon rind
¼   teaspoon black pepper
4   lemon wedges

Mix all ingredients together in a food processor, except lemon wedges. Divide mixture into 4 portions of equal size. With wet hands, mold each portion into a sausage shape 6 inches long by 1½ inches thick, and place on an oiled rack in a broiling pan. Broil 4 inches from the heat for 7 to 8 minutes on each side if you want the meat to be slightly pink in the center. Serve each portion with a small wedge of lemon to be squeezed over the meat at the table.

Indian Spiced Lamb Balls
with *Garam Masala*,
Hot Chili Peppers, and Mint

Makes 9 balls

These tangy lamb balls can be served as a luncheon or dinner dish. Make smaller balls, and you will have a great hors d'oeuvre.

1¼ pounds finely ground lean lamb
⅓ cup finely minced onions (about 1 small onion)
½ teaspoon finely minced garlic (about 1 small clove)
1½ teaspoons finely minced seeded long hot green chili peppers, or more to taste
1 teaspoon finely minced peeled ginger root
¼ teaspoon ground cumin
½ teaspoon grated lemon rind
¼ teaspoon paprika
1 teaspoon *garam masala* (page 12)
⅛ teaspoon black pepper
½ teaspoon Worcestershire sauce
1 teaspoon lemon juice
1 tablespoon finely minced fresh mint
1 egg, slightly beaten

Put meat into a large bowl, and add all the remaining ingredients. Mix very well with a wooden spoon. Cover bowl with plastic wrap, and let stand at room temperature for 2 hours before cooking so that the flavors blend.

Preheat broiler.

Wet hands and form lamb mixture into balls about 2 inches in diameter. If you are using the recipe for hors d'oeuvres, make lamb balls smaller. Place on an oiled rack in a broiling pan, and broil until medium well done, or just slightly pink, about 6 minutes on each side, so that meat will not dry out. (If lamb balls are smaller, broil for less time.) Serve with a wedge of lemon that can be squeezed over the meat at the table.

Lamb *Avgolemono* with Scallions, Walnuts, and Dill

4 servings

Serve this easy-to-prepare, lemony sauced dish with rice or pasta.

     3   tablespoons olive oil
  1¼   pounds lean lamb, cut into
           1½-inch cubes
         whole wheat flour, for dredging
     ¼   teaspoon black pepper
     1   medium-size onion,
           peeled, thinly sliced, and
           separated into rings
  1½   cups chicken stock
     1   small carrot, shredded
     ½   small lemon, thinly sliced
3 to 4 large scallions, trimmed and cut
           diagonally into 1-inch pieces
           (about 1 cup)
     ½   cup walnuts, toasted and broken
           into large pieces
     2   egg yolks
     ⅓   cup heavy cream
     ¼   cup lemon juice
         few grains of cayenne pepper
     2   tablespoons finely minced fresh
           dill

Heat oil in a heavy (preferably cast-iron) skillet. Dredge pieces of lamb in flour lightly. Sprinkle with pepper, and brown meat quickly on all sides over high heat. When meat is browned, transfer pieces with tongs to a heavy casserole or Dutch oven. Add onions to the same skillet, lower heat to medium, and stir, cooking onions until wilted and golden, 7 to 10 minutes. Transfer onions to pot with meat.

Rinse skillet out with chicken stock, scraping up any brown bits, and pour over meat-onion mixture. Add carrots and lemon slices. Bring to a boil, then lower heat, cover, and simmer for 30 minutes.

Add scallions and walnuts, and continue to simmer, covered, for 10 to 15 minutes more, or until meat is tender.

In a small bowl, beat egg yolks, and add cream. Have lemon juice ready in a measuring cup. Add ½ cup of the hot liquid from lamb to lemon juice. Then slowly add this mixture, while beating constantly with a whisk, to egg-cream mixture. Pour slowly over lamb in casserole, stirring to thicken sauce. Do not boil, or sauce will curdle. Transfer to a warm serving dish. Sprinkle with cayenne and dill. Stir once before serving.

Lamb Loaf with Bulgur, Feta Cheese, Parsley, and Dill

6 servings

     1   cup boiling water
     ⅓   cup fine bulgur
     1   tablespoon butter
     1   teaspoon finely minced garlic
     ⅔   cup finely chopped onions
  1¾   pounds ground lean lamb
     2   tablespoons tomato paste
     1   large egg, slightly beaten
     ¼   cup finely minced fresh parsley
     2   tablespoons finely minced fresh dill
     ¼   cup pine nuts, toasted
     ¼   teaspoon black pepper
     2   teaspoons lemon juice
     3   ounces feta cheese, crumbled

Pour boiling water over bulgur, and let stand for 30 minutes. It will swell up by absorbing the water, and should make 1 cup.

Preheat oven to 425°F. Oil a 9 × 5 × 3-inch loaf pan.

Heat butter in a medium-size skillet. Add garlic and onions, and saute until soft, about 5 minutes, stirring to avoid burning. In a large bowl, mix together lamb, cooked onions and garlic, and all the remaining ingredients except feta cheese. Add bulgur, and combine well. Spoon into prepared pan, smooth the surface, and bake for 25 minutes. Remove from oven, scatter feta cheese on top, and continue baking for 15 minutes longer. Let stand for 10 minutes before slicing. If juices have formed, pour them off into a small saucepan, skim any fat from the surface, and boil hard for 1 minute. Serve separately as a natural gravy.

Lamb Shoulder Chops with Barley, Rosemary, and Fennel Seeds

4 servings

This dish is marinated three hours before cooking. You can prepare it ahead and then cook it about an hour before serving. The marinade gives it a tangy, delicious lemon flavor.

- 4 shoulder lamb chops (about ½ pound each)
- 2 lemons
  freshly ground black pepper
- 2 tablespoons olive oil
- 1 cup finely chopped onions (about 1 medium onion)
- 2 carrots, finely chopped (about 1 cup)
- 1 stalk celery, finely chopped (about ¼ cup)
- 1 teaspoon finely minced garlic
- 1 teaspoon fennel seeds, crushed
- 1 tablespoon fresh rosemary leaves
- 1 cup dry white wine
- 2 cups chicken stock
- ¾ cup whole barley
- 1 dried bay leaf
- 1 tablespoon finely minced fresh parsley

Cut each chop lengthwise into 2 pieces, and trim fat. Grate 1 tablespoon rind from lemons, and reserve. Place chops in a non-metallic baking dish, squeeze lemon juice over lamb, and sprinkle with pepper. Marinate for 3 hours, turning once.

Lift out meat, and dry well on paper towels. Reserve lemon-pepper marinade. Heat oil in a 6-quart heavy casserole until very hot, and sear lamb on all sides over high heat until light brown. Lift meat out with tongs, and set aside. Pour off and discard all but a light film of fat from the casserole. Add onions, carrots, and celery to the casserole, and saute over low heat for 8 minutes, stirring until vegetables are soft. Add garlic, fennel seeds, and rosemary, and cook for 1 to 2 minutes more. Stir in wine, stock, and marinade, scraping up any brown bits from the bottom of the pot to include in the liquid. Bring to a boil, lower heat, add barley, and return meat to casserole. Add bay leaf, cover, and cook over very low heat for 1 hour, or until liquid is absorbed and barley is tender. Remove bay leaf, and transfer lamb-barley mixture to a warm serving platter. Sprinkle with parsley and reserved lemon rind, and serve immediately.

Lamb and White Bean Stew with Herbs, Greens, and Turmeric

4 to 6 servings

This is an unusual Iranian lamb and bean stew. The meat simmers on a bed of herbs and spinach.

　3　tablespoons butter, divided
　2　tablespoons olive oil, divided
　⅔　cup finely chopped leeks (about 1 medium leek)
1¼　cups thinly sliced scallions (about 5 large scallions)
　1　teaspoon finely minced garlic (about 1 large clove)
10　ounces spinach, stems removed
　2　cups coarsely chopped fresh parsley (about ¼ pound)
　2　tablespoons coarsely chopped fresh dill
　1　pound lean lamb, cut into ¾-inch cubes
　　　freshly ground black pepper
　1　tablespoon ground turmeric
1¼　cups chicken stock
　2　tablespoons lemon juice (about ½ large lemon)
　1　teaspoon grated lemon rind
　2　cups cooked or 1 can (19 ounces) cannellini beans, rinsed and drained, or ¼ pound dried beans, cooked

Heat 1 tablespoon of the butter and 1 tablespoon of the olive oil in a 5-quart Dutch oven. Add leeks, scallions, and garlic, and saute over medium heat, stirring occasionally, until wilted, about 5 minutes. Do not brown. Add spinach, parsley, and dill, and cook, stirring constantly, only until greens are wilted. Remove from heat, and set aside. In a large skillet, heat remaining butter and olive oil. Add lamb, a few pieces at a time. Sprinkle with pepper. Brown on all sides, and transfer to the Dutch oven with the greens. Repeat until all the meat is browned. Then add turmeric to skillet and cook, while stirring, for a few seconds. Add chicken stock to skillet, scraping up any brown bits that cling to the skillet's surface, and bring to a boil. Transfer to the Dutch oven, cover, and bring to a boil. Lower heat, add lemon juice and lemon rind, cover, and simmer for about 1 hour. Add beans, and continue to cook for 10 to 15 minutes more. Serve with cooked rice or orzo pasta.

Leg of Lamb with Garlic and Rosemary Puree

4 to 6 servings

For garlic lovers, the sauce is pure heaven. Roasting the garlic slowly gives it a much milder flavor.

　　　juice of 1 lemon
　1　tablespoon olive oil
3½　pounds shank-end leg of lamb
　¼　teaspoon black pepper
　½　bulb fennel or 1 stalk celery
　1　carrot
14　cloves garlic, peeled
　2　large sprigs of fresh rosemary (about 1½ tablespoons of leaves)
1½　cups beef stock or water

Preheat oven to 375°F.

Pour lemon juice and olive oil on lamb, and sprinkle with pepper. Cut fennel or celery and carrot into julienne strips, and place on the bottom of a medium-size heavy roasting pan. Scatter garlic cloves over vegetables, and put rosemary on top. Set the leg of lamb over the vegetable bed, and pour stock or water around the edges of the pan. Roast meat, uncovered, for 15 minutes. Then lower heat to 325°F, and continue roasting for 1 hour more, basting frequently with pan juices. (The total time should be 1 hour and 15 minutes for lamb that is slightly pink.)

Remove meat, cover with a foil tent, and keep warm. Let rest for 10 minutes under tent before slicing. Meanwhile, put all the vegetables, garlic, and any remaining liquid into a food processor, and puree. Transfer to a small bowl to be served on the side as a dip for the lamb.

Rosemary was a symbol of fidelity for lovers in sixteenth-century England. History tells us that Anne of Cleves wore a wreath of rosemary when she married Henry VIII. Nevertheless, they were divorced a few months later.

Native American Lamb and Pepper Stew with Juniper Berries and Hominy

4 to 6 servings

A traditional Zuni Indian dish prepared with contemporary cooking techniques. The peppers are broiled first to add a smokey taste.

1½ pounds lean lamb, cut into 1-inch cubes
   whole wheat flour, for dredging
 2 tablespoons corn oil
¼ teaspoon black pepper
 4 dried juniper berries, crushed

 2 teaspoons dried oregano
 1 tablespoon finely minced garlic (about 2 large cloves)
 1 cup coarsely chopped onions (about 2 medium onions)
¼ teaspoon dried red pepper flakes
 1 can (16 ounces) whole hominy with ½ cup liquid
1¼ cups chicken stock
 3 medium-size green peppers, halved
 1 medium-size sweet red pepper, halved
½ cup finely minced fresh parsley

Dredge lamb in flour. Heat oil in a large heavy cast-iron skillet until very hot. Brown lamb (in 2 batches) on all sides over high heat. When browned, lift meat out of skillet with tongs, and put into a 5-quart heavy casserole. Sprinkle lamb with black pepper, juniper berries, and oregano, and stir. Set aside. In the same skillet, add garlic and onions, and saute over low heat, stirring occasionally, for 5 minutes, or until golden. (Do not allow to burn.) Then add to meat and stir. Add red pepper flakes, hominy and its liquid, and chicken stock. Place over medium heat, bring to a boil, then lower heat, and simmer, covered, for 1 hour, stirring occasionally.

While stew is cooking, prepare peppers. Place pepper halves, skin-side up, on a flat baking sheet lined with aluminum foil, and broil until skin is charred and black, about 5 minutes. Then place in a brown paper bag to cool and steam for 10 to 15 minutes. Scrape off skin, and cut each half into 4 pieces. Stir into lamb-hominy mixture, and simmer for 10 minutes more. Stir in parsley just before serving.

FISH AND SEAFOOD

Acini di Pepe with Clams, Zucchini, and Salad Burnet

4 servings

The tiniest size of pasta with shreds of green zucchini is an unusual complement to the briny clams and the lemony salad burnet.

  18 medium-size cherrystone clams in shells, scrubbed
   2 tablespoons butter, divided
   1 teaspoon finely minced garlic
   4 sprigs fresh parsley
   8 ounces acini di pepe pasta
  ½ pound small zucchini, shredded
  ¼ teaspoon black pepper
   1 teaspoon grated lemon rind
  ¼ cup lemon juice
  ¼ cup fresh salad burnet leaves
      pinch of cayenne pepper

Place clams in a large skillet or Dutch oven. Add 1 inch of cold water, cover tightly, bring to a boil, and steam over medium-high heat until shells open, 5 to 8 minutes. Lift clams out of pan with a slotted spoon, and reserve broth. When cool enough to handle, remove clams from shell, cut in half, and set aside. Discard any clams that have not opened. Line a strainer with a man's large linen handkerchief, and strain clam broth to prevent any sand from getting into sauce. Measure liquid, and add enough water to make 2 cups.

In a medium-size saucepan, melt 1 tablespoon of the butter. Add garlic, and saute until soft but not brown. Add reserved clam broth-water mixture and parsley, and bring to a boil. Stir in pasta, lower heat, and simmer, stirring occasionally, for 5 to 8 minutes, or until liquid is almost absorbed. Remove parsley, and stir in zucchini along with remaining butter. Combine well, and cook over low heat for 1 minute. Add reserved clams, black pepper, lemon rind, and lemon juice. Transfer to a warm serving dish, and sprinkle with salad burnet leaves and cayenne. Mix lightly at the table just before serving.

Baked Scrod with Green Peppercorns

4 servings

A lush sauce with the mild sting of pepper enhances the delicacy of the fish.

  1½ pounds scrod fillets (use 1 thick piece)
   ¼ cup finely minced scallions
    2 teaspoons butter
    3 tablespoons water
    3 tablespoons fish or chicken stock
   ¼ cup frozen butter, cut into pieces, divided
    2 teaspoons water-packed green peppercorns, drained, rinsed, and crushed with a mortar and pestle

Preheat oven to 400°F.

Place fish on a large piece of heavy-weight aluminum foil. Remove any remaining bones in the fish by pulling them with your fingers or washed tweezers. Sprinkle fish with scallions, and dot with 2 teaspoons butter. Fold foil to enclose fish, place in a large baking dish, and bake for 20 minutes. Remove from oven, and open foil carefully. Lift fish out with a wide spatula to a warm serving dish, and cover with fresh aluminum foil to keep warm. Pour off accumulated juices into a medium-size saucepan.

Add water and fish or chicken stock, and boil rapidly, uncovered, until sauce is reduced to 2 tablespoons. Remove saucepan from heat. Quickly add the first piece of frozen butter, and beat well with a wire whisk. Add the second piece of butter, and return saucepan to low heat. The idea is not to let the butter melt too quickly, but to whisk it in so that the sauce is creamy, just like a buerre blanc sauce. Whisk in remaining frozen butter piece by piece to keep sauce creamy. Finally, add green peppercorns, and pour sauce over fish. Cut into equal portions when serving.

Baked Stuffed Fish with Chili Powder, Cilantro, and Bananas, Mexican Style

4 servings

 3 tablespoons lime juice, divided
 4 fillets of red snapper, sea bass, or bluefish (about ¼ pound each)
 2 bananas, sliced lengthwise
 ½ cup orange juice
 ½ teaspoon chili powder
 1 tablespoon olive oil
 ¼ cup finely chopped onions
 2 teaspoons finely minced garlic
 ½ teaspoon dried thyme
 ⅛ teaspoon black pepper
 3 tablespoons diced roasted sweet red peppers (page 85)
 1 tablespoon finely minced fresh cilantro

 ½ pound raw shrimp, peeled and deveined
  olive oil, for brushing
 1 teaspoon grated orange rind
 1 teaspoon grated lime rind
 2 sprigs of fresh cilantro

Sprinkle 2 tablespoons of the lime juice over fish. Sprinkle remaining lime juice over bananas. Set both aside. In a cup, mix orange juice and chili powder together, and pour mixture into a large shallow baking dish. Turn fish to coat on both sides, and then let it marinate in the mixture while preparing the stuffing.

Heat oil in a small skillet. Add onions and garlic, and saute until soft. Add thyme, black pepper, and red peppers, and cook, stirring constantly, for 1 minute. Remove from heat, stir in minced cilantro, and cool slightly. Finely chop shrimp in a food processor, and add to onion-pepper-herb mixture.

Preheat oven to 350°F.

Divide stuffing mixture in half, and spread on 2 of the fillets. Top with the other 2 fillets to enclose stuffing. Brush the surface of fish with oil. Place bananas around fish. Tilt pan, and spoon marinade over both. Bake for 30 to 35 minutes, basting occasionally with pan liquid. When fish flakes easily, remove from oven, sprinkle with orange rind and lime rind, and garnish with sprigs of cilantro.

When grilling fish, try brushing it with fennel-flavored oil.

Cold Mussels with Ravigote Sauce

4 servings

Another light, make-ahead luncheon or brunch dish. You can also serve these as an hors d'oeuvre.

MUSSELS

48 mussels in shells, scrubbed and beards removed (1 dozen per person)
½ cup water
1 large shallot, cut in half
3 sprigs of fresh parsley
6 peppercorns

SAUCE

1 tablespoon finely minced shallots
1 tablespoon red wine vinegar
1 tablespoon water
1 teaspoon finely minced fresh tarragon
⅓ cup mayonnaise
½ teaspoon nonpareil capers, rinsed and dried
1 teaspoon minced fresh chives
1 teaspoon finely minced fresh parsley
½ teaspoon French-style mustard freshly ground black pepper, to taste
fresh parsley sprigs

To make the mussels: Combine all ingredients in a Dutch oven with a tight-fitting lid. Bring to a boil, and steam over medium-high heat until shells open, 5 to 8 minutes. Lift mussels out of pan with a slotted spoon. Discard any mussels that have not opened. When cool, discard top half of the shell, and loosen mussel in lower half, but do not remove. Place on a serving dish.

To make the sauce: Combine shallots, vinegar, water, and tarragon in a small saucepan, and cook over high heat for 2 to 3 minutes, or until liquid evaporates. Combine with all the remaining ingredients except parsley sprigs. Place a dab of sauce on each mussel, garnish with parsley sprigs, chill, and serve cold with a salad.

Note: A Serendipity Recipe—When we tested this recipe, we had some ravigote sauce left over. That night, we put the sauce on freshly caught bluefish fillets, placed them in an oven-to-table baking dish with about ½ cup of tomato juice on the bottom, and broiled them for about 7 minutes. They were absolutely superb! Don't limit the idea to bluefish, however. You can try it with flounder, mackerel, or sole if you'd like.

Lemon Sole Yucatan Style with Cumin, Peppers, and Cilantro

4 servings

The light, distinctive sauce in this recipe is also perfect for other delicate fish such as red snapper, fluke, or flounder.

3 tablespoons butter, divided
2 tablespoons finely minced shallots
½ teaspoon finely minced garlic
1 small sweet red pepper, cut into thin strips
1 small green pepper, cut into thin strips

Fresh ingredients for Pot-au-Feu: Short Ribs with Horse-radish Sauce (page 139)

1 teaspoon ground cumin
1½ tablespoons minced fresh cilantro, divided
⅛ teaspoon black pepper
1 teaspoon grated orange rind
½ cup orange juice
1½ pounds lemon sole fillets (4 fillets)
3 to 4 pitted black olives, sliced (optional)
paper-thin slices of lime
3 to 4 slices of avocado, diced

Preheat oven to 350°F.

Melt 2 tablespoons of the butter in a medium-size skillet. Add shallots, garlic, and peppers, and saute until soft. Add cumin, 1 tablespoon of the cilantro, and black pepper. Stir in orange rind and orange juice. Bring to a boil, then lower heat, and simmer for 1 minute. Set aside.

Cut remaining butter into small pieces, and place on the bottom of a large, shallow oven-to-table casserole. Place fish in casserole without overlapping fillets. Pour sauce over fillets, sprinkle with olives (if used), and bake for 10 minutes or more, depending upon thickness of fish, basting occasionally. Garnish fish with lime slices, sprinkle with remaining cilantro, and scatter avocado on top.

Marinated Raw Salmon
with Hot Chili Peppers and Cilantro

4 servings

A welcome light lunch on a summer day or an elegant Sunday brunch.

- ¾ pound salmon fillet, skinned and boned
- 2 tablespoons minced roasted and seeded jalapeno peppers
- 2 scallions, green part only, sliced diagonally into ½-inch pieces
- ⅓ cup lime juice
- 1 teaspoon grated lime rind
- 1 tablespoon olive oil
- 1 tablespoon minced fresh cilantro leaves

Rub fingers over salmon to find any remaining bones, and pull out with fingers or washed tweezers. Cut salmon at an angle into ½-inch slices, and place into a large nonmetallic bowl. Sprinkle peppers, scallions, lime juice, lime rind, olive oil, and cilantro leaves over salmon. Toss, cover, and refrigerate for at least 5 hours or overnight before serving. Serve with whole grain black bread and a crisp green salad.

Oriental Bluefish
with Cilantro and Ginger

4 servings

Complement this dish with Japanese buckwheat noodles or a bowl of steaming rice.

- 2 tablespoons Oriental sesame oil, divided
- 4 bluefish fillets, skinned (1½ to 2 pounds)

- 2 tablespoons rice vinegar
- 1 tablespoon light soy sauce
- 1 teaspoon finely minced peeled ginger root
- ¼ cup finely sliced scallions
- 1½ tablespoons finely minced fresh cilantro leaves

Preheat oven to 425°F.

Brush a shallow oven-to-table baking dish large enough to accommodate fillets in a single layer with 1 tablespoon of the sesame oil. Place fish in the dish. In a cup, mix remaining tablespoon of sesame oil with rice vinegar, soy sauce, and ginger. Pour over fish, and bake for 10 minutes, or until fish turns opaque. Remove from oven, and sprinkle with scallions and cilantro. Serve at once.

Poached Spiced Tilefish
with Mustard and Parsley Sauce

4 servings

TILEFISH

- 4 tilefish steaks, ¾ inch thick (about 2 pounds), cut from the smaller tail end (any firm-fleshed fish steaks may be substituted)
- ½ cup milk
- 2 to 3 cups water
  white pepper, to taste
- 8 sprigs of fresh parsley, tied with string
- 1 dried bay leaf
- 8 peppercorns, crushed

SAUCE

- 2 tablespoons finely minced shallots

2 tablespoons red wine vinegar
1 tablespoon cold water
6 tablespoons butter
1 tablespoon French-style mustard
¼ cup finely minced fresh parsley

To make the tilefish: Place fish in a single layer in a large shallow casserole. Mix together milk, 2 to 3 cups water, and pepper in a medium-size bowl, and pour around fish. The liquid should just barely cover the fish. Add parsley sprigs, bay leaf, and peppercorns. Bring to a boil, then lower heat, cover, and simmer for 6 minutes. Turn off heat, turn steaks over carefully, and let stand in liquid for at least 3 minutes. Lift fish out of casserole, and place on paper towels to drain. Discard poaching liquid and herbs. Transfer fish to a warmed serving platter.

To make the sauce: Put shallots and vinegar into a small heavy saucepan. Cook until most of the vinegar has evaporated. Then cool slightly, and add 1 tablespoon of cold water. Using a wire whisk, gradually add butter, beating vigorously. Don't allow sauce to boil or it will curdle. If it starts to get too hot, adjust by removing saucepan from heat momentarily. When mixture is smooth, creamy, and slightly thickened, add mustard and minced parsley. Spoon sauce over fish.

Sea Bass Baked in Swiss Chard with Tarragon, Yogurt, and Horseradish

4 servings

Since the fish is baked in a blanket of Swiss chard leaves, it retains not only its delicate flavor but also its moist, juicy texture.

4 sea bass fillets (about 1 pound)
  whole wheat flour, for dredging
⅛ teaspoon black pepper
1 tablespoon Oriental sesame oil
4 large Swiss chard leaves, stems removed
4 sprigs of fresh tarragon, dill, or thyme, or 4 large fresh basil leaves
2 thin scallions, sliced diagonally into ½-inch slices
1 tablespoon lemon juice
¼ cup plain yogurt
1 tablespoon prepared horseradish, drained, or grated fresh horseradish, or less to taste
4 lemon wedges (optional)
  paprika (optional)

Preheat oven to 350°F.

Dredge fish lightly in a mixture of flour and pepper. Heat sesame oil in a large heavy skillet. Add fish, and quickly saute for 1 minute on each side. Place Swiss chard leaves on a flat surface and, using a wide spatula, place each fillet on a leaf. Place 1 sprig of tarragon, dill, or thyme, or 1 basil leaf over each fillet. Add a sprinkling of scallions and lemon juice. Wrap fish tightly with Swiss chard, and carefully transfer to a lightly oiled baking dish large enough to accommodate them in a single layer. Cover, and bake for 10 to 15 minutes, depending upon the thickness of the fish.

While fish is baking, mix together yogurt and horseradish in a cup. When fillets are ready, spoon mixture over the center of the fish rolls. Garnish with lemon wedges dipped in paprika for color if you wish.

Marinated Raw Mackerel with Green Peppercorns and Mixed Herbs

4 servings

Serve this dish at a summer luncheon with thin slices of black pumpernickel, or at a party buffet, or as an appetizer. Prepare it two days in advance for an easy, no-cook addition to your menu. This dish can also be made with bluefish fillets. Just trim the dark brown flesh away for a more delicate flavor.

    2 mackerel fillets (about 1 pound)
    ½ cup lemon juice (2 to 3 lemons)
    ¼ cup olive oil
    1 tablespoon water-packed green
         peppercorns, drained, rinsed, and
         crushed
    2 small shallots, coarsely chopped
         (about 1 tablespoon)
    1 tablespoon finely minced fresh
         parsley
    1 tablespoon finely minced fresh
         chervil
    1 teaspoon fresh tarragon leaves

Place fillets into a medium-size baking dish. In a small bowl, mix together lemon juice, olive oil, peppercorns, and shallots, and marinate fillets in this mixture for 2 days in the refrigerator. After 1 day, turn fillets over, and spoon marinade over them. Return to refrigerator. When ready to serve, lift them out of the baking dish, and discard marinade. Scrape off most of the shallots, and sprinkle fillets with fresh herbs. Slice very thinly on the diagonal to serve.

Poached Salmon Steaks in Chive and Mustard Cream Sauce with Shredded Endive

4 servings

SALMON

    4 salmon steaks, 1 inch thick (about
         ½ pound each)
    ½ teaspoon dried thyme
    4 sprigs fresh parsley
    6 peppercorns
    1 dried bay leaf
    2 tablespoons tarragon wine vinegar

SAUCE

    2 tablespoons butter
    1¼ cups shredded endive
    ½ cup heavy cream or creme fraiche
    2 teaspoons French-style mustard
    2 heaping tablespoons finely minced
         fresh chives

To make the salmon: Rub fingers over fish, and pull out any bones you feel in the fleshy part. Place salmon in a single layer in a flat casserole or skillet. Add all the remaining ingredients along with enough water to barely cover. Bring to a simmer, cover tightly with a lid or aluminum foil, and poach for 7 minutes. Lift salmon out of casserole or skillet with a slotted spoon, place on a warm serving platter, and keep warm. Strain poaching liquid, and reserve.

To make the sauce: In a 10-inch skillet, melt butter. Add endive, and saute, stirring until wilted, 2 to 3 minutes. Add cream and mustard, and heat slowly until bubbles form around the edges of the pan. (Do not boil.) Stir in chives, and continue to simmer until sauce is thickened. Add about 2 tablespoons of the poaching liquid and cook, stirring constantly, until sauce is the consistency of light cream, about 1 minute. Spoon over salmon.

Scallops with Ginger and Lemon Verbena

4 servings

Here's another light, tasty, and easy-to-prepare dish. The cooking time is actually about two minutes! If you prefer, you can use a combination of scallops and shrimp in equal amounts. Just peel and devein the shrimp, and then cut them in half lengthwise before cooking.

¼ cup butter
1 pound bay scallops or large sea scallops, cut into quarters
2 tablespoons finely minced peeled ginger root
⅛ teaspoon black pepper
1 tablespoon finely minced fresh parsley
1 tablespoon finely minced fresh lemon verbena
1 tablespoon lime juice

In a large skillet, heat butter until it sizzles, but do not allow to burn. Add scallops and ginger, and cook for 1 to 2 minutes, stirring to coat evenly. Season with pepper, and transfer to a serving dish. Toss with parsley and lemon verbena, sprinkle with lime juice, and serve immediately.

Sauteed Anyfish with Saffron and Vinegar Sauce

8 servings as hors d'oeuvre
4 servings as entree

This Spanish-style cold dish is equally good as an hors d'oeuvre. Use almost any fish that's fresh or in season, prepare it in advance, and keep refrigerated until ready to serve.

1½ pounds fish fillets (haddock, cod, scrod, flounder, halibut, bluefish, bass, or any other firm-fleshed fish)
   whole wheat flour, for dredging
   freshly ground black pepper, to taste
   olive oil
¾ cup apple cider vinegar
1 dried bay leaf
   pinch of saffron
1 small onion, peeled, sliced paper-thin, and separated into rings
1 teaspoon coarsely chopped fresh parsley

Cut fish into 1½-inch slices, and dredge in mixture of flour and pepper. Heat ⅛-inch of olive oil in a large skillet. Add fish, and saute until light brown, turning once. Drain on paper towels. Place on a deep platter. Combine remaining ingredients, except parsley, and pour over fish. Refrigerate for at least 1 hour.

When ready to serve, remove bay leaf, and sprinkle parsley over fish. Lift fish and onion rings from vinegar mixture with a slotted spoon.

Jim Reed

Grove Street Cafe
New York City, New York

For almost six years now, this little 12-table restaurant, located in New York's Greenwich Village, has been our personal favorite. The owners are Gerald Holmes (who does all the desserts and hosts the restaurant) and Jim Reed, the talented chef who manages to change the menu every two weeks. Whenever we dine there we can be sure of enjoying original dishes made with the freshest of ingredients. For example, Jim gives his vegetable timbales a lift by lining each ramekin with blanched, large basil leaves, then adding the vegetable mixture and baking. For serving, the timbale is turned out of the container, revealing an attractive, basil-clad mold, rich in flavor and aroma.

Because he handles the kitchen so well, we were certain that chef Jim Reed had trained under the best instructors France and the United States had to offer, but that is not the case:

Actually, I'm self-trained. As an only child growing up in Detroit, with my mother and my father both working, I had to learn to cook. Actually my formal training was in sociology!

The menu at Grove Street Cafe always reflects what is seasonally available in the markets, and nowadays that invariably includes fresh herbs, which are a feature of Jim's recipes that have delighted us most.

I like to make a sauce for chicken that features coriander and cumin; it somehow has a Mexican ring for me. At one time I had to wait for "coriander season," says Jim, now I get it when I want it!

Jim reminded us that not too long ago, even in New York City, basil was available only twice a year, and imported French tarragon was selling for as much as $18 an ounce.

Today the situation is completely changed. There are new greenhouses springing up all across the country, and many of the herbs sold commercially are being hydroponically grown all year long. Where parsley was once the only fresh herb available in the cold months, today we have no trouble finding all the thyme, savory, tarragon — you name it — we need.

The recipe given here, Seafood Sausage, is one of our favorites at the Grove Street Cafe.

Seafood Sausage

6 to 8 servings

½ pound scallops
½ pound raw shrimp, peeled
    and deveined
½ pound fillet of sole
½ cup heavy cream
⅛ teaspoon ground nutmeg
    dash of cayenne pepper
1½ tablespoons minced fresh
    tarragon
1½ tablespoons minced fresh
    chervil
3 egg whites
6 feet of sausage casing

Using a food processor, process all the ingredients except sausage casing in 3 batches. (The order does not matter.) Combine the processed ingredients in a large bowl. Thoroughly rinse sausage casing in cold running water. Lightly oil a pastry tube, and fit sausage casing over the tube. Tie off the outside end. Fill pastry bag with processed fish, spices, and herbs, and start squeezing the bag until all the fish has been pushed into the casing. Tie off the other end. Be sure to make double knots. Then tie off sausage into desired lengths (6-inch lengths seem to work best).

In a large pot, bring enough water to cover sausage to a boil. Then reduce to a simmer. *The water should be barely simmering. It must not boil.* Add sausage, and simmer for 20 to 30 minutes. While sausage is poaching, prick the skin all over with a needle to prevent it from bursting. Remove from water, and let cool. Cut sausage links at the points where they were tied, remove string, and saute gently in oil in a large skillet until brown. Serve with your favorite light tomato sauce or a beurre blanc sauce. If you wish, try the Basil Beurre Blanc sauce on page 257.

Note: If you can't find sausage casing, wrap filling tightly with plastic wrap. Tie the ends, and *steam* rather than poach. Remove plastic wrap after steaming, and saute sausage as above.

Marinated Raw Mackerel with
Green Peppercorns and
Mixed Herbs (page 172)

Scallops with Vegetables, Thyme, Borage, and Opal Basil

4 servings

This company dish will appeal to any host or hostess because it can be prepared well in advance and kept in the refrigerator until the guests arrive. Although the opal basil gives it a regal look, fresh green basil will work just as well.

- ¼ cup butter, softened
- 2 tablespoons fresh thyme leaves or 1½ tablespoons dried thyme
- ¼ teaspoon black pepper, divided
- 2 leeks, white part only, cut into julienne strips 1¼ inches long
- 2 carrots, cut into julienne strips 1½ inches long
- 1 pound bay scallops
- 1 fresh borage leaf or 1 small cucumber, cut into julienne strips
- 3 tablespoons finely chopped fresh opal basil or green basil juice of 1 lemon

Mash butter, thyme, and ⅛ teaspoon of the pepper together in a small bowl until well blended. Set aside. Pour boiling water over leeks and carrots, and let steep for 3 minutes. Drain, and set aside. Cut 4 12-inch squares of aluminum foil, and distribute equal amounts of leek and carrot strips in the center of each square, reserving a few leek and carrot strips for the top layer. Place equal portions of scallops over vegetables. Sprinkle borage or cucumber and basil over scallops. Add the remainder of the pepper and the lemon juice over each. Place a few reserved strips of leeks and carrots over each portion of scallops, and spoon 1 tablespoon of the thyme butter in the center.

Lift 2 opposite edges of the foil so that they meet in the center, and make an airtight seam along the length of the foil by folding it over a few times. Then fold in the remaining edges several times to form a loose package and to create a seal. Leave some space inside to allow for expansion. These packets can now either be refrigerated until cooking time or cooked at once in a preheated 450°F oven. Place on a baking sheet and bake for 12 to 15 minutes. Serve packets alongside cooked angel's hair pasta or cooked rice, and let your guests open them right at the table. They look quite beautiful!

Shrimp and Sea Scallops in Green Sauce

6 servings

A special make-ahead lunch or supper dish. Or present it at a party buffet.

SAUCE

½ clove garlic
½ cup chopped fresh spinach (5 to 6 large leaves)
¼ cup chopped fresh parsley (12 to 14 sprigs)
2 tablespoons minced fresh chives
⅓ cup chopped watercress leaves (about ¼ bunch)
1 tablespoon chopped fresh dill
2 teaspoons lemon juice
¼ teaspoon black pepper
¾ cup sour cream
2 tablespoons mayonnaise

SEAFOOD

4 cups water
1 teaspoon tarragon vinegar
2 tablespoons pickling spices
1 pound medium-size raw shrimp in shells
1 pound sea scallops

To make the sauce: In a food processor, chop garlic first, then add spinach and herbs, and process until fine. Add all the remaining ingredients, and process until smooth. Refrigerate for 2 hours to blend flavors, or overnight if you wish.

To make the seafood: Bring water, vinegar, and pickling spices to a boil in a large nonaluminum pot. Add shrimp and scallops, cover, and bring to a boil again. Remove from heat, and let seafood cool in liquid for 5 minutes. Then drain well, discarding spices. Let cool for easier handling. Peel and devein shrimp, and slice scallops horizontally into 2 or 3 slices, depending upon thickness. Serve with green sauce as a dip, or toss with green sauce and serve on a bed of red lettuce or raddichio.

Shrimp Baked with Tomatoes, Feta Cheese, Oregano, and Fennel

4 servings

Serve this traditional Greek dish with a tiny pasta, such as orzo, or rice.

1 can (35 ounces) Italian plum tomatoes, drained
1½ pounds medium-size raw shrimp (about 8 per person)
1 cup water
2 tablespoons olive oil
1 tablespoon butter
1½ teaspoons finely minced garlic
2 tablespoons cognac or brandy, warmed
1 tablespoon finely minced fresh oregano
 scant ½ teaspoon dried red pepper flakes
1 tablespoon capers, rinsed and dried (optional)
1 tablespoon fennel seeds, crushed
¼ pound feta cheese, crumbled
2 tablespoons finely minced fresh parsley

Preheat oven to 350°F.

Crush and cook tomatoes in a nonstick skillet, stirring occasionally, until reduced to 2 cups. Transfer to a bowl, and reserve. Wipe out skillet. Peel and devein shrimp, reserving shells. Place shells only into a medium-size saucepan, add water, and cook for 10 minutes. Strain liquid, and reserve. This becomes the shrimp stock.

Heat oil and butter in the wiped out skillet. Add garlic and shrimp, and saute, stirring constantly, for about 1 minute. Then add warm cognac or brandy, and ignite with a match to allow the alcohol to burn away. Remove skillet from heat, and add reserved tomatoes along with ¼ cup of the shrimp stock, oregano, red pepper flakes, capers (if used), and fennel seeds. Place in a flat casserole or in individual baking dishes, crumble feta cheese on top, and bake for 10 to 12 minutes. Sprinkle with parsley, and serve over orzo pasta or rice.

Sole Venetian Style with Mint, Parsley, and Lemon

4 servings

4 small fillets of sole
3 tablespoons butter, softened
1 tablespoon finely minced fresh mint
2 tablespoons finely minced fresh parsley
¼ teaspoon finely minced garlic (about ½ medium-size clove)
⅛ teaspoon black pepper
4 lemon wedges
 cayenne pepper

Wash and dry fish well with paper towels. In a small bowl, combine butter, mint, parsley, garlic, and pepper until mixture is smooth. Divide into 5 equal portions. Using a spatula, spread 1 portion of herb butter evenly on each fillet, reserving 1 portion.

Preheat broiler.

Place fillets, herb-side down, in an oven-to-table baking dish large enough to accommodate them in a single layer. Broil for about 7 minutes, or until fish flakes easily when the point of a knife is inserted into the thickest part. Remove fish, and spread remaining herb butter equally on top of each fillet. Sprinkle lemon wedges with a few grains of cayenne, and top each fillet with a lemon wedge.

Striped Bass
with Tarragon and Saffron Sauce

4 servings

A hint of tarragon perfumes the golden saffron-flavored sauce.

STRIPED BASS

2 cups water
1½ pounds striped bass fillet
4 tablespoons lemon juice
6 peppercorns
1 small onion, peeled and sliced
1 dried bay leaf
4 fennel seeds
1 whole clove

SAUCE

2 tablespoons butter
1 tablespoon minced shallots
1 cup strained reserved stock
⅛ teaspoon saffron threads, crushed
½ cup heavy cream
⅛ teaspoon dried tarragon, crushed
white pepper, to taste

To make the bass: In a large shallow casserole, bring water to boil. Add fish and remaining ingredients, lower heat, and simmer, uncovered, for 8 minutes. Turn off heat, cover casserole with aluminum foil, and let fish rest in stock for 5 minutes. Drain fish, reserving the stock, and transfer to a warm serving platter.

To make the sauce: Heat butter in a medium-size saucepan. Add shallots, and saute. Add stock, and cook over high heat until sauce is reduced by half. Add saffron, cream, tarragon, and pepper. Cook over low heat for 1 to 2 minutes, stirring constantly. Spoon over fish, and serve hot.

Steamed Seafood
with Individual Fresh
Herb Bouquets

4 servings

A simple and luxurious feast. If you own a Chinese bamboo basket steamer, this dish can be made and served in the same container.

12 cherrystone clams in shells, scrubbed
12 large mussels, scrubbed and beards removed
8 large sea scallops
8 large raw shrimp, in shells
5 small bunches fresh herbs, 4 tied with string and 1 bunch finely minced and reserved. For each bunch: 2 sprigs each of fennel or dill; 2 sprigs each of thyme and parsley; 1 sprig each of oregano and sage; 1 large basil leaf
¼ cup butter, melted
2 teaspoons lemon juice

Place all the seafood in a large steamer (clams and mussels on the bottom, scallops and shrimp on top), and lay the 4 herb bouquets over all. (Or use a large skillet such as a chicken fryer with 3-inch-high sides and a tight-fitting lid.) Add 2 inches of water, cover, bring to a boil, and steam over medium-high heat for 3 to 4 minutes, or until clams and mussels have opened and shrimp is pink. Do not overcook. It is best to remove shrimp and scallops first if clams need additional steaming to make them open.

To serve, place 3 clams, 3 mussels, 2 scallops, and 2 shrimp on each plate along with an herb bouquet as a garnish. Heat melted butter in a small saucepan with reserved minced herbs, and then add lemon juice. Spoon into individual small dishes as a dipping sauce.

As a change from crushed peppercorns in Steak au Poivre, crush dried rosemary and press the herb into the meat along with, or instead of, the peppercorns.

LIVER

Beef Liver with Red Onions, Oranges, and Parsley

4 servings

The oranges and sweet-flavored red onions give sparkle to this easy, new way to serve liver. If you prefer, it's equally good with calf's liver. Serve with rice or orzo pasta.

- 1 pound beef liver, ½ inch thick, trimmed of membranes and cut into 1-inch squares
- 2 medium-size red onions, peeled and cut into ½-inch slices
- 2 small navel oranges
- 2 tablespoons lemon juice
- 3 tablespoons safflower oil
- 1 tablespoon olive oil
- ½ teaspoon finely minced garlic
- ⅛ teaspoon black pepper
- 1 tablespoon finely minced fresh parsley

Place liver into a large, shallow non-aluminum casserole. Finely mince 1 slice of the onion, and put it into a small bowl. Arrange remaining onion slices in casserole. Grate the rind of 1 orange, and add it to bowl. Then thickly slice oranges, and arrange in casserole along with onions and liver. Add lemon juice, both oils, garlic, and pepper to onions in bowl, mix well, and spoon over the liver-orange mixture. Marinate for 30 min-

utes, occasionally tilting pan and spooning mixture over ingredients in casserole.

When ready to cook, preheat broiler, and broil for 4 minutes. Remove casserole, turn only the liver pieces to the other side, baste with pan liquid, and return to broiler for 4 more minutes. Scatter parsley over all before serving.

Chicken Liver Souffle with Sage and Parsley

4 to 6 servings

It looks like a souffle, but it tastes like a pate with a lighter texture. It's lovely for lunch or for a light supper.

- 6 tablespoons butter, divided
- ¼ cup finely minced onions (about 1 small onion)
- 6 tablespoons whole wheat flour
- ¼ teaspoon black pepper
- ¾ cup milk
- ¼ pound chicken livers (about 5 livers)
- 1 teaspoon finely minced garlic (1 to 2 cloves)
- 1 teaspoon finely minced fresh sage
- ¼ cup finely minced fresh parsley
- 4 eggs, separated

In a small skillet, melt 2 tablespoons of the butter over medium heat. Add onions, and saute over low heat, stirring occasionally, until wilted and golden, about 10 minutes.

Meanwhile, in a 2-quart nonstick saucepan, melt remaining butter over medium heat, add flour and pepper, and stir with a wire whisk, cooking until bubbly but not brown. Gradually whisk in milk and cook slowly, stirring constantly, until very thick, about 5 minutes. Remove from heat and add sauteed onions. Set aside to cool slightly.

In a food processor, blend uncooked livers, garlic, sage, and parsley until smooth. Add this mixture to the sauce along with egg yolks.

Preheat oven to 325°F. Butter a 2½-quart souffle dish.

When oven is hot, beat egg whites in a medium-size bowl until stiff peaks form. Carefully fold whites into liver mixture. Spoon and scrape into prepared souffle dish, and bake for 50 to 55 minutes, or until cake tester inserted in the center comes out clean. Serve at once. Like all souffles, it deflates quickly.

Marinated and Grilled Chicken Livers with Summer Savory and Thyme

4 servings

1½ teaspoons fresh summer savory
1 teaspoon fresh thyme leaves
2 tablespoons olive oil
⅛ teaspoon black pepper
10 to 12 chicken livers (depending upon size)

In a medium-size bowl, mix herbs, olive oil, and pepper with the livers, and let marinate for at least 2 hours in the refrigerator, turning a few times.

Preheat broiler.

Broil livers 4 to 5 inches from heat for 5 minutes on one side, basting once or twice. Turn, and broil on other side for 2 to 3 minutes. Serve on a bed of rice.

Sauteed Chicken Livers with Sage

4 servings

2 tablespoons butter
1 tablespoon olive oil
3 tablespoons finely minced shallots
1 pound chicken livers, cut in half and dried well on paper towels
2 tablespoons finely minced fresh sage
¼ cup dry Marsala wine

Heat butter and oil in a large skillet over medium-high heat. Add shallots, and stir for a few seconds. Add livers, and cook for 3 to 4 minutes, turning livers with tongs so that they cook on all sides. Do not overcook—they will become tough. Remove from heat, and stir in sage. Transfer livers with a slotted spoon onto a warmed serving dish. Return skillet to heat, add wine, and bring to a boil, scraping pan and stirring with a wooden spoon until sauce is reduced by half. Pour over livers, and serve over a bed of cooked fine noodles, orzo, or rice.

Thyme cures melancholy, according to the ancient Romans; they recommended stuffing beds and pillows with it.

Stuffed Chicken Breasts with
Honey-Sesame Seed Glaze
and Sugar Snap Peas
(page 133)

Venetian-Style Calf's Liver with Onions and Parsley

4 servings

Almost every restaurant in Venice serves this popular specialty, quickly sauteed for optimum tenderness.

  1 tablespoon olive oil
  1 sweet Spanish onion (about ¾ pound), peeled, thinly sliced, and separated into rings
  2 tablespoons corn oil
3 to 4 thin slices of calf's liver (about 1¼ pounds), trimmed of membranes and cut into ¼-inch-wide strips
     whole wheat flour, for dredging
  ¼ teaspoon black pepper
  2 teaspoons capers, rinsed and dried (optional)
  1 tablespoon red wine vinegar
  2 tablespoons finely minced fresh parsley

Heat olive oil in a large cast-iron skillet. Add onion rings, and saute for 15 to 20 minutes over medium-low heat, stirring often, until golden (do not burn or onions will be bitter). Remove onions with a slotted spoon, and set aside. Wipe out skillet with paper towels, add oil, and heat until very hot. While oil is heating, dredge liver strips in flour, and sprinkle with pepper. Add to skillet, and cook very quickly, about 1 minute on each side. Turn strips with tongs or stir with a wooden spoon. Lower heat, and quickly return reserved onions to skillet, stirring to mix well. Add capers (if used) and vinegar. Transfer to a warm serving plate, sprinkle with parsley, and stir once to distribute parsley throughout. Serve at once.

Stewed Chicken Livers with Sweet Marjoram, Thyme, and Basil

4 servings

A rich, dark stew that goes particularly well with cooked barley.

2 cups chicken stock
½ cup coarsely chopped onions
1 dried bay leaf
⅛ teaspoon black pepper
¾ pound chicken gizzards, cut in half
¼ pound chicken hearts (optional)
1 pound chicken livers, cut into bite-size pieces
  whole wheat flour, for dredging
1 tablespoon butter
2 tablespoons olive oil
½ teaspoon finely minced garlic
¼ pound fresh mushrooms, thinly sliced
1 cup finely chopped celery (3 to 4 stalks)
1 cup finely chopped carrots (2 to 3 carrots)

1 tablespoon fresh bush basil or 1 tablespoon finely minced fresh basil
2 teaspoons whole fresh marjoram leaves
1 tablespoon whole fresh thyme leaves

In a 4-quart heavy pot, combine chicken stock, onions, bay leaf, pepper, chicken gizzards, and chicken hearts (if used), and bring to a boil. Cover, reduce heat, and simmer for 45 minutes to 1 hour, or until gizzards and hearts (if used) are tender. Remove and discard bay leaf. Lift out gizzards and hearts (if used) and coarsely chop. Reserve stock.

Dredge livers in flour. In a large skillet, heat butter and oil until foamy. Add livers, and saute for 1 minute on each side. Lift out with a slotted spoon and reserve. In the same skillet, add garlic and mushrooms, and stir for about 2 minutes over medium heat. Stir in celery and carrots, and cook for 2 to 3 minutes more. Add reserved stock, gizzards, and hearts (if used) to vegetables. Bring to a boil, cover, lower heat, and simmer for about 10 minutes. Add reserved livers, herbs (and additional pepper, if you wish), and heat, stirring occasionally, until sauce is thickened slightly, 3 to 5 minutes. Serve over cooked barley, rice, or pasta.

EGG DISHES

Basil and Parmesan Cheese Frittata

4 servings

This Italian-style "omelet" is a perfect companion for grilled sweet Italian fennel sausages, either for brunch or a quick Sunday supper.

2 tablespoons butter, divided
¼ cup thinly sliced scallions
2 tablespoons finely minced sweet
　　red peppers
⅓ cup sour cream
6 eggs
2 tablespoons finely minced fresh
　　basil leaves
¼ teaspoon black pepper
⅓ cup grated Parmesan cheese

　　Melt 1 tablespoon of the butter in a small skillet. Add scallions and red peppers, and saute over low heat until soft, 1 to 2 minutes. Place sour cream into a medium-size bowl, and add eggs, one at a time, beating with an egg beater or a wire whisk. Stir in basil, black pepper, scallions, and red peppers. Melt remaining butter in a 10-inch cast-iron skillet or any skillet with an ovenproof handle. Pour in egg mixture, and cook slowly until eggs are just set and the surface is still moist. Remove from heat, and sprinkle with Parmesan cheese, and place under broiler just until cheese melts and the edges of the frittata puff, about 1 minute. Cut into wedges, and serve in the skillet.

Emerald Herb Flan

4 to 6 servings

2 teaspoons butter, softened
3 cups milk
½ teaspoon black pepper
½ teaspoon dried crushed tarragon
¼ cup cold milk
1 tablespoon cornstarch
1 teaspoon Worcestershire sauce
2 to 3 drops of hot pepper sauce
1 teaspoon grated lemon rind
6 eggs
¼ cup finely minced fresh
　　watercress
⅓ cup finely minced scallions
1 tablespoon finely minced fresh
　　parsley

　　Preheat oven to 350°F. Butter a 6-cup ovenproof souffle dish (preferably glass).
　　Boil a tea kettle of water, and set aside. In a medium-size nonstick saucepan, heat the 3 cups of milk slowly, adding pepper and tarragon, and cook until bubbles form around the edges of the pan. In a small cup, mix together the ¼ cup of cold milk and cornstarch, and add mixture to hot milk. Add Worcestershire sauce, hot pepper sauce, and lemon rind to milk, and remove from heat. In a large deep bowl, beat eggs with an egg beater until light and foamy. Remove a ladleful of the hot milk mixture, and slowly add to eggs, beating with a wire whisk as you add it.

Return egg-milk mixture to saucepan of hot milk, beating constantly while adding it. Stir in watercress, scallions, and parsley, and pour into prepared souffle dish. Set the dish in a larger pan, pour boiled water into the outer pan one-third of the way up the sides of the souffle dish, making a "bath" in which the souffle dish will bake, and bake for 1 to 1¼ hours. To test, insert a knife in the center. It should come out clean when the flan is done. The flan will shrink a bit from the sides of the pan, and the herbs will have floated to the surface to form a green topping. Let cool, then chill, and serve.

Note: If you don't have a glass souffle dish, use a regular mold or souffle dish. When the flan is finished, let it chill in the refrigerator. Then loosen the edges, unmold, and turn it right side up on another plate so that the herb crust is on the top.

Hard-Boiled Eggs with Three-Herb Sauce

4 servings

The sauce for this brunch or luncheon dish also goes well with fish or chicken breasts. It is delicious, delicate, and a favorite of ours.

 6 hard-boiled eggs, peeled and cut in half lengthwise
1½ tablespoons finely minced shallots (about 2 medium-size shallots)

 1 teaspoon grated lemon rind
 2 tablespoons finely minced fresh parsley
 2 tablespoons finely minced fresh chervil
 1 teaspoon finely minced fresh tarragon
 3 tablespoons butter, softened
 1 teaspoon whole wheat flour
 1 egg yolk, beaten
 ½ cup heavy cream
 1 teaspoon French-style mustard
2 or 3 drops of hot pepper sauce or few grains of cayenne pepper pinch of freshly ground black pepper
 1 tablespoon lemon juice

Place 3 egg halves on each serving plate, and set aside. In the top of a double boiler, mix together shallots, lemon rind, parsley, chervil, and tarragon, and place over simmering water. In a cup, combine butter and flour, and add to double boiler, stirring occasionally with a wooden spoon, until butter is melted and mixed with herbs and shallots, 1 to 2 minutes. In a small bowl, mix egg yolk with cream, mustard, hot pepper sauce or cayenne, and black pepper, and add to herb mixture. Stir constantly for 5 minutes, or until sauce is thickened. Do not allow to boil. Remove from heat, and cool slightly. Stir in lemon juice. Spoon 2 to 3 tablespoons of sauce over eggs. Serve at room temperature.

Poached Eggs Florentine with Sweet and Hot Pepper Sauce

4 servings

Colorful, delicate, yet hearty, this is a brunch, supper, or luncheon dish with extra sauce for another use. The sauce is also excellent on fish, chicken, or vegetables.

SAUCE

1 large sweet red pepper, roasted (page 85)
1 jalapeno pepper, roasted, peeled and seeded
3 cloves garlic, peeled and sliced
1 small potato, peeled and cooked until soft (preferably cook in chicken stock)
2 tablespoons olive oil

SPINACH

1 pound fresh spinach or 1 package (10 ounces) frozen spinach
1 teaspoon butter
   few gratings of nutmeg

EGGS

1 teaspoon white vinegar
4 eggs

To make the sauce: In a blender, puree peppers, garlic, and potato, slowly adding olive oil while blender is running. Let sauce stand to develop flavors, or prepare it the day before.

To make the spinach: If using fresh spinach, steam until wilted. If using frozen spinach, cook according to package directions. Drain spinach, and press out remaining liquid in a strainer with the back of a wooden spoon. Chop spinach. Distribute equally among 4 buttered individual oven-to-table baking dishes, sprinkle with nutmeg, and keep warm while preparing eggs.

To make the eggs: Fill a large, nonstick skillet three-quarters full of water, and bring to a boil. Add vinegar, and lower heat to a simmer. Break an egg into a teacup. Tilt the teacup, and place cup gently into simmering water, letting hot water run into the cup to begin to set egg whites. Then slip egg into water. Repeat with all the eggs. When whites are firm and yolks have a white film over them, but are still soft, lift eggs out carefully with a slotted spoon. With the egg still on the spoon, place it for a moment on paper towels to drain any excess moisture. Then slide the egg on to the spinach in one of the baking dishes. Spoon 1 tablespoon of the sauce down the center of each egg, and serve immediately. Pass the rest of the sauce at the table. Serve with crusty bread.

Poached Eggs in Yogurt with Paprika and Cayenne Pepper

4 servings

These eggs are poached and floated on yogurt, Turkish style. They're simple but unusual, and you can serve them for lunch or for a festive breakfast.

  1 cup plain yogurt
  1 very small clove garlic, peeled
     sprinkling of freshly ground black
        pepper
  4 eggs
  ½ teaspoon white vinegar
  1 tablespoon butter
  ½ teaspoon paprika
     dash of cayenne pepper
  1 tablespoon finely minced fresh
        parsley

Pour yogurt into the top of a double boiler, and warm over simmering water. Do not overheat or yogurt will curdle. Squeeze garlic through a garlic press, and stir it into yogurt. Add pepper, and keep yogurt mixture warm while eggs poach.

Poach eggs with vinegar in simmering water in a nonstick skillet. (For detailed directions, see page 186.) In a small saucepan, melt butter along with paprika and cayenne. When eggs are ready, spoon ¼ cup of warm yogurt into individual shallow serving bowls, lift eggs out of skillet with a slotted spoon, and place carefully over yogurt, one in each bowl. Quickly trickle a bit of the paprika sauce over each portion from the tip of a spoon. Then sprinkle the edges of the bowl with parsley. Serve with toast or crusty bread.

When you're in the mood for something different, try herb toast for breakfast or lunch. Toast a slice of whole wheat bread and spread it with soft herb butter. It's delicious by itself, and it makes a good base for sauteed mushrooms or poached eggs.

Chapter 9

GRAINS, BEANS, & PASTA

← Penne with Broccoli di Rape, Hot Pepper, and Nutmeg (page 204)

The rice of China and the Orient, the wheat and millet of Africa, the corn of South America, have served for centuries as the core ingredients for the cuisines of those areas. Natives depend upon tasty sauces laced with spices and herbs to vary the basic flavors. As you will see, the neutral character of grains and beans makes a perfect foil for a wide variety of seasonings.

The East Indians are especially adept at flavoring grains and legumes. A standard dish couples lentils with fresh dill leaves; another brightens red kidney beans with green chilies, garlic, ginger, and turmeric. Of course, the enchanting combination of saffron and rice whose origin is attributed to the Indians puts us forever in their debt.

North Africans perform culinary miracles with bulgur in their traditional couscous, covered with a lamb stew redolent of garlic, ginger, cumin, cloves, and coriander. The opportunities for variety when cooking with grains and legumes are endless. What's more, a 4-ounce serving of cooked beans contains only about 135 calories, and these carbohydrate foods are very satisfying.

The same holds true for pasta and noodle dishes. Who among us doesn't like pasta? Ah, those sauces! (An important tip: Never overwhelm the delicate flavor of pasta with large quantities of sauce. The sauce is intended to add aroma, flavor, and color—and to keep the pieces from sticking together. Serve extra sauce in a pitcher for those who want more.) If you think you've tried it all with pastas, we promise some exciting surprises in this section. Even the names of some of the dishes here will make you want to begin your dinner preparation at once: Linguine di Passeri with Six Herbs; Penne with Broccoli di Rape, Hot Pepper, and Nutmeg; Vietnamese Noodles with Pork, Shrimp, Cilantro, and Shredded Lettuce.

And how about these dishes that feature beans—Cannellini Beans with Sage and Garlic *(Fagioli all'Uccelletto)* and French Flageolets with Summer Savory and Thyme! Because they contain relatively little meat, the amount of saturated fat in such treats is lower than in most main courses. Better yet, their nutritional value is very high.

189

Black Beans with Roasted Red Peppers and Oregano

4 servings

The Cubans add a few tablespoons of dark rum to the black beans, and the Brazilians mash half the beans with garlic to form a sauce for the rest. Our colorful version features aromatic vegetables and herbs.

1	cup dried black beans
3	whole cloves
1	large onion, peeled
2	cloves garlic, peeled
1	carrot
1	dried bay leaf
2	stalks celery
5 to 6	sprigs fresh parsley, tied with string
3	cups chicken stock
2	tablespoons olive oil
1	tablespoon red wine vinegar
1½	tablespoons coarsely chopped fresh oregano, divided
½	cup sour cream
1	large sweet red pepper, roasted and cut into ½-inch strips (page 85)

Soak beans in 3 to 4 cups water overnight. Then drain and rinse beans. Put beans into a 5-quart Dutch oven (preferably nonstick). Insert cloves into onion, and add to beans along with garlic, carrot, bay leaf, celery, and parsley. Then add chicken stock, bring to a boil, cover, lower heat, and simmer for 1½ hours, or until tender. During the last 20 minutes of cooking, remove cover, and check on the amount of liquid. If there is too much, keep the cover off for the remainder of the cooking time. If there is too little liquid, add a bit of boiling water. When beans are cooked most of the liquid should be absorbed.

Remove all the vegetables and the bay leaf, and discard. Add olive oil and vinegar, and stir well. Then add 1 tablespoon of the oregano. Spoon beans onto a warm serving platter, add 2 dollops of sour cream, sprinkle with remaining oregano, and lay strips of roasted pepper over the top.

Buckwheat Noodles with Sesame Seeds and Cilantro

4 to 6 servings

A spicy, cold noodle dish to serve on a hot summer day, or *any* day. With a few shreds of cooked chicken, it's a whole meal; and it can be made several hours ahead of time.

NOODLES

8	ounces uncooked Japanese buckwheat noodles *(soba)*
1	tablespoon Oriental sesame oil
2	tablespoons finely sliced scallions, green part only
1	carrot, scored deeply on 4 sides with tip of knife and then sliced paper-thin crosswise to make carrot "flowers"
2	tablespoons sesame seeds, toasted
1	cup shredded cooked chicken
1	heaping tablespoon fresh cilantro leaves
4	large scallions, white parts only, cut into 2½-inch pieces

DRESSING

¼	cup rice vinegar
1	tablespoon sesame paste
2	tablespoons peanut butter
2	teaspoons French-style mustard

2 teaspoons light honey

2 tablespoons light soy sauce

1 scant tablespoon Oriental hot chili oil

¼ cup Oriental sesame oil

2 tablespoons corn oil

¼ cup orange or tangerine juice

1 tablespoon grated orange or tangerine rind

the dish. When chilled, the scallions form into delicate "brushes." Prepare dressing.

To make the dressing: In a small bowl, mix all the ingredients together with a wire whisk. Pour over noodles and toss well.

When ready to serve, arrange reserved carrot flowers and scallion brushes around noodles on a large serving platter, and scatter reserved chicken and cilantro leaves on top.

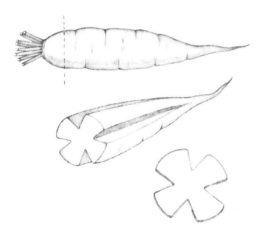

To make the noodles: Cook noodles in a large quantity of boiling water for 5 minutes. Drain, and run under cold water at once to cool. Toss in a bowl with sesame oil to prevent noodles from sticking together, and then add sliced scallion greens and carrot flowers, reserving some for garnish later on. Toss with sesame seeds. Reserve chicken and cilantro leaves until it is time to serve the dish. Put noodles in the refrigerator to chill, and prepare scallion "brushes" that will be used as garnish.

Trim bulb ends off scallions. Slice top ends lengthwise so that they look like "brushes." Place scallions into ice water, and place in refrigerator until it is time to serve

Brown Rice and Bulgur with Fennel and Swiss Cheese

4 to 6 servings

    2 tablespoons butter
    ½ cup finely chopped onions
    2 cups coarsely chopped fennel bulb
           plus ¼ cup finely chopped feathery
           leaves, divided
    ½ cup long-grain brown rice
    ½ cup medium bulgur
    2 cups chicken stock
    ¼ teaspoon black pepper
    ½ cup grated Swiss or Gruyere cheese

Preheat oven to 375°F.

In a medium-size heatproof casserole, melt butter. Add onions and saute over medium heat on top of stove until soft but not brown. Add chopped fennel, rice, and bulgur, and stir for 1 to 2 minutes. Add chicken stock and pepper, bring to a boil, lower heat, and cover tightly with aluminum foil. Place in oven, and bake until all the liquid has been absorbed, about 30 minutes. Remove foil, and bake, uncovered, for 10 minutes more. Remove from oven, and stir in fennel leaves and cheese. Cover again, and set aside for 5 minutes to allow the heat of the rice and bulgur to melt the cheese. Uncover, and serve immediately.

Cannellini Beans with Sage and Garlic
(*Fagioli all'Uccelletto*)

4 servings

    1½ cups dried cannellini beans
    2 tablespoons olive oil
    1 tablespoon finely minced garlic
           (about 2 cloves)
    1 can (14 ounces) Italian plum
           tomatoes, drained and chopped,
           or 1 cup chopped, peeled, ripe
           fresh plum tomatoes
    2 tablespoons coarsely chopped fresh
           sage leaves (about 10 large
           leaves)
    ½ teaspoon poivre aromatique*
    2 tablespoons minced fresh
           parsley

Soak cannellini beans in 4 cups water overnight. Drain and rinse beans. Cook in 6 cups fresh water for 1 hour, and then drain again.

In a large Dutch oven, heat oil and garlic and saute for 1 minute, stirring constantly. Do not brown. Add tomatoes, sage, beans, and poivre aromatique. Simmer, uncovered, for 10 minutes, stirring occasionally. Add more pepper to taste if you'd like, and sprinkle with parsley before serving.

*Poivre aromatique is a mixture of mostly malabar peppercorns and allspice. If you have difficulty obtaining this blend, try a mixture of ¼ teaspoon allspice and ¼ teaspoon freshly ground pepper.

Egg Noodles with Watercress and Pot Cheese

4 servings

This dish, without the watercress, was Sheryl's favorite supper when she was a child. When we tested it, she said it brought back memories of her mother serving it hot and steaming.

10 ounces uncooked medium-size egg noodles
3 tablespoons butter
8 ounces pot cheese
1½ cups coarsely chopped watercress
¼ teaspoon black pepper
2 tablespoons grated Parmesan cheese

Cook noodles for 8 to 10 minutes in 7 quarts of boiling water. Drain, and put into a large, warmed serving bowl in which butter has been melted. Toss well. Add pot cheese, and toss again. Then add watercress, toss again, and sprinkle with black pepper and Parmesan cheese. Serve at once.

French Flageolets with Summer Savory and Thyme

4 servings

This is the traditional accompaniment to *gigot,* a leg of lamb.

1 cup dried flageolet beans
6 cups water
2 whole cloves
1 medium-size onion, peeled
1 large carrot
1 stalk celery
4 sprigs of fresh parsley
3 sprigs of fresh thyme
1 dried bay leaf
1 tablespoon butter
1 teaspoon finely minced garlic
1 tablespoon finely minced shallots

¼ cup light cream
1 tablespoon finely minced fresh summer savory
1 large ripe tomato, peeled and diced
1 tablespoon finely minced fresh parsley

Soak beans overnight in 3 cups water. (The surface of the water should be about 2 inches over the tops of the beans.)

Drain and rinse beans, and put into a large pot with the fresh water. Insert cloves into onion, add to beans along with carrot, and celery, and bring to a boil. Lower heat. Tie parsley sprigs, thyme sprigs, and bay leaf with string, and add to the pot. Simmer with cover ajar for 1½ to 2 hours, or until beans are tender. Check after 1 hour to see if additional water needs to be added. When beans are cooked, remove onion, carrot, celery, and herbs.

In a small skillet, melt butter. Add garlic and shallots, stir and cook until soft. Add to beans, along with cream, summer savory, and tomato, and simmer until hot, stirring occasionally, 3 to 5 minutes. Serve with minced parsley sprinkled on top.

Tradition says that thyme was the herb used to line the creche of Jesus Christ.

Green Fusilli with Cranberry Beans, Sausage, Herbs, and Tomatoes

4 to 6 servings

1 pound fresh cranberry beans, shelled (about 1½ cups)
2 fresh sweet Italian sausages, removed from casings and crumbled
1 cup finely chopped onions
1 tablespoon finely minced garlic
1 can (14 ounces) Italian tomatoes (about 1⅔ cups)
1 dried bay leaf
1 teaspoon fresh oregano
1 teaspoon finely chopped fresh sage
½ teaspoon chopped fresh rosemary
4 fresh basil leaves, shredded
1 teaspoon tomato paste
¼ teaspoon dried red pepper flakes
12 ounces uncooked spinach fusilli pasta
1 tablespoon olive oil
2 tablespoons grated Romano or Parmesan cheese
1 tablespoon chopped fresh parsley

Place beans in a 3-quart saucepan with enough water to cover, and simmer for 20 to 25 minutes, covered. Cook until beans are tender. Drain, and set beans aside.

In a 12-inch skillet, saute sausage until it loses its color, stirring over medium heat for about 3 minutes. (If you wish to leave sausage in casing, saute links over low heat for 30 minutes, turning occasionally.) Add onions and garlic, and continue to cook, stirring occasionally, until onions wilt. Stir in tomatoes, and bring to a boil. Lower heat, add bay leaf, oregano, sage, rosemary, basil, tomato paste, and red pepper flakes, stir, and simmer, uncovered, while pasta cooks.

Cook fusilli in a large quantity of boiling water until al dente (10 to 12 minutes). Drain, place into a large serving bowl, and toss with olive oil to prevent pasta from sticking together. Remove bay leaf from sauce. Add cranberry beans to sauce, and spoon over pasta. Sprinkle Romano or Parmesan cheese over pasta, and then add parsley. Serve at once.

Hominy Grits and Shrimp Paste with Lemon Thyme, Parsley, and Chives

6 servings

Here are two versions of the same dish. The first one is lovely to serve as an accompaniment to plain broiled fish or as the stuffing for a rolled fish fillet. As an alternative, you can also smooth it into a flat pie plate, cut it into squares or rounds, and saute it in a bit of corn oil to serve as a side dish.

The second version is made into patties, dipped in corn flour, and sauteed. The patties go particularly well with Watercress, Lemon Balm, Parsley, and Chive Sauce (page 266).

4 cups water
juice of ½ lemon
1 dried bay leaf
6 sprigs of fresh lemon thyme or regular fresh thyme
10 to 12 sprigs of fresh parsley
1 pound medium-size raw shrimp
½ cup butter, softened
3 tablespoons lemon juice
1 tablespoon finely minced fresh chives

Green Fusilli with Cranberry Beans, Sausage, Herbs, and Tomatoes (page 194)

2 tablespoons finely minced fresh parsley
1 tablespoon fresh lemon thyme leaves
⅛ teaspoon hot pepper sauce
1 cup stone-ground hominy grits

In a 5-quart nonaluminum Dutch oven, combine water, lemon juice, bay leaf, thyme sprigs, and parsley sprigs. Cover, and bring to a boil. Add shrimp, and bring to a boil again. Remove from heat. Let shrimp stand for 5 minutes in liquid. Then drain and reserve liquid, discard herbs, and cool shrimp under cold water. Peel and devein shrimp. Add shrimp and all the remaining ingredients, except shrimp stock and hominy grits, to a food processor, and process until pastelike in consistency. Spoon and scrape paste into a bowl, and chill for 1 hour to blend flavors.

When ready to cook, bring reserved shrimp stock to a boil in a 4-quart nonstick saucepan or Dutch oven. (There should be 4 cups of stock. If necessary, add enough water to make 4 cups liquid.) When stock boils, gradually add hominy grits, stirring constantly with a wooden spoon. While stirring, bring to a boil, and then lower heat. Cover, and simmer, stirring once or twice, for 20 to 25 minutes, or until grits are cooked and liquid is absorbed. Stir in reserved shrimp paste, and simmer for 1 minute, stirring constantly, or until heated through.

VERSION TWO

Using the hominy grits-shrimp paste mixture described above, make pancake-shaped patties, and dip the patties into corn flour on both sides. Melt some butter or corn oil (or a combination of both) in a large cast-iron skillet. Saute the cakes until cooked through on both sides, being careful to turn them gently with a spatula. When finished, serve hot with Watercress, Lemon Balm, Parsley, and Chive Sauce (page 266). This will make 4 to 6 servings.

195

Herb and Tomato Pancake Noodles with Borage Flowers

4 servings

The pancake batter is prepared and refrigerated for two to three hours before cooking. The thin, crepe-like pancakes are then cut into fine "noodles."

2	eggs
1	cup tomato juice
1	teaspoon tomato paste
2 or 3	drops of hot pepper sauce
¼	cup whole wheat flour
1	cup unbleached white flour
2	tablespoons butter, melted
1	tablespoon finely minced fresh basil
1	tablespoon finely minced fresh chives
	clarified butter or oil, for brushing pan
2	tablespoons butter
¼	cup grated Romano or Parmesan cheese
5 or 6	fresh basil leaves
8	borage flowers or other herb blossoms

In a food processor, mix together eggs, tomato juice, tomato paste, hot pepper sauce, whole wheat flour, unbleached white flour, melted butter, minced basil, and chives, and blend until very smooth. Transfer to a medium-size bowl, cover with plastic wrap, and refrigerate for at least 2 hours.

Heat a crepe pan, whose base measures 7 inches in diameter, over medium-high heat, and brush the pan lightly with clarified butter or oil. Pour ¼ cup of the batter into a corner of the pan, quickly lifting and tilting pan in a circular motion, so that batter coats the bottom of the pan thinly and evenly. Return to heat, and cook until edges of pancake look dry and pull away slightly from the edge of the pan and the top looks as if it has lost its sheen. Loosen edges of pancake slightly, and turn pan over on sheet of waxed paper. Repeat until all the batter is used up. There should be about 10 pancakes. Stack each pancake between sheets of waxed paper. When all 10 are cooked on one side, peel off waxed paper and cook each pancake for 1 minute on the other side, again stacking them between waxed paper sheets. This will keep them pliable as well as keeping them from sticking together.

When ready to serve, roll up pancakes individually, and cut into noodles ⅛ inch wide. Warm an oven-to-table serving dish with the butter in it. When butter is melted, put noodles into dish, tossing to coat, and warm in a 350°F oven for about 10 minutes. Sprinkle cheese on noodles before serving, and toss. Cut basil leaves into fine shreds, and scatter over the top. Add borage flowers or other herb blossoms when ready to serve.

Note: We cook all the pancakes on one side, then return them to the pan to cook on the other side. This avoids trying to turn them while hot after cooking them on one side only.

Kasha with Carrots, Mushrooms, and Mint

4 servings

Serve as a side dish or use as a stuffing for poultry.

1	tablespoon corn oil
2	tablespoons butter, divided
¼	cup coarsely chopped scallions

2 cups coarsely chopped carrots
(3 to 4 carrots)
¼ pound fresh mushrooms, coarsely
chopped
¼ teaspoon black pepper
1 egg
½ cup whole or medium kasha
1½ cups chicken stock
1 heaping tablespoon coarsely
chopped fresh mint

In a 10-inch skillet, heat oil and 1 tablespoon of the butter. Add scallions, and saute over medium-high heat for 1 minute, stirring constantly. Add carrots, mushrooms, and pepper. Cook and stir for 2 to 3 minutes more. Transfer vegetables to a bowl, and set aside.

Melt remaining butter in the same skillet. In a small bowl, beat egg slightly, and then combine well with kasha. Add to skillet, and cook, stirring constantly, until grains separate. Return vegetables to skillet, and add stock. Bring to a boil, then lower heat to a simmer, cover, and cook for 15 to 20 minutes, or until liquid is absorbed. Turn off heat, stir in mint, cover again, and let stand for 5 minutes before serving in a warmed serving dish.

Lasagna Rolls with Spinach, Sorrel, Raisins, and Mace

4 servings

½ pound sorrel, center stems
removed
1 pound fresh spinach, coarse stems
removed
2 tablespoons butter
1 medium onion, peeled and finely
minced (about 3 tablespoons),
divided
½ teaspoon ground mace

2 tablespoons golden raisins
¼ teaspoon black pepper
8 ounces uncooked lasagna or wide
noodles (12 pieces)
1¾ cups low-fat milk
2 eggs, slightly beaten
1½ cups grated Gruyere cheese
(6 ounces)
⅛ teaspoon white pepper
cayenne pepper

Coarsely chop sorrel and spinach. Steam for 4 to 5 minutes, or until wilted. Drain in a sieve, pressing excess moisture out with a wooden spoon. Transfer to a medium-size bowl. In a large skillet, melt butter. Add 1 tablespoon of the onions, and saute until wilted. Then add to spinach-sorrel mixture. Stir in mace, raisins, and black pepper. Puree in a food processor for a few seconds, or until finely chopped. Set aside.

Cook lasagna for 10 to 12 minutes in a large amount of boiling water with a few drops of olive oil added to keep pasta from sticking. Stir occasionally. Drain in a colander, rinse under cold water, and carefully lay noodles between 2 pieces of waxed paper. Butter a 9 × 12-inch oven-to-table baking pan, and set oven temperature to 350°F. Place 2 teaspoons of reserved spinach-sorrel mixture on each noodle and spread evenly with a small spatula. Roll up each noodle, and place seam-side down in prepared pan.

In a large saucepan, combine milk, eggs, remaining onions, cheese, and white pepper. Cook over low heat, stirring constantly, for 8 to 10 minutes, or until cheese is melted and sauce is slightly thickened. Spoon over rolls, sprinkle with cayenne, and bake for 25 minutes. Place under broiler for a few minutes to brown top slightly. Serve at once.

Lemon Lentils with Cinnamon Sticks, Ginger, Cilantro, and Powdered Bay Leaves

4 to 6 servings

This spicy and lemony treatment of the plain lentil takes this dish out of the ordinary. Try it with plain brown rice for a vegetarian meal or with a simply grilled lamb steak.

  1 lemon
¼ cup plus 1 tablespoon corn oil, divided
  1 medium onion, peeled, cut in half, and thinly sliced (about ¾ cup)
  1 pound green lentils
  2 2-inch pieces of cinnamon stick
¾ tablespoon finely minced peeled ginger root
3½ cups chicken stock
½ teaspoon cayenne pepper (or less if you prefer)
¼ cup finely chopped onions
  1 clove garlic, peeled and finely minced
½ small hot pepper, seeded and minced (optional)
¼ teaspoon powdered bay leaves or 2 whole dried bay leaves
¼ cup coarsely chopped fresh cilantro leaves

Grate rind of lemon, squeeze juice, and set aside.

Heat ¼ cup of the oil in a 10-inch skillet. Add sliced onions, and saute over medium heat until wilted. Stir in lentils, cinnamon, and ginger, and cook, stirring often, for about 5 minutes. Add stock and cayenne, bring to a boil, cover, lower heat, and simmer for 15 minutes. Stir in reserved lemon rind and juice, and cook for 10 to 15 minutes more, or until lentils are tender, adding additional stock if lentils seem dry.

While lentils are cooking, heat remaining oil in another small skillet. Add chopped onions, garlic, and hot pepper (if used). Sprinkle with powdered bay leaves or whole dried bay leaves, and saute over low heat until onions begin to brown slightly. Remove whole dried bay leaves (if used), and stir mixture into lentils. Transfer to a serving dish, and sprinkle with cilantro before serving.

Lemon Rice with Dill and Toasted Pine Nuts

6 servings

  2 cups chicken stock
⅛ teaspoon black pepper
  1 tablespoon butter
    juice of 1 lemon plus enough water to make ½ cup
  1 teaspoon grated lemon rind
  1 cup long-grain brown rice
  2 tablespoons pine nuts, toasted
1½ tablespoons coarsely chopped fresh dill

In a 5-quart nonstick Dutch oven, bring chicken stock, pepper, butter, and lemon-water to a boil. Add lemon rind and rice, reduce heat, cover, and simmer for 40 to 45 minutes, or until rice is tender. Place a paper towel between the pot and the lid to absorb excess moisture, and let rice stand for 5 minutes. Sprinkle with pine nuts and dill, and toss to fluff. Transfer to a warm serving dish, and serve while hot.

Lentil and Rice Pilaf with Hot Sausage and Fennel

6 servings

The peppery bite of the hot sausage is cooled by the natural sweetness of the fennel leaves. You can serve it as a main luncheon dish or as an accompaniment to any lamb dish.

2 tablespoons olive oil
2 fresh hot Italian sausages (about ¼ pound), removed from casings and crumbled
⅔ cup coarsely chopped scallions
¾ cup brown rice
½ cup lentils
3 large plum tomatoes, peeled and cubed
3 cups chicken stock
¼ teaspoon lemon pepper or black pepper
¼ cup finely minced fresh parsley
1 tablespoon finely minced fresh oregano
1 tablespoon finely minced fresh fennel leaves

In a 5-quart nonstick saucepan, heat olive oil. Add sausage, and saute, stirring constantly, for 1 to 2 minutes. Lift out with a slotted spoon, place in a small dish, and reserve. In the same pan, add scallions, and cook, stirring constantly, for 1 to 2 minutes, or until wilted. Add rice and lentils, and stir until coated with the oil in the pan. Return reserved sausage to pot, stir in tomatoes and chicken stock, and bring to a boil. Lower heat, add pepper and half of all the herbs, cover, and simmer for 30 minutes, stirring occasionally. Transfer to a warm serving dish, sprinkle with remaining herbs, and mix at the table before serving.

Linguine di Passeri with Six Herbs

4 servings

A hint of fresh tomato plus the taste of fresh herbs in a light, quick, uncooked sauce.

1 teaspoon finely minced fresh rosemary
1 tablespoon finely minced fresh sage
1 tablespoon finely minced fresh mint
2 tablespoons finely minced fresh parsley
2 tablespoons finely minced fresh chives
1 teaspoon finely minced fresh oregano
2 large ripe tomatoes, peeled and cubed
2 cloves garlic, peeled and finely minced
1 teaspoon grated lemon rind
12 ounces uncooked linguine di passeri pasta
¼ cup olive oil
¼ teaspoon black pepper

In a large bowl or oven-to-table serving dish, mix together all the ingredients except pasta, olive oil, and pepper. Cook pasta in a large quantity of boiling water for 8 to 10 minutes. While pasta is cooking for the last few minutes, slowly heat olive oil in a small skillet until it is very hot. Pour hot olive oil into herb-tomato mixture so that hot oil makes herbs sizzle. Drain pasta, add to hot herb-tomato-oil mixture, and toss, sprinkling with pepper. Serve at once.

Lynne Springer

Lynne's Restaurant
Sebastopol, California

If there is a quintessential California restaurant, Lynne's must be it. Lynne Springer came to California many years ago, by way of New York and the Culinary Institute of America, and has found that it offers all a dedicated chef could ask for.

When I cook I use fresh everything, and the reason I stayed in California is the availability of fresh fruits, vegetables, wine, and seafood — without chemicals, without nitrates. It's phenomenal!

After four years as executive chef at the huge 5,000-acre resort Coto de Caza in California's Trabuco Canyon, she and her husband Mark went north to open their own place about two years ago. Lynne's is on a two-lane road right outside of Santa Rosa, about an hour's drive north of San Francisco. It's surrounded by willow trees and large apple trees, and the Springers grow all of their fresh produce for the restaurant in a garden out in back.

I guess you could say that this area is just like the Napa Valley before it was discovered. We have several wineries just up the road, and many of our customers come here after visiting the vineyards. Another couple of miles past the wineries we have a turkey farm, so we have access to a supply of fresh birds. Our butcher, just two miles away, dresses his own meat.

What about herbs?

We grow our own basil, rosemary, thyme, cilantro, parsley, and summer savory. Try fresh tarragon or chervil in a cheese and tomato quiche. Either herb is a welcome change from the usual oregano and marries well with the cheese-tomato combination. Last year I was addicted to dill and shallots. This year I've been discovering cumin and thyme. A particular favorite of mine is cumin combined with fresh tomatoes in a cream sauce. The flavors come together magnificently when served over salmon.

Lynne prefers marjoram over oregano in cooked dishes because oregano is sometimes bitter. She puts poppy seeds in her blue cheese salad dressing because it provides a pleasant surprise in taste and texture. For the same reason, she adds fresh basil and wild radishes (picked in the fields of northern California) to salads of various lettuce greens.

Next year I hope to grow mizuna, a Japanese mustard green. I've been trying it in salads as a flavoring rather than an herb with excellent results.

The restaurant itself has been growing, though Lynne's does not advertise. It's word of mouth that brings in plenty of new customers to try the fresh ingredients so skillfully blended in the restaurant's delicious specialties. Here is Lynne's recipe for the fettuccini with mussels she serves. This marvelous dish is flavored with garlic and herbs.

Fresh Herb Fettuccine with Garlic and Mussels

4 servings as entree
8 servings as appetizer

PASTA

1½ cups semolina
1½ cups unbleached white flour
½ cup finely chopped fresh dill
4 eggs, at room temperature, slightly beaten
1½ tablespoons olive oil
2 tablespoons lukewarm milk or water
8 cloves garlic, peeled and pureed

MUSSELS

48 mussels
3 cups clam juice or 2½ cups water mixed with ½ cup lemon juice and 2 cloves garlic, peeled and minced
2 tablespoons butter, melted
2 tablespoon chopped fresh parsley

To make the pasta: In a large bowl, mix together semolina, flour, and dill.

Transfer to a bread board or flat surface, and make a well in the center. Combine eggs, oil, milk or water, and garlic, and pour into well. Mix by hand until well blended. Knead for 10 to 15 minutes, or until smooth and elastic. Dough will be lemon colored. Let rest for 20 to 30 minutes.

Divide dough into 4 sections. Roll out each section paper-thin. Cut fettuccine-size strips about ¼ inch wide. Dust with semolina, and roll loosely. Place on a plate, cover with plastic wrap, and chill until ready to cook.

To cook, bring 4 quarts of water to a rolling boil. Add pasta, stir, and cook for 4 to 5 minutes. Test for doneness by breaking 1 strand and looking for an uncooked line.

To prepare the mussels: Cover mussels with water, and let stand for 1 hour so that mussels will open and most of the sand inside will wash out. Lift mussels out of water, remove beards, and put into a large saucepan. Add clam juice. If not using clam juice, combine water, lemon juice, and garlic, and add to mussels. Bring to a boil, lower heat, cover, and simmer until all shells open. Discard any mussels that do not open. Set aside mussels and cooking liquid, covered.

When ready to serve, toss cooked and drained fettuccine with melted butter and parsley. Divide pasta among 4 plates. Arrange 12 mussels attractively on each plate, and pour 1 to 2 tablespoons reserved mussel cooking liquid over each serving. Provide separate bowls for discarding mussel shells.

Linguine with Scallops, Saffron, and Thyme

4 servings

1 pound uncooked linguine pasta
¼ cup butter, divided
¼ cup dry white wine
2 tablespoons lemon juice
1 teaspoon grated lemon rind
¼ pound fresh mushrooms, thinly sliced
¼ teaspoon black pepper
2 teaspoons finely minced garlic
1 pound whole bay scallops or sea scallops cut into small pieces
1 cup cubed peeled tomatoes (about 1 large tomato)
½ cup creme fraiche
½ teaspoon saffron threads
1½ tablespoons fresh thyme leaves
1½ tablespoons finely minced fresh parsley

Cook linguine in a large amount of boiling water for 8 to 10 minutes while preparing sauce.

Combine 1 tablespoon of the butter and the wine in a large skillet. Simmer until butter melts. Add lemon juice, lemon rind, mushrooms, and pepper, and saute for 5 minutes. Remove to a large bowl along with accumulated liquid, and set aside. Wipe out skillet with a paper towel, and melt remaining butter. Add garlic and scallops, and cook, stirring constantly, until scallops become opaque, 1 to 2 minutes. Lift out scallops with a slotted spoon, and reserve.

Add tomatoes to pan, and cook over medium heat for 2 minutes. Add creme fraiche, saffron, and thyme to skillet. Then pour off any accumulated juices from mushrooms and scallops, and add to skillet. Cook for 4 to 5 minutes more, and then return mushrooms and scallops to skillet to heat through. Drain linguine, pour sauce over it, and sprinkle with parsley. Toss with extra black pepper at the table, if desired.

Navy Bean Puree with Garlic, Chili Powder, and Mint

4 to 6 servings

This puree can be served as a side dish or as a spread with corn crackers. You might also want to try it served over brown rice, topped with a few tomato cubes that have been marinated in vinegar and oil.

½ pound navy beans
5 cups cold water
10 cloves garlic, peeled
1 tablespoon butter
1 tablespoon olive oil
1 tablespoon safflower oil
¼ teaspoon chili powder
1 tablespoon balsamic vinegar or red wine vinegar
2 tablespoons finely minced fresh mint

Soak beans overnight in enough water to cover.

Drain and rinse beans, place into a medium-size pot, and add cold water. Bring to a boil, lower heat, and simmer, covered, for 45 minutes. Add garlic, and simmer for 45 minutes longer. When beans are tender, drain in a strainer, reserving any cooking liquid. There should be about ¼ cup. Puree beans in a food processor, adding enough of the bean liquid to form a fairly thick puree. Mix in all the remaining ingredients, and serve at room temperature.

◄ Fresh ingredients for Vietnamese Noodles with Pork, Shrimp, Cilantro, and Shredded Lettuce (page 208)

Penne with Broccoli di Rape, Hot Pepper, and Nutmeg

4 servings

An Italian favorite, Broccoli di Rape tastes like a cross between broccoli and mustard greens.

1½ pounds broccoli di rape
¼ cup olive oil
1 tablespoon finely minced garlic
½ cup chicken stock
¼ to ½ teaspoon dried red pepper flakes
⅛ teaspoon nutmeg
1 teaspoon lemon juice or balsamic vinegar
⅛ teaspoon black pepper
12 ounces penne pasta, cooked
¼ cup grated Parmesan cheese

Trim and discard the tough bottom stalks of the broccoli di rape, leaving the tender leaves, stems, and buds intact. Wash, dry, and coarsely shred. Make sure it is dried very well or it will splatter while cooking. In a large skillet, heat olive oil. Add garlic, and quickly cook for a few seconds. Do not brown garlic or it will be bitter. Add broccoli di rape, and stir with a wooden spoon. Stir in chicken stock and red pepper flakes, cover, and cook over medium heat for 5 minutes, or until vegetable is tender. Stir in nutmeg, lemon juice or vinegar, and pepper. Spoon over cooked pasta, toss, add cheese, and toss again. Serve at once.

For a new taste in pasta or vegetables, try drizzling aromatic oils (for example, basil oil or hot chili oil) over them.

Spaghetti with Mussels, Basil, and Oregano

4 servings

The mussels in this dish are steamed first, and then the broth is added to the pasta sauce to enrich and flavor the fresh herbs and tomatoes.

2 pounds mussels (about 40), scrubbed and beards removed
1 dried bay leaf
2 whole cloves
6 to 8 peppercorns
4 sprigs of fresh parsley
¼ cup white wine vinegar
12 ounces uncooked spaghetti
2 tablespoons olive oil
¼ cup finely chopped onions
¼ cup finely chopped leeks
1 tablespoon finely minced garlic
1 pound ripe tomatoes, peeled and cubed (about 2 cups)
1 pinch of saffron threads (optional)
1 teaspoon fennel seeds
⅛ teaspoon dried red pepper flakes
1 teaspoon fresh thyme leaves
1 tablespoon chopped fresh oregano leaves
2 tablespoons finely chopped fresh parsley, divided
2 tablespoons whole small fresh basil leaves or chopped large basil leaves, divided
1 teaspoon grated lemon rind

In a 4-quart wide-bottomed nonaluminum pot with a tight-fitting lid, combine mussels, bay leaf, cloves, peppercorns, parsley, and wine vinegar. Steam over high heat until mussels open (5 to 10 minutes depending upon their size). Let mussels stand for a few minutes in the pot, and then strain stock. Add enough water to stock to equal 1¼ cups, and reserve. Discard herbs and spices. Reserve mussels in their shells, discarding any that have not opened.

Cook spaghetti in a large quantity of boiling water for 8 to 10 minutes.

Meanwhile, in a 10-inch skillet, heat olive oil. Add onions, leeks, and garlic, and saute until soft but not brown, stirring occasionally. Add tomatoes and reserved mussel stock, and cook over medium-high heat for 5 minutes. Stir in saffron (if used), fennel seeds, red pepper flakes, thyme, oregano, and half the parsley and basil. Lower heat, and simmer sauce while spaghetti cooks.

When ready to serve, spoon sauce into a large warmed serving bowl. Drain spaghetti, and toss with sauce. Arrange reserved mussels on top, sprinkle with remaining parsley and basil, and top with lemon rind.

Spiced Sweet Rice with Toasted Cashew Nuts

4 to 6 servings

This is another tasty dish, spicy with the flavor of ginger, cardamom, mace, and cloves and sweetened by the addition of carrots, raisins, and honey.

 2 tablespoons light honey
 1 teaspoon water
2½ cups hot chicken stock
 3 tablespoons butter
 ¼ cup finely minced scallions (about 1 scallion)
 ½ teaspoon finely minced garlic
 ⅓ cup finely chopped carrots (about 1 carrot)
 2 tablespoons golden raisins
 ⅛ teaspoon each of cardamom, mace, and ground cloves
 1 teaspoon finely chopped peeled ginger root
 ¼ teaspoon black pepper
 1 cup long-grain brown rice
 2 tablespoons coarsely chopped cashew nuts, toasted
 1 tablespoon shredded orange rind
 1 tablespoon coarsely chopped fresh parsley

Heat honey and water in a 5-quart nonstick Dutch oven, and cook over medium heat until dark and bubbly, about 1 minute. Add hot chicken stock, and bring to a boil. Remove from heat, and set aside.

In a 10-inch nonstick skillet, melt butter. Add scallions, garlic, and carrots, and saute for about 5 minutes, stirring often. Stir in raisins and spices, and cook, while stirring, for about 1 minute. Add rice, stir to coat with seasoned vegetables, and cook for 1 minute. Meanwhile, heat reserved stock to boiling, and then stir in rice mixture. Bring to a boil again, then lower heat, cover, and simmer for 45 minutes, or until rice is tender and liquid is absorbed. When ready to serve, mound rice in a warm serving dish, and sprinkle with nuts, orange rind, and parsley. Mix at the table just before serving.

Spinach Fettuccine with Nasturtium Blossoms

4 servings

2 tablespoons olive oil
1 large clove garlic, peeled and finely minced
4 plum tomatoes, peeled and coarsely chopped
2 tablespoons finely chopped fresh oregano
10 ounces uncooked green fettuccine pasta
2 tablespoons butter
12 nasturtium blossoms, cut in half
3 to 4 tablespoons grated Parmesan cheese
freshly ground black pepper, to taste
2 or 3 nasturtium blossoms with leaves

Heat oil in a large skillet. Add garlic, and cook, stirring constantly, until soft, but not browned. Add tomatoes, and cook over medium-high heat, stirring occasionally, for 5 minutes, or until excess liquid evaporates. Remove from heat, add oregano, and set aside.

Cook fettuccine in a large quantity of boiling water for 5 to 10 minutes, or until al dente. Homemade fettuccine will generally take less time to cook than the packaged commercial varieties. Melt butter in a warmed oven-to-table serving dish. When pasta is cooked, drain, and toss quickly with butter. Add tomato-oregano sauce, and toss again. Scatter cut blossoms over surface, sprinkle with cheese and pepper, and add the blossoms with leaves for garnish. Toss again at the table before serving.

Split Peas with Shallots, Marjoram, Tarragon, and Cloves

4 servings

1 cup split peas (½ pound)
2½ cups chicken stock
4 whole cloves
4 large shallots
1 small dried hot pepper
½ teaspoon dried marjoram
¼ teaspoon dried tarragon
¼ teaspoon black pepper
3 tablespoons butter

Rinse peas in cold water, and drain. Put them into a large nonstick saucepan, and add stock. Insert 1 clove into each shallot, and add to pot along with hot pepper. Bring to a boil, lower heat, cover, and simmer for 50 minutes. Take off heat. Remove hot pepper and cloves, and discard. Return shallots to pot, and beat vigorously with a wooden spoon to incorporate shallots. Add marjoram, tarragon, pepper, and butter, return to heat, and simmer for 10 minutes, stirring occasionally. The mixture should be very thick, and all the liquid should be absorbed. Serve in a warmed, shallow casserole.

Tube Pasta with Fresh Tomatoes, Zucchini, and Basil

4 servings

¼ cup plus 1 tablespoon olive oil, divided
1 teaspoon finely minced garlic

Linguini with Scallops, Saffron, and Thyme (page 203)

¾	cup coarsely chopped fresh basil
¼	cup coarsely chopped fresh parsley
1½	pounds ripe tomatoes, peeled and cut into chunks
1	teaspoon grated lemon rind
1	teaspoon nonpareil capers, rinsed and dried
¼	teaspoon black pepper
1	pound uncooked tube pasta (penne, ziti, or mostaccioli)
1	cup shredded zucchini (about 1 small zucchini)
2 to 3	tablespoons grated Romano or Parmesan cheese

Heat ¼ cup of the oil in a small skillet until hot. Add garlic, and saute for 1 minute. Do not brown. Remove from heat, and let cool to room temperature.

In a food processor, chop basil and parsley until fine. Add tomatoes, and process, but not too much. Allow some tomato pieces to remain intact. Remove to a medium-size bowl, and add lemon rind, capers, and pepper. Let stand for 20 minutes to blend flavors.

Then, cook pasta in a large quantity of water for 8 to 10 minutes; drain, and toss with remaining oil.

When ready to serve, spoon fresh tomato sauce over the hot pasta, and mix well. Scatter zucchini and cheese on top, and mix again at the table before serving.

Vietnamese Noodles with Pork, Shrimp, Cilantro, and Shredded Lettuce

4 servings

Hot, sweet, cool, and pungent—all at the same time! This is a treat for the taste buds and just perfect for a warm summer evening, since the actual cooking time is only about five minutes!

SAUCE

    4 limes
    2 teaspoons light honey
    3 tablespoons light soy sauce
¼ to ½ teaspoon dried red pepper flakes, depending upon your taste

NOODLES

    6 ounces uncooked bean thread noodles
    1 teaspoon Oriental sesame oil

FILLING

    1 tablespoon corn or peanut oil
    ½ pound lean ground pork
    1 large clove garlic, finely minced
    ¼ pound large raw shrimp, peeled, deveined, and cut in half (small whole shrimp may be substituted)
    ½ cup thinly sliced scallions
    6 romaine lettuce leaves, shredded
4 to 8 sprigs of fresh cilantro

To make the sauce: Shred rind of 1 lime. Cut another lime into small wedges (for garnish), and squeeze juice of 3 limes to get ½ cup lime juice. In a small bowl, mix all the ingredients with the lime rind, and stir until honey dissolves. Set aside to develop flavor.

To make the noodles: Bring a large pot of water to a boil. Add noodles, and stir. Remove from heat. Let noodles stand in the water until they are transparent, about 10 minutes. Drain, rinsing well with cold water. Cut noodles into 6-inch lengths for easier handling, since they are quite slippery when cooked. Place in a bowl, and toss with the oil to prevent them from sticking together. Set aside.

To make the filling: In a 10-inch skillet, heat oil. Add pork and garlic, and saute, stirring constantly, over medium heat until pork is brown, about 3 minutes. Add shrimp and cook, stirring constantly, for 1 minute more. Remove skillet from heat, add reserved noodles and lime sauce, and mix well to combine. Spoon into the center of a large serving platter, and top with scallions. Place shredded lettuce on the outer rim of the platter, and garnish with wedges of lime. Scatter sprigs of cilantro over the top. The lettuce is eaten with the noodles. It is a crisp and cooling part of the dish.

Note: Traditionally, the noodles are spooned into whole leaves of soft lettuce and eaten as a finger food. Westerners find this version easier to manage.

Chapter 10
STUFFINGS

Some time ago, the *New York Times* carried a story about a child who asked for "some more of that bread that the turkey ate." Many of us have indulged in feasts at Thanksgiving or Christmas that are more memorable for the stuffing than the bird.

A good stuffing supplies a contrast in textures and a complementary taste for the bird or the fish or the meat. Stuffings can range from delicate to rib-sticking, and they all have the make-ahead advantage, which takes some of the pressure off at cooking time. In fact, stuffings are better when prepared in advance, allowing plenty of time to let the flavors blend and to reach the peak of taste perfection. Here are some things to keep in mind when you're preparing stuffings:

&❧ All the stuffings in this chapter can also be used as a side dish, served as an accompaniment to the main course. If you decide to use them that way put the stuffing in a shallow casserole dish, cover it with foil, and bake at 350°F for about 35 minutes. During the last 5 minutes, uncover the dish to let a crust form.

&❧ Stuffings expand considerably during cooking, so stuff lightly. Be sure to stuff just before cooking, even though you have prepared the stuffing in advance to let it develop flavor and have kept it in the refrigerator.

&❧ Before storing the leftovers of a cooked, stuffed bird, remove the stuffing from the cavity and wrap it separately in foil.

&❧ To calculate the quantity of stuffing you will need, allow roughly 1 cup per pound for poultry and 2/3 cup per pound for meat or fish. This is a generous allowance, since stuffings do expand during cooking.

&❧ When preparing stuffings, don't stint. Extra stuffing can be baked separately (as per instructions above) or frozen and used to stuff vegetables, such as peppers, eggplant, zucchini, or summer or winter squash.

Apricot and Pecan Brown Rice Stuffing

Makes 12 cups

This recipe makes enough stuffing for a 12- to 14-pound turkey. Or bake separately in a 3-quart oven-to-table casserole for 35 minutes at 350°F, and serve as a side dish.

- 6 tablespoons butter, divided
- 2 cups coarsely broken pecans
- 1 cup finely chopped onions (about 2 medium-size onions)
- 1 cup finely diced celery (about 2 large stalks with leaves)
-   turkey liver and giblets, finely chopped (optional)
- 6 cups cooked long-grain brown rice
- 1 pound dried apricots, coarsely cut
- ½ cup finely minced fresh parsley
- 1 tablespoon dried thyme
- 1½ teaspoons dried sage
- ¼ teaspoon black pepper
- 1⅔ cups chicken stock

In a large skillet, melt 2 tablespoons of the butter. Add nuts, and toast for 2 to 3 minutes. Transfer nuts with a slotted spoon to a large bowl, and set aside. Heat remaining butter in the same skillet. Add onions and celery, and saute for about 3 minutes, or until onions are wilted, stirring occasionally. Do not brown. If using giblets, add at this point, and saute for 3 minutes more. Add mixture to nuts, and then add all the remaining ingredients except chicken stock. Stir well. Add stock to moisten, and mix thoroughly.

Kasha, Chicken Liver, and Chestnut Stuffing

Makes about 7 cups

This recipe makes enough stuffing for a capon, a goose, two ducks, a large chicken, or a small turkey.

- 1 pound chestnuts
- 2 cups chicken stock
- 2 tablespoons butter
- 3 tablespoons finely minced shallots (4 to 5 shallots)
- 1 cup finely diced celery (3 to 4 stalks)
- 2 large chicken livers, diced
- 4 cups cooked kasha
- 2 tablespoons finely chopped fresh parsley
- 1 egg, slightly beaten
- ½ teaspoon black pepper

Make an *X*-shaped incision on the curved side of the chestnuts, and steam for about 10 minutes. Shell and peel chestnuts while hot (using rubber gloves to protect your fingers). The shell and the membrane should come off easily. Do a few at a time while keeping the other chestnuts hot in the steamer with the cover on. When all the chestnuts are peeled, coarsely chop them, and simmer in chicken stock in a medium-size saucepan until they are tender and almost all the chicken stock has been absorbed, about 30 minutes. Set aside.

Melt butter in a medium-size skillet. Add shallots and celery, and saute until soft. Add chicken livers and cook, stirring constantly, for 1 to 2 minutes, or until livers lose their color. Set aside. In a large bowl, combine kasha, chestnuts and stock, and celery-liver mixture. Mix well, add all the remaining ingredients, and mix again.

Leek and Mushroom Low-Calorie Stuffing

Makes about 6 cups

This recipe makes enough stuffing for an 8- to 9-pound turkey or a crown roast of pork.

4	pounds large leeks (10 to 12 thin leeks)
1/3	cup butter
1	teaspoon finely minced garlic (2 cloves)
2½	pounds fresh mushrooms, thickly sliced
1	teaspoon grated lemon rind
½	teaspoon black pepper
1	teaspoon dried thyme
1½	tablespoons lemon juice

Cut off root ends of leeks, and trim off tough tops, leaving about 1½ inches of green part. Split leeks in half lengthwise. Separating each leaf, rinse well under cold running water, and drain on paper towels. Cut crosswise into thin slices, and set aside.

In a 12-inch skillet, melt butter over medium-high heat. Add garlic, and stir for 30 seconds. Then add mushrooms, and cook until limp. Add leeks. Cook, stirring occasionally, until all the liquid evaporates. Stir in all the remaining ingredients. Cool before using, or store in refrigerator for up to 3 days.

Lemon and Dried Herb Stuffing

Makes about 2 cups

This recipe makes enough stuffing for a boned and rolled leg of lamb or a 3½-pound chicken.

6	tablespoons butter, softened
½	teaspoon dried marjoram
½	teaspoon dried mint
¼	teaspoon dried oregano
¼	teaspoon dried sage
¼	teaspoon dried rosemary
⅛	teaspoon powdered bay leaves
½	teaspoon black pepper
1½	cups soft whole grain bread crumbs (about 3 slices)
2	tablespoons lemon juice
1	teaspoon grated lemon rind

Beat butter in a small bowl until very smooth. Place all the herbs and the pepper in a blender, or use a mortar and pestle, and crush until finely pulverized. Add to butter along with bread crumbs, lemon juice, and lemon rind. Blend well.

To release the aromatic oils of herbs, bruise them, or rub dried herbs between the palms of your hands before adding them to a dish. You'll smell the delightful difference at once.

Onion, Apple, Sausage, and Walnut Stuffing

Makes 3½ to 4 cups

This recipe makes enough stuffing for a capon, a small turkey, or a pheasant.

 1 pound fresh sweet Italian sausage, removed from casing
 1 tablespoon butter
 ¾ cup finely chopped onions (about 1 large onion)
 ½ teaspoon finely minced garlic
 ¼ cup finely minced celery (about 1 stalk with leaves)
 3 green apples, peeled, cored, and diced
 1 cup soft whole grain bread crumbs
 ½ cup milk
 1 egg, slightly beaten
 ½ cup finely minced fresh parsley
 2 to 3 fresh sage leaves, finely minced, or 1 teaspoon dried sage
 ¼ teaspoon dried thyme
 ¼ teaspoon black pepper
 ½ cup coarsely broken walnuts, toasted

Cook sausage in a large skillet, stirring with wooden spoon until meat loses its color. Lift out of skillet with a slotted spoon, and set aside. Pour off and discard any accumulated fat, and wipe out skillet. Then melt butter. Add onions, garlic, and celery, and saute until onions are wilted, stirring occasionally, 3 to 4 minutes. Add apples, and cook for 3 minutes more, stirring occasionally. Meanwhile, put bread crumbs into a large bowl, add milk, and mix well. Add sauteed apple mixture, reserved sausage, and all the remaining ingredients, and mix thoroughly.

Mushroom and Dried Herb Bread Stuffing

Makes about 6 to 7 cups

Use this stuffing for a 6- to 7-pound oven-stuffer chicken or a boned and rolled veal shoulder.

 3 tablespoons butter
 1 small onion, peeled and minced
 1 cup coarsely chopped mushrooms
 1 to 2 teaspoons dried sage
 1 teaspoon dried summer savory
 1 teaspoon dried thyme
 1 tablespoon finely minced celery leaves
 ½ teaspoon white pepper
 6 cups soft whole grain bread crumbs
 1 egg, well beaten
 1 tablespoon finely minced fresh parsley
 small amount of chicken stock or milk (optional)

Melt butter in a medium-size skillet. Add onions, and saute until wilted, 3 to 5 minutes. Add mushrooms and dried herbs, and continue to cook just until mushrooms give up and then reabsorb their juices. Transfer to a large bowl, and cool. Add all the remaining ingredients (include chicken stock or milk if you prefer a moist stuffing), and mix well.

Spinach and Pork Stuffing

Makes 8 cups

This recipe makes enough stuffing for a 12-pound turkey, a boned and rolled loin of veal, or a crown roast of pork.

6 tablespoons butter, divided
1 teaspoon finely minced garlic (about 2 cloves)
1 cup finely chopped onions (about 1 large onion)
  turkey giblets, finely chopped (optional)
1 pound lean ground pork
  turkey liver, finely chopped (optional)
2 packages (10 ounces each) frozen chopped spinach, thawed and drained well
6 slices stale whole grain bread, cut into small cubes
3 eggs, slightly beaten
2 teaspoons dried thyme
1 teaspoon dried marjoram
½ teaspoon black pepper
½ cup finely minced fresh parsley
1 tablespoon grated orange rind

Melt 3 tablespoons of the butter in a large skillet. Add garlic and onions, and saute, while stirring, for about 3 minutes. Transfer to a large bowl, and set aside. In the same skillet, melt remaining butter, and saute giblets (if used), for 10 minutes over low heat, or until tender. Add pork, and cook for 7 to 10 minutes, or until it loses its pink color, break-ing up meat with a wooden spoon. Add liver (if used), at this point, and continue to cook for 2 minutes more. Then add to onion-garlic mixture. Add all the remaining ingredients, and mix well.

Wild Rice Stuffing

Makes 4 to 4½ cups

This recipe makes enough for two 5-pound ducks or a large chicken.

⅓ cup corn oil
1 cup uncooked wild rice
½ green pepper, cut into large pieces
2 medium-size onions, peeled and quartered
3 stalks celery, cut into chunks
¼ pound mushrooms, coarsely chopped
4 cups chicken stock
½ teaspoon black pepper
1 teaspoon grated lemon rind

Heat oil in a large nonstick skillet. Add rice, and toast over low heat for about 8 minutes. Set aside.

In 2 batches, puree in a blender, the green peppers, onions, celery, mushrooms, and chicken stock. Over a bowl, strain mix-ture, pressing solids against strainer, and reserve both vegetables and stock. Return skillet with rice to heat, stir in reserved stock, and bring to a boil. Cover, lower heat, and simmer for 45 minutes, adding more stock if necessary. When rice is tender, stir in reserved vegeta-bles, pepper, and lemon rind.

Chapter 11

VEGETABLES

There was a time when most people simply boiled the life out of any vegetable before they considered it fit to serve. Today's cooks make it a point to cook vegetables lightly whenever possible so that they remain crisp and nutritious, with their brilliant and inviting colors intact. Our own attitude toward vegetables became more appreciative after we became avid gardeners. Now we have discovered how delicious vegetables can really be, newly harvested and at their peak of flavor.

With the addition of fresh herbs and spices, vegetables can take on a stature that moves them from side dish to a central role in any menu. For example, grilled tomatoes served with basil are a world-renowned culinary treasure. We love them that way. But, by adding a trickle of honey and a touch of fresh mint in place of the basil, grilled tomatoes take on yet another taste dimension. Now we have *two* treasures. Another example is cauliflower. Most cooks can't think of cauliflower without thinking of buttered bread crumbs sprinkled over its creamy head. We add garlic, yogurt, and dill to our cauliflower for a newer, lighter approach.

In two recipes in this section, we combine carrots with ginger, but we add cilantro in one instance and lime plus mace in the other. The variations can be endless. In one recipe we bake onions with potatoes and rosemary; in another we puree the onions with nutmeg, cloves, and Gruyere cheese. Quite an improvement over the plain, overboiled vegetables we once knew!

Baked Asparagus Custard with Parmesan Cheese and Chervil

6 to 8 servings

This dish can be served as a spring luncheon main course along with a green salad in a lemony vinaigrette.

¾ pound asparagus, trimmed and cut into 1-inch pieces (reserve 6 to 8 asparagus tips for garnish)
4   eggs
1   cup milk
½   cup heavy cream
⅛   teaspoon freshly grated nutmeg
⅛   teaspoon white pepper
½   cup grated Parmesan cheese
2   tablespoons finely minced fresh chervil
    melted butter
    additional grated Parmesan cheese
    fresh chervil sprigs

Preheat oven to 375°F. Generously butter 6 to 8 individual custard cups or ½-cup dariole molds, or use 1 large 4-cup mold.

Steam asparagus until very soft, about 25 minutes. Puree in a food processor or blender, remove puree, and set aside. In the same food processor, beat eggs, and then add milk, cream, nutmeg, pepper, Parmesan cheese, and minced chervil, and blend well. Blend in asparagus puree, and pour into prepared molds. Place molds (or mold) into a large pan, and pour boiling water into the pan until it reaches three-quarters of the way up the sides of the molds. Bake for 40 to 45 minutes, or until the knife point inserted into the center of the custards comes out clean.

Cool on a wire rack for 10 minutes before running a knife around the edges of the cus-tards. Invert molds; on top of each one, spoon some melted butter and sprinkle a few pinches of cheese. Garnish with an asparagus tip and a sprig of fresh chervil.

Baked Butternut Squash with Prunes, Walnuts, and Cardamom

4 to 6 servings

A light accompaniment for poultry or pork. It has a rich, delicious flavor reminiscent of the yam dishes Grandmother used to make.

1   3-pound butternut squash, peeled, strings and seeds removed, and cut into chunks
¼   cup maple syrup
½   teaspoon ground cardamom
1   tablespoon butter
⅓   cup coarsely chopped walnuts, toasted
8   pitted prunes, coarsely chopped
1   teaspoon grated orange rind

Steam squash until tender, about 30 minutes.

Preheat oven to 350°F. Butter a medium-size baking dish.

When squash is tender, mash in a large bowl. There should be about 3 cups. Combine all the remaining ingredients and spoon into prepared baking dish. Bake for 15 minutes, and serve hot.

Cardamom is widely used in Saudi Arabia, for three important reasons: It has a cooling effect on the body, it's good for the digestion, and it is considered an aphrodisiac.

Baked Eggplant Fans
on a Bed of Tomatoes and Herbs

4 servings

TOMATO COULIS *(Makes 1¼ cups)*

- 6 cups coarsely cut peeled tomatoes
- 2 shallots, peeled and thinly sliced
- 1 clove garlic, peeled
- 2 tablespoons mixed fresh herbs (thyme, basil, oregano, rosemary)

EGGPLANT FANS

- 8 small, long eggplants (Japanese)
- ¼ teaspoon black pepper
- ¼ teaspoon fresh thyme
- 6 tablespoons fine whole grain bread crumbs
- 4 tablespoons grated Parmesan cheese
- 6 tablespoons olive oil

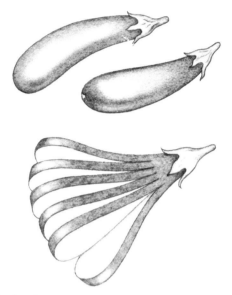

To make the coulis: Put tomatoes, shallots, and garlic into a large nonstick skillet. Bring to a boil, and cook, uncovered, over medium-high heat for about 40 minutes, stirring occasionally. Add herbs, and cook for a few seconds more. Then force through a strainer or put through a food mill. Set aside.

To make the eggplant fans: Preheat oven to 375°F. Line a baking sheet with foil.

With a sharp knife, cut eggplants lengthwise into 6 slices, keeping stem end intact. Then spread out eggplant slices like a fan. (The uncut top will hold them together as you fan the slices out.) Season with pepper.

In a small bowl, mix thyme, bread crumbs, and cheese together. Dip eggplants in oil, and then press crumb mixture onto the spread-out slices. Bake 15 to 20 minutes, or until crisp and golden. When ready to serve, spoon some tomato coulis on 4 plates, and place 2 "fans" on each plate.

Baked Potatoes
with Red Onions and Rosemary

4 servings

- 4 large Idaho baking potatoes
- 1 small red onion, peeled and thinly sliced
  several sprigs of fresh rosemary
  freshly ground black pepper
- ¼ cup butter, melted

Preheat oven to 350°F. Cut each potato into thick slices, and place onions and rosemary between each slice. Set assembled potatoes on aluminum foil sheets. Sprinkle with pepper, and trickle a tablespoon of melted butter over each potato. Wrap tightly in the foil, and bake for 1½ hours. For the last 15 minutes of baking, open the foil, but do not unwrap potatoes completely or slices may separate. To serve, roll back the foil halfway, allowing potato-onion combination to keep its shape.

Baked Stuffed Cucumbers with Tarragon

4 servings

Another light summer luncheon dish with a delicate chicken-almond filling, heightened by the flavor of tarragon.

  2 to 3 large burpless cucumbers
       3 tablespoons tarragon vinegar
       3 tablespoons finely sliced scallions, green part only
       5 tablespoons whole grain bread crumbs
       1 cup finely minced cooked chicken
       1 tablespoon chopped almonds, toasted
     1/8 teaspoon black pepper
  2 to 3 drops hot pepper sauce
       1 tablespoon finely minced fresh tarragon
     1/4 cup butter, melted, divided
     3/4 cup plus 2 tablespoons chicken stock, divided

Preheat oven to 375°F.

Cut cucumbers into 1½-inch pieces, and core the center of each piece with an apple corer, making "tubes" of the pieces. Coarsely chop cores, and place tubes and chopped cores into a medium-size oven-to-table casserole. Pour vinegar over cucumbers, and let marinate while preparing stuffing.

In a small bowl, mix scallions, bread crumbs, chicken, almonds, pepper, hot pepper sauce, and tarragon together. Moisten with 2 tablespoons of the melted butter and 2 tablespoons of the chicken stock. Stuff tubes with mixture. Make sure tubes are upright. Pour remaining melted butter and chicken stock around cucumbers, and bake for 20 minutes, or until crisp-tender, basting occasionally. Serve hot.

Braised Belgian Endive and Italian Radicchio with Mushrooms and Marjoram

4 servings

If radicchio is not available, you can use eight small Belgian endives as the main ingredient for this dish.

       4 medium-size heads of Belgian endive
       1 small head of radicchio, cut into quarters
       5 tablespoons butter, melted, divided
     1/3 cup chicken stock
       1 tablespoon lemon juice
       2 tablespoons finely minced shallots
       6 fresh mushrooms, thinly sliced
     1/4 teaspoon black pepper
       1 teaspoon fresh marjoram leaves
       3 tablespoons grated Gruyere cheese

Wash, dry, and trim endives and radicchio. Spread 1 tablespoon of the melted butter evenly in a shallow oven-to-table baking dish that can also be used on top of stove and is large enough to accommodate the endive and radicchio in a single layer. Arrange greens in prepared baking dish. Add chicken stock and lemon juice. Spoon another tablespoon of the melted butter over the top of the endives and radicchio. Cover tightly with foil, and simmer over low heat for 8 to 10 minutes. Then uncover, and simmer for 5 minutes more.

While endives and radicchio are cooking, heat 1 tablespoon of the melted butter in a medium-size skillet. Add shallots, and saute for 1 minute. Add mushrooms, and saute for 5 minutes more, stirring constantly. Stir in pepper and marjoram. Then place mushroom mixture around endives and radicchio along with remaining butter and the grated cheese. Place under the broiler for a few minutes to brown. Serve hot.

Braised Celery with Tarragon

4 to 5 servings

Another easy-to-prepare vegetable dish that can be ready in 10 to 15 minutes.

4 to 5   stalks celery, cut into 1½-inch pieces
  3   tablespoons butter, divided
  2   tablespoons finely minced scallions, white part only
  1   cup chicken stock
  1   tablespoon minced fresh tarragon, divided
      pinch of paprika
      pinch of freshly ground black pepper

Cut celery pieces lengthwise into 2 or 3 slices.

Melt 2 tablespoons of the butter in a large skillet. Saute scallions until wilted. Add celery, chicken stock, and 1 teaspoon of the tarragon. Simmer for about 5 minutes. Add remaining butter, and sprinkle with paprika and pepper. Simmer, basting occasionally, until

liquid has been absorbed. Transfer to a serving dish, and sprinkle with remaining tarragon before serving.

Broccoli and Swiss Cheese Loaf with Nasturtium Blossoms

6 servings

This light vegetable pate can be served as a luncheon dish or as an hors d'oeuvre. Roasted Red Pepper and Borage Sauce (page 264), though optional, gives it an extra elegance.

1½   pounds broccoli, trimmed of coarse stems and steamed
  2   eggs, beaten
  4   ounces Swiss cheese, grated (about ½ cup)
  ½   cup creme fraiche
  ½   teaspoon black pepper
  ¼   cup grated onions
  ½   teaspoon ground nutmeg
      pinch of cayenne pepper
  ¼   cup finely chopped almonds, toasted
  3   nasturtium blossoms, coarsely cut

Preheat oven to 350°F. Butter an 8½ × 4½-inch loaf pan.

In a food processor, puree broccoli. Turn broccoli into a large bowl. Add all the remaining ingredients, and mix very well. Spoon into prepared pan, and set loaf in a larger pan, adding 1 inch of boiling water to the larger pan. Cover top of loaf pan loosely with aluminum foil, and bake for 1 hour. Let stand for 15 minutes. Then loosen edges, and invert onto a serving dish. Garnish with additional nasturtium blossoms if you wish.

Cauliflower Puree
with Yogurt, Garlic, and Dill

4 servings

Both of us love cauliflower, and usually we steam it for just a few minutes to keep it crisp and tasty. Here is another way to serve this nutritious vegetable, bringing out the flavor of the dill.

1   medium head of cauliflower
2   large cloves garlic, peeled
¼   cup plain yogurt
¼   cup coarsely cut dill
⅛   teaspoon black pepper
    few gratings of nutmeg

Trim and separate cauliflower into florets, and then steam with garlic for about 8 minutes. Puree cauliflower and garlic in a food processor. Add yogurt, dill, pepper, and nutmeg, and blend. Spoon into a serving dish.

Cherry Tomatoes
in Cucumber Herb Cream

4 servings

Cherry tomatoes are always excellent eaten out of hand, but prepared this way they become an elegant accompaniment to simply broiled chicken or fish.

2   tablespoons butter
2   tablespoons finely minced shallots
¼   cup creme fraiche
1   cup julienne cucumbers
1   teaspoon fresh thyme leaves

2   cups whole or halved cherry
    tomatoes
⅛   teaspoon black pepper
1   tablespoon minced fresh dill

Heat butter in a large skillet, add shallots, and saute for a few minutes. Add creme fraiche, cucumbers, thyme, tomatoes, and pepper, and cook over medium-high heat for 5 minutes. Transfer to a serving dish, and sprinkle with dill.

Collard Greens Tart
(Kale, Mustard Greens,
or Turnip Greens)

6 to 8 servings

A luncheon, first course, or supper dish, this tart has a satisfying bite of hot pepper to complement the stronger tasting greens.

PASTRY

¾   cup whole wheat pastry flour
1   teaspoon dry yeast
2   tablespoons olive oil
1   egg, beaten

FILLING

1¼ cups milk
⅓   cup brown rice
1   pound fresh collard greens (kale,
    mustard greens, or turnip
    greens), coarse stems removed
1   tablespoon olive oil
2   cloves garlic, peeled

⅛ teaspoon dried red pepper flakes
2 tablespoons finely minced fresh parsley
2 eggs, beaten
⅔ cup milk
⅓ cup heavy cream
3 tablespoons Parmesan cheese
  few gratings of nutmeg

To make the pastry: Put flour and yeast into a medium-size bowl, and mix. Make a well in the center, and add oil and egg to the well. Mix together with floured hands. Dough will be sticky. Turn out onto a floured surface, and knead a few times. Let rest for 10 minutes, and then roll paper-thin. Use a 10-inch tart pan, and roll dough so that it will extend about 1 inch beyond the edge of the pan.

To make the filling: Preheat oven to 350°F.

Heat milk in a large saucepan. Add rice, and simmer slowly until all the milk is absorbed. Set aside.

Coarsely cut greens, and steam for 3 minutes. Finely chop in a food processor, and then squeeze out excess moisture between your palms. There should be about 1¼ cups of greens. Add to rice, and mix well.

In a small skillet, heat oil. Add garlic, and saute until soft. Add red pepper flakes and parsley, and stir into rice-greens mixture. Mix all the remaining ingredients together in a medium-size bowl, and then add to rice-greens mixture. Turn into pastry-lined pan, and turn edges of pastry over to partially enclose filling. Bake for 40 to 45 minutes, or until top is golden.

Cranberry Glazed Yams with Ginger and Pecans

4 servings

Golden yams are dotted with berries and laced with ginger and crisp, toasted pecans—a perfect accompaniment to a holiday bird or pork chops.

4 yams, peeled and cut in half lengthwise
1 cup fresh cranberries
¼ cup water
¼ cup honey
1 tablespoon grated orange rind
1 teaspoon grated peeled ginger root
3 tablespoons butter, melted
½ cup pecans, toasted

Steam yams for 15 minutes, or until tender. They should not be so soft that they fall apart, but should keep their shape.

Preheat oven to 350°F, and butter an oven-to-table baking dish large enough to hold yams in a single layer.

In a medium-size saucepan, mix together cranberries, water, honey, orange rind, and ginger. Bring to a boil, then lower heat to medium, and cook, stirring occasionally, for 5 minutes, or until berries pop. Put yams into prepared baking dish, and spoon cranberry sauce over them. Spoon melted butter on top, and bake for 15 minutes, basting with the glaze every 5 minutes. During the last 5 minutes, sprinkle with pecans. Serve at once.

Deep-Dish Mushroom Pie with Cheese and Herb Crust

4 to 6 servings

You can serve this either as an accompaniment to lunch or dinner, or as a main course. We think you'll like the very special taste and texture of the wild mushrooms.

CRUST

- ¼ cup whole grain bread crumbs
- 2 tablespoons grated Parmesan cheese
- ¼ cup grated Gruyere or Swiss cheese
- 1 tablespoon finely minced fresh parsley
- 1 tablespoon finely minced fresh basil
- 1 teaspoon fresh marjoram leaves

FILLING

- ¾ pound fresh mushrooms
- 2 ounces dried mushrooms* (Porcini, Chantarel, or Cepes), reconstituted
- 2 tablespoons butter
- 2 tablespoons finely minced shallots
- 1 teaspoon finely minced garlic
- 2 tablespoons sherry
- ⅔ cup creme fraiche
    freshly ground black pepper

To make the crust: Combine all ingredients in a small bowl and set aside.

To make the filling: Cut fresh and dried mushrooms into large, bite-size pieces. (Remember that they shrink a bit when cooked.)

Heat butter in a large skillet. Add shallots and garlic, and cook, stirring, until soft. Add mushrooms, and cook until liquid forms. Continue cooking until liquid evaporates, 5 to 8 minutes. Transfer mushrooms to a medium-size bowl, and set aside.

In the same skillet, add sherry, creme fraiche, and pepper, and cook over medium heat for 5 to 10 minutes, or until sauce is reduced to ½ cup. Stir into reserved mushrooms, and spoon into a 9½ × 2-inch round baking dish. Cover with crumb mixture, and place under preheated broiler only until crust is nicely browned. Serve hot.

*Dried mushrooms are more intensely flavored than fresh ones, therefore it's advisable to use fewer of them than if they were fresh. Since they must be reconstituted and are usually gritty, follow this procedure before using them in a recipe: Pour ½ cup boiling water over 2 ounces dried mushrooms, and let stand for 30 minutes. Line a small strainer with a man's linen handkerchief. Pour off mushroom liquid, and reserve to flavor another dish, or use to replace some of the liquid in the dish being prepared. Then rinse mushrooms under cold running water to make sure they are free of grit. Dry on paper towels, and cut into small pieces.

Fennel with Thyme, Coriander Seeds, and Peppercorns

4 to 6 servings

Serve this dish as a vegetable or as a salad at room temperature.

- 2 cups water
- ¼ cup olive oil
- ¼ cup lemon juice (about 1 large lemon)
- 1 tablespoon finely minced shallots (about 2 shallots)

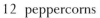

12 peppercorns
12 coriander seeds
 6 sprigs of fresh parsley
¼ teaspoon fennel seeds
 3 sprigs of fresh thyme
 4 small bulbs fennel (1½ to 2
      pounds), cut into halves, feathery
      leaves reserved
 1 tablespoon finely minced fresh
      parsley

In a large heavy saucepan, combine water, oil, lemon juice, and shallots. Put peppercorns, coriander seeds, parsley sprigs, fennel seeds, and thyme into a cheesecloth bag, tie with string, and add to pot. Cover, bring to a boil, lower heat, and simmer for 10 minutes. Then add fennel bulbs, and continue to simmer, covered, for 30 minutes, or until fennel is tender. Lift out fennel with a slotted spoon, and place into a serving dish. Remove cheesecloth bag, and discard. Reduce sauce, uncovered, over high heat until there is ½ cup remaining. Pour sauce over fennel, and chill. Before serving, bring to room temperature, and sprinkle with minced parsley.

Gingered Carrots
with Tofu and Cilantro

4 servings

 1 tablespoon corn oil
 1 tablespoon finely minced garlic
      (3 to 4 cloves)
 1 ½-inch piece of ginger root,
      peeled and finely minced (about
      2 teaspoons)

 1 medium onion, peeled and thinly
      sliced
¾ pound carrots (3 to 5 carrots), cut
      into 2-inch-long, thin strips
½ teaspoon dried red pepper flakes,
      or less to taste
 1 teaspoon grated lemon rind
 2 teaspoons soy sauce
½ cup water
 1 teaspoon honey
 1 teaspoon Oriental sesame oil
 1 pound tofu, cut into 1 × ½-inch
      pieces
½ cup finely minced fresh cilantro, with
      stems

Heat corn oil in a large skillet or wok. Add garlic and ginger, and cook, stirring constantly, for 1 minute. Do not brown or garlic will be bitter. Add onions, and cook, continuing to stir, for 2 to 3 minutes, or until wilted. Then add carrots, and cook, stirring constantly, for 1 minute more. Stir in red pepper flakes and lemon rind. Mix soy sauce, water, honey, and sesame oil together in a cup, and stir into vegetables. Lower heat, cover, and simmer for 3 to 4 minutes, or until carrots are tender but still crisp. Stir in tofu, cover, and cook for about 1 minute, or until tofu is heated through. Add cilantro, and transfer to a warm serving dish.

Peppercorns were used to pay rent, taxes, debts, and tolls in the thirteenth century. The spice was valuable enough to be included in the dowry of young brides.

Gingered Carrots with Lime and Mace

4 servings

A fresh vegetable dish that takes under five minutes to prepare.

- ¾ pound carrots, cut into julienne strips
- 2 tablespoons butter
- 1 teaspoon grated peeled ginger root
- 1 tablespoon lime juice
- ¼ teaspoon black pepper
- ¼ teaspoon ground mace
- 1 teaspoon finely shredded lime rind

Steam carrots for 2 to 3 minutes, or until crisp and tender.

In a 10-inch skillet, mix together all the remaining ingredients except lime rind. Place skillet over medium heat. Toss carrots in the skillet for 30 seconds, or until butter is melted. Transfer to a serving dish, and sprinkle with lime rind.

Green Cabbage with Caraway Seeds and Mustard

4 to 6 servings

This quick and tangy vegetable perks up any pork dish.

- 1 head of cabbage (1½ to 2 pounds), finely shredded
- ¾ teaspoon caraway seeds
- 2 tablespoons butter
- 1 medium onion, coarsely chopped
- 3 scallions, finely sliced (1 tablespoon reserved)
- 1 tablespoon dijon mustard
- 1 tablespoon lemon juice
- ¼ cup plain yogurt
- ¼ teaspoon black pepper

In a steamer, cook cabbage sprinkled with caraway seeds for 5 minutes.

Meanwhile, melt butter in a large skillet. Add onions and scallions, and saute, stirring often, for 2 to 3 minutes. Add steamed cabbage, and continue sauteeing for 5 minutes more, stirring occasionally so that the bottom does not brown.

In a cup, mix together mustard, lemon juice, and yogurt. Lower heat under skillet, add yogurt mixture to cabbage mixture, sprinkle with pepper, and cook for a minute more. Sprinkle with reserved scallions before serving.

Grilled Tomatoes with Garlic, Honey, and Mint

4 servings

Tart, cool, sweet, and piqued with garlic, these tomatoes will complement lamb chops or roasted lamb beautifully.

- 2 large ripe tomatoes, stem end cored
- 2 cloves garlic, peeled and cut into slivers
- ⅛ teaspoon black pepper
- 1 tablespoon olive oil
- 1 tablespoon light honey
- 1 tablespoon finely minced fresh mint

Cut tomatoes in half horizontally. Arrange halves in an oven-to-table baking dish so that they support each other by touching. Slip slivers of garlic into the soft, fleshy parts of the tomatoes. Sprinkle with pepper. Trickle olive oil and then honey evenly over the top. Place tomatoes under the broiler, and broil until bubbly. Remove slivers of garlic, and sprinkle with mint.

Japanese Eggplants with Ginger Root and Sesame Seed Sauce

4 servings

SAUCE

- ¼ cup soy sauce
- ¼ cup chicken stock
- 1 teaspoon shredded peeled ginger root
- 1 tablespoon sesame seeds, toasted
- 1 teaspoon rice wine vinegar

EGGPLANT

- 8 unpeeled small, long eggplants (about 2 pounds)
  corn oil, for frying

To make the sauce: Mix all the ingredients together in a cup, and transfer to a small serving bowl.

To prepare the eggplant: Trim off stem end of each eggplant. Wash and then dry eggplants thoroughly with paper towels. Make 4 lengthwise slashes, equally spaced, in each eggplant. The slashes will release the steam and speed the cooking.

Heat ½ inch oil in a large enough skillet to hold all the eggplants at one time without their touching one another. When oil is very hot (about 350°F), add eggplants, and cook until soft, turning carefully with tongs so that all sides are cooked, 8 to 10 minutes. Drain well on paper towels. Transfer to a warm serving dish. Spread open one of the slits on

the top of each eggplant to form a pocket. At the table, pass the sauce to be spooned into each pocket.

Okra with Tomatoes and Rosemary

4 servings

Okra, one of our favorite vegetables, sometimes gets "bad press" because of its slippery texture if cooked incorrectly. The secret of cooking okra is to use *small* pods and *keep them whole*. Trim only the tiniest sliver from the stem end, and do not cut into the okra itself.

- 2 tablespoons olive oil
- ¼ cup finely chopped onions
- 1 teaspoon finely minced garlic
- ¾ pound okra (1 to 1½ inches long), stem end trimmed
- ½ pound fresh plum tomatoes, peeled, or canned Italian plum tomatoes, cut into chunks (4 to 5 chunks per tomato)
- 1 tablespoon lemon juice
- 1½ tablespoons coarsely chopped fresh rosemary
- ⅛ teaspoon black pepper
  dash of cayenne pepper

Heat oil in a medium-size skillet. Add onions and garlic, and saute, stirring often, until onions are wilted. Add okra and cook, stirring occasionally, for about 5 minutes. Stir in tomatoes, cover, lower heat, and simmer for 10 minutes, or until okra is tender. Stir in lemon juice, rosemary, and black pepper, and cook for 1 minute more.

When ready to serve, sprinkle with cayenne. This dish can be served at room temperature if you prefer.

Onion and Gruyere Cheese with Nutmeg and Cloves

4 to 6 servings

This onion puree is perfect with roasted meats.

3 tablespoons butter, softened, divided
1½ pounds medium-size onions, peeled and halved
¼ teaspoon black pepper
¼ teaspoon ground nutmeg
⅛ teaspoon ground cloves
3 to 4 thin slices of whole grain bread
½ cup grated Gruyere cheese, divided
¼ cup heavy cream
2 tablespoons dry white wine

Butter a shallow oven-to-table casserole with 1 teaspoon of the butter, and set aside. Steam onions until soft, about 20 minutes.

Preheat oven to 400°F.

Puree onions in a blender or food processor. There should be about 2 cups of puree. Mix onion puree with pepper, nutmeg, cloves, and 1 tablespoon of the butter. Toast and butter bread with 1 tablespoon of the butter, and arrange slices on the bottom of the casserole. Sprinkle with ¼ cup of the cheese. Spread onion puree over bread and cheese. In a cup, mix cream and wine together, and pour over all. Sprinkle with remaining cheese, and dot with remaining butter. Bake for 25 minutes, then place under broiler for 1 minute to brown the top. Serve hot.

Poke holes into an unpeeled onion, put a sprig of herbs into each hole (rosemary or thyme for example), steam or roast, and peel before eating.

Parsnip Fritters with Orange Rind and Lemon Verbena

4 servings

The nutty sweetness of this underrated vegetable is complemented by the tang of citrus.

¾ pound parsnips, peeled and cut into 1-inch cubes
2 tablespoons butter, divided
1 tablespoon finely minced fresh lemon verbena
1 teaspoon finely minced orange rind
½ cup whole wheat flour
½ beaten whole egg
¼ teaspoon black pepper
additional flour
2 tablespoons corn oil

In a large saucepan, cook parsnips in boiling water for 15 minutes, or until very tender. Drain, place into a large bowl, and mash well with 1 tablespoon of the butter. Add all the remaining ingredients except additional flour, oil, and remaining butter, and mix thoroughly. Chill mixture for 10 minutes.

Put some additional flour on waxed paper, and using floured hands, form mixture into small cakes, using about 1 tablespoon of mixture for each. Dip cakes in additional flour, place on a plate lined with waxed paper, and chill for 5 minutes more.

Melt oil and remaining butter together in a heavy cast-iron skillet. When hot, add parsnip fritters, and brown on both sides, turning to brown evenly. Drain on paper towels. Serve warm.

Deep-Dish Mushroom Pie with Cheese and Herb Crust (page 224) ➤

Cherry Tomatoes in Cucumber Herb Cream (page 222)

Parsleyed Brussels Sprouts with Shallots, Red Peppers, and Pecans

4 servings

A festive and tasty way to serve brussels sprouts. The tiny diced red peppers make a colorful accent, and the toasted pecans add crunch.

1 cup chicken stock
1 pound brussels sprouts (about 4 cups)
2 tablespoons butter
1 tablespoon finely chopped shallots (about 1 large shallot)
⅔ cup diced sweet red peppers
2 tablespoons sour cream
⅛ teaspoon black pepper
½ cup pecans, toasted
2 tablespoons finely minced fresh parsley

Bring chicken stock to a boil in a medium-size saucepan. Add sprouts, and cook for 7 to 8 minutes. Drain sprouts, reserving 2 tablespoons of the liquid, and set aside.

Melt butter in a 12-inch skillet. Add shallots and red peppers, and saute for 3 to 5 minutes. Mix sour cream with reserved liquid, stir in black pepper, and add to skillet. Mix in sprouts, and heat through. Scatter pecans and parsley over all, and serve at once.

Potato and Carrot Balls Stuffed with Sorrel Puree

4 servings

1 pound Idaho or Russet potatoes
3 tablespoons plus 1 teaspoon butter, divided
⅛ teaspoon black pepper
½ cup grated carrots
1½ tablespoons finely minced fresh chives
¼ pound sorrel

Peel potatoes, and cut into chunks. Boil potatoes for 15 to 20 minutes, and while hot, mash in a large bowl with 3 tablespoons of the butter, pepper, and then carrots and chives. Set aside.

Remove center stems of sorrel leaves by folding each leaf so that the stem is on the outside and running a sharp knife along the stem edge. Discard the stem. Finely shred the leaves.

In a medium-size skillet, melt 1 teaspoon of the butter. Add sorrel, and stir and cook over medium heat until sorrel is wilted and its color has changed from bright green to olive green. There should be about ¼ cup of puree.

With your hands, form potato mixture into 8 2-inch balls. Then make an indentation in each ball with your index finger, and put about ½ teaspoon of puree into the indentation. Pinch a piece of potato from the bottom of the ball to cover the top, and re-form the ball with your hands. Chill for 1 hour or more.

When ready to serve, preheat oven to 450°F, and butter a small oven-to-table serving dish. Carefully transfer balls to dish, and bake for 15 to 20 minutes. Serve hot.

Potato and Carrot Pancakes with Parsley

Makes 30 pancakes

These lacy pancakes are traditionally served for *Chanukah*, but you can enjoy them any time — and you don't have to be Jewish to love them!

2 carrots
3 unpeeled potatoes
1 medium-size onion, peeled
1 teaspoon lemon juice
½ cup finely chopped fresh parsley
2 eggs, slightly beaten
½ teaspoon black pepper
¼ cup whole wheat flour or matzoh meal
¾ cup corn oil
sour cream

Using the shredder blade of a food processor, shred carrots (you should have 1 cup). Place into a bowl, and set aside. In the same food processor bowl, shred potatoes and onion. Sprinkle with lemon juice, place into a strainer over a bowl, and drain for 15 minutes. Press excess liquid from potatoes with the back of a wooden spoon. Add potato-onion mixture to carrots, and then add parsley, eggs, pepper, and flour or matzoh meal. Stir well.

Heat ¼ cup of the oil in a cast-iron skillet until very hot. Add a heaping tablespoon of potato-carrot mixture to the skillet. Flatten it a bit with the back of the spoon. Turn once when edges are golden brown, and cook on the other side. Drain on paper towels, and keep warm in 300°F oven. Repeat until all the mixture is used up, adding more oil as needed. Stir mixture well before frying each batch. Serve hot. Top with sour cream at the table.

Edward Merard
Executive Chef
Beaver Club
Queen Elizabeth Hotel
Montreal, Quebec, Canada

In summertime here in Montreal, we have an herb garden on the roof of the hotel and we grow everything — tarragon, rosemary, chives — everything! And, of course, we use only fresh herbs. I add them at the last minute in preparing the dish, whenever possible. The flavor of fresh herbs is so delicate that it is quickly diminished in cooking. Often, I simply chop the herb and sprinkle it over the dish just before serving.

But Montreal is a city that has severe winters, so we wondered about the supply of fresh herbs during the snowy months.

I have a friend in Morocco. He grows herbs there and sends them by air to me here at the hotel.

We first became acquainted with Chef Merard when we were sent to Montreal to conduct a seminar about aging at the Queen Elizabeth Hotel, where he reigns as executive chef over a staff that numbers 125. Our first lunch at the hotel's renowned Beaver Club made us resolve to include at least one of his recipes in this book. We found it amazing that, in spite of the huge numbers of people that Chef Merard serves each day — a recent banquet for 850 people included the prime minister and the governor general — the food at the Queen Elizabeth is superbly prepared, and accented with the zest of fresh herbs throughout. We asked Chef Merard for a tip we might use at home to add an herbal plus to our cooking, as he does at the hotel.

A simple thing professional chefs often do is to echo the herb used in cooking a dish in the cream sauce or buerre blanc used to dress the dish — fresh dill in the sauce served with fish baked with dill, for example.

Edward Merard has been involved with cooking since he was a young boy in France:

I had no choice. I was an orphan and I had to find a job. When I was 14, I started working in restaurant kitchens after school.

His experience took him through France, England, the United States, and finally to Montreal at the Queen Elizabeth. And, like many chefs we've known, he has very definite opinions about flavors.

I am very careful about using spices. Herbs are gentle, but a spice will take over a dish so that one can taste nothing else. Always begin with a minimal amount. More can be added if necessary.

How does Edward Merard feel about the career he has followed?

You have to be crazy to be a chef. But I love it! I feel lucky to be allowed to do it!

Cream of Fresh Vegetable Soup with Sorrel

4 servings

¼ pound leeks, white parts only, finely chopped
¼ pound celery, finely chopped
¼ pound carrots, finely chopped
¼ pound turnips, peeled and finely chopped
2 tablespoons butter
3 cups chicken stock
4 medium-size potatoes, quartered
  dash of white pepper
  black pepper, to taste
2 tablespoons light cream
  butter
½ cup finely shredded sorrel

In a 4-quart pot, saute leeks, celery, carrots, and turnips in the 2 tablespoons of butter until moisture appears. Then add chicken stock, and bring to a boil. Add potatoes, season with white and black pepper, and cook for about 35 minutes. Let cool, and then process in a blender or food processor. Return to pot, and bring to a boil again. Remove from heat, and add cream.

When ready to serve, melt a small amount of butter in a medium-size skillet, saute sorrel, and then garnish each serving with it.

NEW HERBAL IDEAS

Break out of the traditional combinations of herbs and the foods that "match" them best. Try some new herbal ideas:

- ❧ marjoram with roasted onions, in place of sage
- ❧ summer savory to flavor turkey stuffing as a change from using it always with beans
- ❧ basil to season pork chops (an excellent blend)
- ❧ peas with basil to replace the old standby, mint
- ❧ tarragon with beets for an earthy sweetness, instead of mint
- ❧ chervil with fish for a change from dill

Spinach and Ricotta Gnocchi with Chives and Mint

4 servings

These little dumplings are so light that they practically float off your plate. They're a bit tricky to prepare, but well worth the effort. They make a lovely lunch or supper dish, and they're perfect for the visiting vegetarian guest.

- 1 pound fresh spinach, coarse stems removed
- 1 pound ricotta cheese
- 2 egg yolks
- 3 tablespoons finely minced fresh chives
- 1 tablespoon finely minced fresh mint leaves
- ½ cup plus 3 tablespoons grated Parmesan cheese, divided
- ½ cup whole wheat pastry flour
- ⅛ teaspoon black pepper
  pinch of nutmeg
  pinch of ground cloves
  additional flour
- 3 tablespoons butter, melted

In a large pot with a cover, bring ½ cup water to a boil. Add spinach, and cook for 3 minutes, or until spinach is wilted but still green, stirring occasionally.

Line a colander with dampened cheesecloth. Add spinach, and let drain while cooling. When cool enough to handle, gather together the edges of the cheesecloth, and squeeze out as much liquid as possible. Chop for a few seconds in a food processor. Then, add remaining ingredients except 3 tablespoons of the Parmesan cheese, additional flour, and melted butter, and process until smooth. Spoon mixture into a bowl, using a rubber spatula, and chill for 20 minutes.

Place additional flour in a mound on a piece of waxed paper, and spoon 1 teaspoon of the spinach mixture onto the flour. (The easiest way is to scrape the mixture off the spoon with a rubber spatula.) Sprinkle some flour on top, and then lift it gently and roll it between your fingers until it forms a small oval shape. Place on a platter lined with waxed paper, and continue this process until the entire mixture is used up. Chill for 15 minutes or longer. (You may prepare these several hours in advance if you wish.)

When ready to cook, fill a wide-bottomed (about 10 inches) 5-quart pot with water, and keep at a simmer. Pour melted butter into an oven-to-table serving dish, and keep warm in the oven. Add 8 to 10 gnocchi at a time to the simmering water. They will sink to the bottom and then rise to the top. Let them simmer for 3 to 5 minutes. Then lift out with a slotted spoon, and put them in the serving dish with the melted butter. Repeat in batches of 8 to 10 until all of the gnocchi are cooked. Tilt the serving dish and spoon butter that accumulates over the gnocchi. Sprinkle with 3 tablespoons of the Parmesan cheese, and grind some additional black pepper over all. Serve at once.

Steamed Mixed Vegetables with Mixed Herbs, Hot Pepper, and Garlic Olive Oil

6 servings

You may try our choice of vegetables or your own favorites. Use different colors for the most attractive presentation.

    1   small head of cauliflower, broken into bite-size pieces
    ½   bunch broccoli, cut into bite-size pieces
    2   carrots, cut into long strips
    ¼   pound sugar snap peas or snow peas
    1   small yellow summer squash, cut into ½-inch disks
    3 to 4   tiny whole turnips, peeled and quartered
    1   small zucchini, cut into ½-inch disks
    6   cherry tomatoes
    ¼   pound green beans
        Mixed Herbs, Hot Pepper, and Garlic Olive Oil (page 259)

Steam vegetables, a few batches at a time, just until crisp and tender. Arrange on a large platter, drizzle sauce over the warm vegetables, and serve.

Sweet and Sour Red Cabbage with Cloves and Allspice

4 to 6 servings

We make this the day before and reheat after the flavors meld.

    1   head of red cabbage (1¾ pounds)
    ¼   cup butter
    1   medium-size onion, peeled and chopped (about ⅔ cup)
    ½   teaspoon black pepper
    2   tablespoons honey, or more to taste
    2   tablespons red wine vinegar
    ¼   cup water, or more as needed
    2   large tart green apples, peeled, cored, and sliced (about 4 cups)
    ½   teaspoon ground allspice
    ⅛   teaspoon ground cloves
    1   tablespoon lemon juice (optional)

Cut cabbage into quarters lengthwise. Cut out and discard the tough ribs and the core. Coarsely shred cabbage in a food processor. There should be 5 to 6 cups.

Melt butter in a heavy 4- or 5-quart Dutch oven (either stainless steel or enameled cast iron) with a tight lid. Add onions and pepper, and saute, stirring constantly, for 2 minutes. Add cabbage, honey, vinegar, and ¼ cup of the water. Stir well, cover pot, and cook over low heat for 10 minutes. Stir in sliced apples and spices, and continue to simmer, covered, for 1 hour, or until apples have dissolved into cabbage. Add more water if cabbage seems dry. Taste, and add either lemon juice or honey to adjust the sweet-sour flavor.

Sugar Snap Peas with Pine
Nuts and Mustard (page 237)

Sweet Corn and Peppers with Chili Powder and Cilantro

4 servings

Prepare this colorful dish with a peppery bite ahead of time, and pop it into the oven for 10 minutes just before serving.

- 4 ears of corn
- 2 tablespoons butter
- ¼ cup coarsely sliced scallions
- ½ cup diced green peppers
- ½ cup diced sweet red peppers
- 1 teaspoon finely minced seeded jalapeno peppers or ⅛ teaspoon dried red pepper flakes, or to taste
- 2 tablespoons sour cream
- ¾ teaspoon chili powder few grindings of fresh black pepper
- 1 tablespoon coarsely chopped fresh cilantro leaves
- ⅓ cup grated sharp cheddar cheese

Bring a large pot of water to a boil. Remove the pot from the stove, and add corn. Let stand in the water for 10 minutes. Lift out with tongs, and when cool enough to handle, scrape corn kernels into a large bowl. There should be about 3 cups. Set aside.

Preheat oven to 425°F. Butter a small oven-to-table baking dish.

In a medium-size skillet, melt butter. Add scallions, green peppers, and red peppers. Cook until scallions are wilted, stirring occasionally, 3 to 4 minutes. Mix with corn and all the other ingredients except cheese. Spoon into prepared baking dish, sprinkle with cheese, and bake for 10 minutes.

Cloves were the breath sweetener of choice for the Chinese of the third century B.C. All courtiers were required to have the spice in their mouths to avoid offending when they addressed the emperor.

Sweet and Sour Lettuce with Dill

4 servings

This dish proves that you don't have to eat lettuce raw or in a salad to enjoy it. Try it as a vegetable. You'll be pleasantly surprised.

    3 tablespoons sour cream or creme
        fraiche
    1 teaspoon tarragon vinegar
    2 teaspoons honey
    1 tablespoon capers, rinsed and dried
    2 tablespoons butter
    1 small onion, peeled and minced
    1 large head of romaine or iceberg
        lettuce, shredded (about 12 cups)
    ⅛ teaspoon black pepper
    1 tablespoon minced fresh dill

    In a small bowl, mix together sour cream or creme fraiche, vinegar, honey, and capers, and set aside.
    In a 5-quart Dutch oven or large pot, heat butter. Add onions, and saute until wilted.

Do not brown onions. Add lettuce, and cook over low heat until completely wilted, about 5 minutes. When lettuce is wilted, remove to a strainer, and squeeze out excess liquid. Return to pot.
    Sprinkle pepper over lettuce and onion mixture, and then stir in reserved sour cream mixture. Cook over low heat, uncovered, for about 5 minutes more. Stir occasionally, and be sure to keep the heat low enough to prevent the sour cream from curdling. Remove to a serving dish, and sprinkle dill on top. Serve at once.

Sugar Snap Peas
with Pine Nuts and Mustard

4 servings

When sugar snap peas are out of season, you may substitute snow peas, which are available year round now. The touch of mustard brings out the natural flavor and sweetness of the peas.

    2 tablespoons butter
    1 small clove garlic, peeled and cut in
        half lengthwise
    1 teaspoon French-style mustard
    ¼ cup water
    4 cups sugar snap peas
    2 tablespoons pine nuts, toasted

    Melt butter in a medium-size saucepan over medium-high heat. Add garlic, and stir for a few seconds. Add mustard and water, and stir. Mix in peas, cover, and cook for 2 minutes. Remove garlic, and spoon peas into a warm serving dish. Sprinkle with toasted pine nuts.

Warm Asparagus in Herbed
Vinaigrette Sauce (page 240)

Tiny Turnips with Orange and Tarragon

4 servings

Delicate, naturally sweet, and colorful. A good accompaniment to poached or broiled chicken.

¾ pound small white turnips, peeled
     (the turnips should be the size of
     table tennis balls or smaller)
 2 tablespoons butter
 2 tablespoons finely minced shallots
 2 teaspoons light honey

½ teaspoon dijon mustard
⅓ unpeeled orange, coarsely chopped
¼ teaspoon black pepper
 2 teaspoons finely minced fresh
     tarragon

Steam turnips for 8 to 10 minutes.

Melt butter in a large skillet. Add shallots, and saute, stirring constantly, for about 1 minute. Add honey, mustard, and turnips, and toss for 30 seconds. Add orange, and cook for 1 minute more, stirring often. Sprinkle with pepper and tarragon. Serve at once.

◄ Tiny Turnips with Orange and Tarragon (page 239)

Warm Asparagus
in Herbed Vinaigrette Sauce

4 servings

This bright green spring and early summer treat can be a luncheon main dish, a salad, or a first course.

  1 hard-boiled egg
  2 tablespoons red wine vinegar
  2 teaspoons dijon mustard
  5 tablespoons olive oil
  2 shallots, peeled and finely minced
     (about 1 tablespoon)
  1 teaspoon nonpareil capers, rinsed
     and dried
 ½ cup finely minced mixed fresh
     herbs (¼ cup parsley, 1 teaspoon
     dill, and the remainder consisting
     of basil, mint, thyme, and
     tarragon)
 ⅛ teaspoon black pepper
  1 pound asparagus

Separate egg white from yolk, and finely chop white. Force yolk through a sieve. Set both aside.

In a small bowl, mix all ingredients together except egg and asparagus. Add 1 tablespoon each of the prepared egg white and yolk, and beat well with a wire whisk or a wooden spoon. Set aside.

Steam the asparagus until just tender-crisp, and place on a serving platter. While they are still hot, spoon sauce over them. Using reserved egg white and egg yolk, sprin-kle an alternating white and yellow design on the surface of the asparagus. Do not chill. Serve at room temperature.

White Turnip Puff with Chives

4 servings

This is a simple but attractive vegetable served in a souffle dish: It looks like a green-speckled white cloud.

  8 medium-size turnips, peeled and
     thinly sliced
  1 small onion, peeled and quartered
  1 tablespoon butter
  2 tablespoons milk
     dash of white pepper
 ⅛ teaspoon ground nutmeg
  2 tablespoons finely minced fresh
     chives
  2 egg whites, stiffly beaten
     cayenne pepper

Preheat oven to 350°F. Butter a 1-quart souffle dish.

Steam turnips and onions together in a steamer for 7 to 8 minutes. Set aside to cool slightly. Put all ingredients except egg whites and cayenne pepper into a food processor or blender, and process until smooth. Fold into beaten egg whites, and transfer to prepared souffle dish. Sprinkle with a few grains of cayenne pepper, and bake for 20 to 25 minutes, or until souffle is slightly brown. Serve at once.

Zucchini, Summer Squash, Tomatoes, and Goat Cheese with Midsummer Herbs

4 to 6 servings

Eight or nine slices of each ingredient are arranged in a tart pan and then baked with olive oil and sprinkled with fresh herbs. This can be a simple hors d'oeuvre or a light luncheon.

  1 small yellow squash, cut into ¼-inch slices
  1 small zucchini, cut into ¼-inch slices
  3 plum tomatoes, cut into ¼-inch slices
  8 slices (each ¼ inch thick) Montrachet goat cheese
  3 tablespoons olive oil
  ¼ teaspoon black pepper
  1 teaspoon grated lemon rind
  4 tablespoons mixed fresh herbs (chives, basil, thyme, oregano, and dill)

Preheat oven to 325°F.

Arrange 8 or 9 slices of squash, zucchini, tomatoes, and cheese alternately in an attractive pattern in a 12-inch round ovenproof baking dish. Trickle olive oil over vegetables and cheese, and sprinkle with pepper. Bake for 15 minutes.

Remove from oven, and while hot, sprinkle lemon rind and mixed herbs over the top. Serve at room temperature.

Plant fresh herbs near your customary paths: by your entrance doorway, for example, or along the walk to the garage. As you brush by or crush them with your feet their fragrance will cheer you up.

Chapter 12

BREADS

We had been planning the bread chapter for this book for some weeks, and with July rounding the corner, many of our fresh herbs were ready for harvesting—*all at the same time!* The feathery dill flowers stirred lazily in the breeze near the shore; the basil was shiny and tempting. We began to wonder how we could ever take advantage of the harvest in order to test all the recipes at exactly the right moment.

On the beach, over the Fourth of July weekend, we told of our timing dilemma to a group of bread bakers who had contributed to Mel's two bread books, *Bread Winners* and *Bread Winners Too.* In the face of a seductive beach and cool, blue ocean, we had the temerity to suggest that *they* might like to become our test bakers. Maybe *they* would be willing to divide the recipes among them and report to us on the results? Surprisingly, these gracious people consented.

The next day, July 5th, broke cloudy and misty and cool. It was certainly no day for the beach. At noon the telephone rang. It was Andy Esberg. His bread was coming out of the oven right now!—the Shallot and Herb Bread Swirl. Would we come over to taste? We would. We did. We ate too much—enough to ruin lunch—and we went home.

We had barely arrived when George Meluso came by to announce that the Basil Walnut Bread with Romano Cheese was just about ready for a taste test. Would we come over and taste? We would. But, just as we got on our bicycles, the phone rang again. It was Gerry Franklin, who laughingly commented that he just could not wait until the end of the summer. The Czechoslovakian Vanocka with Aniseeds, Lemon, and Almonds would be ready in half an hour. Would we come over and taste? We would, of course, as soon as we could leave George's house.

And so it went for the entire weekend, with 11 bake-offs and taste tests. Len Silver waited until the following week for his testing, which turned out for the best, since we were by that time quite sated with warm, fresh-baked bread.

And so, the breads in this chapter are all tested through the courtesy and the expertise of our Fire Island bakers. May their ovens always be the right temperature!

A Few Bread Baking Tips

For readers who have never tried baking their own breads, here are a few basic tips about the procedures. As those of you who have read our other books know, there are no real rules for bread baking—something

243

you will discover for yourselves once you try it. Some bakers put the flour in first and then the liquid; others are inclined to do the reverse. Some bakers use loaf pans, others make free-form shapes, and still others use flowerpots. However, there are some tips that we'd like to pass on that will encourage creativity in baking your own breads:

❧ Salt helps control the rise. Use your judgment about the amount. Breads will work with no salt, a small amount of salt, or lots of salt. The salt shaker is in your hands. We use a small amount.
❧ Baking times and amounts are approximate. Flour will handle differently in drier climates than it will at the seaside. Learn to judge by the "feel" of the dough and what the bread looks like when it's done. It spite of the baking time given, when a bread is done, it's done—usually judged by tapping the loaf on the bottom. If it sounds hollow, it's finished.
❧ Ovens vary in temperature from place to place. Don't be afraid to move breads to other levels and other spots in the oven as they bake.
❧ Creating steam can help set the crust and make it crisp, and that's what the French do. When the oven reaches the proper temperature and the loaves are ready to be put in, toss about three ice cubes on the floor of the oven. This will create a steam bath for your breads.
❧ Don't be afraid to slash the loaves before baking. They will not fall, and slashing will prevent them from splitting open at various unplanned spots while they bake. Use a razor blade or a sharp knife to do the job.
❧ To keep seeds or other toppings from falling off during and after baking, moisten the top of your breads with the glaze called for (water or egg yolk and water), and then sprinkle the seeds on top. Lightly press them in with your fingers before putting the breads into the oven.

Of course, these are just a few of many more tips. You may even develop your own as you become more adept.

ABOUT FLOURS AND HERBS

Those of you who have read our other books already know that we use whole grains wherever possible. Except for traditional breads, you will discover that we generally use whole wheat flour or other whole grain flours for our baking. However, in testing the recipes for this book, we found that the exclusive use of whole grains tended to cover the flavor and aroma of the herbs. Thus, in some of the bread recipes that follow, we combine whole wheat with white flour to allow the taste of the herbs to come through.

Basil Walnut Bread with Romano Cheese

Makes 2 loaves

This is a pretty bread with an unusual shape. We describe it as a melted upside-down ice cream cone. The Romano cheese adds a tang to this delicious bread.

  3 cups whole wheat flour
4½ cups unbleached white flour, divided
  2 teaspoons honey
  1 package dry yeast
2½ cups warm water, divided
  ½ cup finely minced fresh basil
  ½ cup finely minced fresh parsley
  1 tablespoon lemon juice
  ¼ cup finely chopped walnuts
  ⅓ cup grated Romano cheese
  1 egg yolk, beaten with 1 teaspoon water
  2 fresh basil leaves (optional)

In a large bowl, combine whole wheat flour and 3½ cups of the unbleached white flour. Mix honey, yeast, and 1 cup of the warm water together in a small bowl, and set aside to proof for 10 minutes. Add yeast mixture to flour, gradually beating it in with a wooden spoon. Gradually, add just enough of remaining water and remaining flour to make a soft dough. Turn out onto a lightly floured surface, and knead for 8 to 10 minutes, or until smooth and elastic, adding more flour if needed to prevent dough from sticking. Form into a ball, and put into an oiled bowl, turning to coat all sides. Cover with a towel, and let rise in a warm place until doubled in bulk, about 1 hour. Punch down dough, turn out onto a lightly floured surface, knead a few times, and then invert bowl over dough to let rest for 10 minutes.

Combine basil, parsley, lemon juice, walnuts, and Romano cheese in a medium-size bowl. Divide dough in half, keeping one half under bowl to prevent it from drying out. Roll out dough into a 12 × 16-inch rectangle. Spread with half the basil-parsley mixture, and roll up from the long side like a jellyroll, stretching it to make a 20-inch roll. Repeat the process with the other half of the dough and remaining filling.

Oil a large baking sheet. Take 1 of the 20-inch rolls, and, using less than half of the baking sheet, coil it into a circle about 6 inches in diameter. Keep coiling it by winding the dough onto the top of the first circle, tapering inward to make a coil about 4 inches in diameter. Tuck the remainder of the dough into the hole in the middle. Where the coils touch, use your finger to moisten the seams with water. As we described it at the beginning, it should resemble a flattened cone. Repeat with the other half of the dough on the other side of the baking sheet, leaving enough room between them to allow space for a rise. Cover with a towel, and let rise in a warm place until doubled in bulk, about 45 minutes.

Preheat oven to 375°F.

Brush loaves with egg mixture. Bake for 30 to 35 minutes, or until breads are golden and sound hollow when tapped on the bottoms. Slide off to wire racks and cool. Before serving, tuck a fresh basil leaf on top as a garnish if desired.

In some parts of Italy, men still wear a sprig of basil in their lapel if they are looking for a mate.

Butternut Squash Spice Bread with Walnuts and Raisins

Makes 2 loaves

These breads, baked in coffee cans, were tested by Fire Island friend Len Silver. When he cut them, we were delighted by the raisin-walnut pattern within the round slices.

  1 cup raisins
  1 cup water
  2 eggs
  1 cup mashed cooked butternut
      squash
  ½ cup corn oil
  ¾ cup honey
  1¼ cups whole wheat flour
  ¾ cup unbleached white flour
  1 tablespoon baking powder
  ½ teaspoon baking soda
  ½ teaspoon ground nutmeg
  ½ teaspoon ground cinnamon
  ½ cup chopped walnuts

Preheat oven to 350°F. Butter and flour 2 1-pound coffee cans.

Put raisins and water in a medium-size saucepan, and bring to a boil. Remove from heat, cool to room temperature, drain, and reserve both raisins and liquid. In a medium-size bowl, mix eggs, squash, oil, ⅓ cup of the raisin liquid, and honey together. In a large bowl, mix whole wheat flour, unbleached white flour, baking powder, baking soda, nutmeg, and cinnamon together. Stir in squash mixture. Add raisins and walnuts, and beat well. Divide batter between prepared coffee cans. Bake for 1 hour, or until a cake tester or toothpick inserted into the center comes out clean. If breads seem to be getting too brown on top, cover

cans with aluminum foil for the last 10 to 15 minutes of baking. Cool for 20 minutes on wire racks, and then invert cans to remove loaves. If breads will not come out easily, you can open the bottom of the cans, and push the loaves through to the racks. Cool before slicing.

Caraway Cottage Cheese Bread with Chives

Makes 2 loaves

  2 cups whole wheat flour
  2½ cups unbleached white flour
  2 tablespoons honey
  1½ tablespoons caraway seeds
  2 packages dry yeast
  ½ teaspoon salt
  ½ cup water
  2 tablespoons butter
  1 pound cottage cheese, at room
      temperature
  6 heaping tablespoons finely minced
      fresh chives

In a large bowl, mix together 1 cup of the whole wheat flour and 1 cup of the unbleached white flour, honey, caraway seeds, yeast, and salt, and set aside. In a small saucepan, heat water and butter together until water is warm and butter melts. Gradually stir liquid into flour mixture, adding cottage cheese and minced chives. Stir in enough flour to make a stiff, but flexible dough. Turn out onto a lightly floured surface, and knead for 8 to 10 minutes, or until smooth and elastic. If dough becomes sticky, add more flour as you knead. Place into an oiled bowl, turn to coat all sides, cover with a towel, and let rise in a warm place until doubled in bulk, about 1 hour. Punch down dough, turn out onto a floured surface, and knead for 1 to 2 minutes. Divide dough in half, shape with your hands, and place each half into a buttered 8 × 4 × 2-inch loaf pan. Cover with a towel, and let rise in a warm place until doubled in bulk, about 45 minutes.

Preheat oven to 375°F.

Bake for 40 to 45 minutes, or until loaves are browned. Test by turning a loaf out onto a gloved hand and tapping the bottom. If it sounds hollow, it's done. Remove from pans, and cool on wire racks.

Cheddar Cheese and Dill Scones

Makes 16 scones

These were tested by Len Silver. When he telephoned to say that he was ready, we bicycled to his house, and we quickly finished *ten* of the hot scones!

1¼ cups grated extra sharp cheddar cheese
¼ cup finely minced fresh dill
1 cup whole wheat pastry flour
1 cup unbleached white flour
1 tablespoon baking powder
¼ cup cold butter, diced
2 eggs, beaten
½ cup heavy cream, divided
1 egg yolk

Preheat oven to 450°F. Butter a baking sheet.

Mix cheese and dill together in a small bowl, and set aside. In a food processor, mix whole wheat pastry flour, unbleached white flour, and baking powder together. Add butter, and process until mixture is the texture of cornmeal. Add eggs, reserved cheese-dill mixture, and all but 1 tablespoon of the cream. Do not overprocess, but mix lightly to make a soft dough.

Turn out onto a lightly floured board, and knead for another 1 to 2 minutes. Pat dough into a square shape. Then, lightly roll out dough into an 8-inch square about 1 inch thick. Cut dough into 4-inch squares, and then cut each square twice diagonally to make 4 triangles. Place triangles about 2 inches apart on prepared baking sheet. Mix egg yolk with remaining cream, and brush mixture on the tops of the triangles. Bake for 15 to 18 minutes, or until golden. Cool for about 10 minutes before serving.

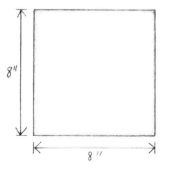
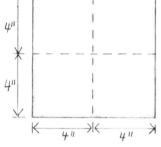

Czechoslovakian Vanocka with Aniseeds, Lemon, and Almonds

Makes 2 loaves

Gerry Franklin loves to make braided breads just like this traditional Czech Christmas bread. "When I was an altar boy," he explains, "I had to braid the fringes of the altar cloth. I never used the skill again until I learned to bake *Challah* many years later!" Since this is a traditional bread, we use all unbleached white flour.

 7 cups unbleached white flour
 2 packages dry yeast
1¼ cups milk
 ½ cup honey
 6 tablespoons butter
 ½ teaspoon salt
 2 eggs
 1 egg white
 1 teaspoon aniseeds, crushed
  grated rind of 1 lemon
1½ cups raisins
 1 egg yolk, beaten, divided
 ¼ cup sliced almonds, divided

In a large bowl, combine 3 cups of the flour and dry yeast. In a saucepan, heat milk, honey, butter, and salt until butter melts, and then add to flour mixture. Add eggs, egg white, aniseeds, and lemon rind. Stir in the rest of the flour to make a moderately stiff dough. Coat raisins with flour, and stir them into dough. Turn out onto a floured surface, and knead for 8 to 10 minutes, or until the dough is smooth and elastic. Shape into a large ball, place into an oiled bowl, turning to coat all sides, cover with a towel, and let rise in a warm place until doubled in bulk, about 1 hour.

Divide dough in half, reserving the second half for the second loaf. Divide the first portion into halves. Cut one piece into thirds. Roll each third into an 18-inch rope. Braid loosely. Place on an oiled baking sheet.

Divide remaining piece into fourths. Roll 3 of these into 14-inch ropes. Braid loosely, and place atop the first braid, tucking ends under. Cut remaining piece of dough into thirds. Roll each into a 12-inch rope. Braid, and place atop the second braid, tucking ends under. Brush loaf with half the beaten egg yolk. Top with half the almonds, gently pressing them in one by one so that they do not come loose during baking or slicing.

Repeat the process for the second loaf. Cover both loaves with a towel, and let rise in a warm place until doubled in bulk, about 45 minutes. During this last rise, the braid may shift slightly. Lift the covering occasionally, and readjust the braids.

Preheat oven to 350°F.

Bake for 25 to 30 minutes, or until braided loaves are done. Cool on wire racks.

Fragrant Rosemary and Onion Bread

Makes 1 loaf

 1 cup warm water, divided
 1 package dry yeast
 ½ teaspoon honey
 2 teaspoons dried rosemary, divided
 2 cups whole wheat flour
 2 cups unbleached white flour
 ½ teaspoon salt
 ¼ cup grated onions
 1 teaspoon olive oil
 1 egg yolk, beaten with 1 teaspoon
  water

In a small bowl, mix together ¼ cup of the warm water, yeast, honey, and 1½ teaspoons of the rosemary, and set aside to proof for 5 to 10 minutes. Using a food processor, mix the whole wheat flour and 1½ cups of the unbleached white flour together, reserving ½ cup of the white flour to work in after the rise, if needed. Add salt, grated onions, yeast-water mixture, and enough of the remaining water to make a dough that leaves the sides of the bowl. Do not overprocess. Turn dough out onto a floured surface, and shape into a smooth ball. Oil a large bowl. Put the dough into the bowl, cover with a towel, and let rise in a warm place until doubled in bulk, 1 to 1½ hours. Punch down dough, and knead briefly. Turn out onto a floured surface, and shape into a smooth loaf. Place into 9 × 5 × 3-inch loaf pan, brush with olive oil, cover with a towel, and let rise in pan until doubled in bulk, 1 to 1½ hours.

Preheat oven to 350°F.

Brush top of loaf with egg yolk mixture, sprinkle with remaining rosemary, and bake for 45 minutes. Lower oven to 325°F, and bake for another 30 minutes, or until the top is brown and the bread sounds hollow when tapped. Turn out of pan, and cool completely on a wire rack.

Italian Rye Bread with Olive Oil and Fennel Seeds

Makes 3 long loaves

1¾ cups lukewarm water, divided
2 packages dry yeast
1 teaspoon honey
2 tablespoons plus 1 teaspoon olive oil, divided
2 cups whole wheat flour
3 cups unbleached white flour
1 cup rye flour
½ teaspoon salt
3 teaspoons fennel seeds, divided
1 tablespoon cornmeal
1 egg, beaten with 1 teaspoon water

Put ¼ cup of the warm water, yeast, honey and 2 tablespoons of the olive oil into the bowl of a food processor, and mix for 5 seconds. Add whole wheat flour, unbleached white flour, rye flour, salt, and 2 teaspoons of the fennel seeds plus the remaining water a little at a time, and process until you have a firm dough. Turn dough out onto a lightly floured surface, and knead for 8 to 10 minutes. Shape into a ball, place into an oiled bowl, cover with a towel, and let rise in a warm place until doubled in bulk, about 1½ hours. Punch down dough, knead briefly on a floured surface again, and shape into a ball. Return to oiled bowl, cover, and let rise again in a warm place for about 1 hour.

Divide dough into 3 parts, and roll out each part into an 8 × 12-inch rectangle. Roll up each part like a long jellyroll, pressing lightly to seal the bottom seam. Tuck the ends in, and press to make them smooth. Lightly oil a baking sheet with the remaining oil, and sprinkle with cornmeal. Arrange loaves on prepared baking sheet, cover with a towel, and let rise until nearly doubled in bulk, about 30 minutes.

Preheat oven to 425°F.

Brush the surface of the breads with the egg mixture. Sprinkle with remaining fennel seeds, and press in gently with the tips of your fingers so that they adhere to the loaf. Using a sharp knife or a razor blade, slash the breads at 3 or 4 places along the top. Bake for 20 to 25 minutes, or until the loaves sound hollow when tapped. Cool on wire racks.

Lemon and Saffron Tea Bread

Makes 1 loaf

After Len Silver had tested this delicious bread, Sheryl remarked, "It's too bad that people don't have afternoon tea any longer. This would be a great accompaniment!" Well, if you don't have afternoon tea, try it with morning coffee. It will taste just as good.

BREAD

   1 cup whole wheat flour
1¾ cups unbleached white flour
   2 teaspoons baking powder
  ¼ teaspoon baking soda
  ⅓ cup butter, softened
  ¾ cup light honey
   2 eggs
1½ tablespoons grated lemon rind
      (from about 3 lemons)
  ¼ teaspoon saffron threads, crushed
      to a powder in a mortar and
      pestle
  ¾ cup milk

TOPPING

  ⅓ cup light honey
   2 tablespoons lemon juice
   1 teaspoon grated lemon rind

Preheat oven to 350°F.

Butter a 9 × 5 × 3-inch loaf pan. Line bottom of pan with waxed paper, and butter again.

To make the bread: Mix whole wheat flour, unbleached white flour, baking powder, and baking soda in a large bowl, and set aside. In a medium-size bowl, cream butter. Add honey, eggs, lemon rind, saffron, and milk, and let stand for 5 minutes. The mixture may look curdled; but don't worry, it will smooth out during the next step. Slowly add milk mixture to flour mixture, stirring to blend. Scrape and pour batter into prepared pan, smoothing the top with a spatula. Bake for 50 to 60 minutes, or until a cake tester or toothpick inserted into the center comes out clean. Run a knife around the edges of the bread, and turn out onto a wire rack that is standing on waxed paper to catch the drippings from the topping.

To make the topping: In a cup, mix honey with lemon juice, and brush mixture on top of the bread while it is still hot. Sprinkle lemon rind on the surface. Place bread on a baking sheet, and place it under the broiler for 1 to 2 minutes, or until the top caramelizes. Do not put it too close to the flame, and watch it carefully to avoid burning. Cool on a wire rack.

◄ Cheddar Cheese and Dill Scones (page 247)

Basil Walnut Bread with
Romano Cheese (page 245)

Shallot and Herb Bread Swirl

Makes 1 loaf

This is one of the breads tested by Andy Esberg. When we cut the bread, the first thing that impressed us was the beauty of the green swirl in the loaf, the second was the taste!

1½ packages dry yeast
¼ cup lukewarm water
½ teaspoon honey
¼ cup butter, divided
¾ cup water
3½ cups whole wheat flour
½ teaspoon salt

1¾ cups finely minced fresh parsley, divided
1 teaspoon finely minced garlic
1 tablespoon finely minced shallots
¼ teaspoon black pepper
1 tablespoon finely minced fresh oregano
1 large egg, beaten but not frothy
2 tablespoons grated Parmesan cheese

In a cup, mix yeast with lukewarm water and honey, and set aside in a warm place for 10 minutes to proof. Mix 2 tablespoons of the butter with water in a small saucepan, and heat briefly over very low heat until butter melts. Don't let it get too hot. Place flour and salt into a food processor. Add yeast and butter mixtures, and ¾ cup parsley, and blend until a ball of dough forms. Turn dough out onto a lightly floured surface, knead briefly, and shape into a ball. Place into a lightly oiled bowl, turn to coat all sides, cover with a towel, and let rise in a warm place until doubled in bulk, about 1 hour.

Heat remaining butter in a small skillet. Add garlic and shallots, and cook, while stirring, for 1 to 2 minutes, or until shallots are wilted. Add remaining parsley, pepper, and oregano. Remove from heat, and cool slightly.

Butter a baking sheet. Turn the dough out again onto a floured surface, and roll out dough into a 13 × 7-inch rectangle. Brush the top of the rectangle with a little of the beaten egg. Add some of the remaining egg to the parsley mixture, and reserve a bit of the egg to mix with a few drops of water to make an egg wash for the top of the bread later on. Spoon parsley and shallot mixture on top of the rectangle, leaving a 2-inch border. Sprinkle with Parmesan cheese, and then roll up, jellyroll fashion, from the short side. Pinch the edges to seal. Place bread on baking sheet, seam-side down, cover with a towel, and let rise once more in a warm place until doubled in bulk, about 1 hour.

Preheat oven to 400°F.

Brush top of bread with reserved egg and water wash, and bake for 30 minutes. Reduce heat to 375°F, and bake for 15 minutes longer. Let cool on a wire rack before slicing.

Chapter 13
SAUCES

Clockwise from top right:
Mixed Herbs, Hot Pepper, and Garlic Olive Oil (page 259)
Low-Calorie Sauce Louis (page 258)
Roasted Red Pepper and Borage Sauce (page 264)
Horseradish and Soy Dipping Sauce (page 258)
Oriental Ginger and Cilantro Butter (page 260)
← Watercress, Lemon Balm, Parsley, and Chive Sauce (page 266)

We read somewhere that making sauces is probably the most challenging and most creative part of cooking. Many chefs in some of the great restaurant kitchens would probably agree wholeheartedly. A great sauce calls for harmony, flavor, voluptuousness, and — on the part of the chef — vigilance. Sauces are at the heart of thousands of superb dishes and inspired menus. Think carefully — what is it you remember most about that great dinner you had at the absolutely superb restaurant? Probably the *sauce* that blanketed the veal or the fish or the chicken.

Like herbs and spices, sauces were first used as a merciful disguise for the lack of refrigeration. The French were particularly good at this; today, many of our favorites are variations on their classic sauces. We lighten them by using less butter, less cream. We also depend more upon reductions, simmering down sauces for more intense flavor, and we use herbs even more liberally than before. There is a current Near Eastern and Far Eastern influence in eating, and many of our sauces reflect that, too. The use of cilantro and ginger, and the access to the more exotic varieties of hot peppers introduces yet other dimensions. What follows is but a sampling from a world of possibilities.

If we had to choose one essential tip concerning sauces it would be this: Use sauces discreetly. Remember, a sauce is actually a seasoning for the dish, a complement to the basic flavor of the food it dresses. The essence of a delicate fish such as sole can easily be overpowered, so clever chefs are careful to use something on the order of a hot butter and cilantro sauce which provides a subtle lift to the fish, yet lets the character of the food prevail. On the other hand, the robust flavor of bluefish can take an herby tomato sauce without a diminution of the rich fish flavor. Think carefully about the appropriateness of the sauce you choose.

In preparing any cooked sauces, spices and herbs should not be added until just before the sauce is finished, so that their flavors are released, but not lost. Be especially careful to hold black pepper until the end; it tends to become bitter if cooked too long.

255

HERB BUTTERS

Combine 4 tablespoons of softened butter with 1 tablespoon finely minced fresh herbs or 1 teaspoon dried herbs plus ⅛ teaspoon black pepper. Form into a bar or cylinder shape and wrap with aluminum foil. Refrigerate from several hours to several days to let the butter absorb the flavor of the herbs. Add herb butters to hot cooked foods, but do not use for sauteeing or the herbs will burn and discolor.

The following are only a few suggestions for the many ways you can use these wonderful butters:

❧ When serving an herb butter on a buffet table, you can identify it as such by pressing a sprig of the flavoring herb lightly onto the top of the butter.

❧ A pretty idea: Spread herb or flower butters smooth and flat on a sheet of waxed paper and chill. Then cut into shapes with a cookie cutter to serve on the bread and butter plate.

❧ When making herb butters with dried herbs, first soak the herbs in 1 teaspoon of lemon juice for 15 minutes to bring out their flavors, then add them to the butter.

❧ You can add spicy fragrance to ¼ pound of softened butter by adding ¼ cup of flower petals (for example, rose, carnation, violet, or lilac), blending the two, and refrigerate overnight.

❧ A drop of two of Worcestershire sauce added to herb butters adds nuance for use with meats. A bit of lemon juice does the same for herb butters that are used with fish.

❧ Basil butter is delicious as an addition to steamed carrots, beets, or summer squash, as a spread for cucumber sandwiches, or British fashion, as a topping for raw radishes.

❧ Use sage or rosemary butter with pork, onions, chicken, or potatoes.

❧ Herb butters forced up under the skin of a chicken before roasting will flavor the entire bird.

❧ Try tarragon butter with fish, eggs (poached, boiled, or scrambled), and lamb chops.

❧ Lemon balm butter imparts a unique quality when it tops steamed, shelled shrimp or poached bay scallops.

Basil Beurre Blanc

Makes ¾ cup

This elegant, traditional sauce is lovely with poached fish or lobster, or spooned over a poached chicken breast. The sauce must be made and used at once or it will separate.

1 tablespoon butter
¼ cup finely minced shallots
3 tablespoons white wine vinegar
2 tablespoons water
⅓ cup heavy cream
  small pinch of powdered bay leaves
  small pinch of white pepper
¼ pound butter, cut into 12 pieces
6 to 8 large fresh basil leaves, finely minced (2 tablespoons of minced mixed fresh herbs may be substituted)

Heat butter in a small heavy saucepan. Add shallots, and cook, stirring constantly, for 1 minute. Stir in vinegar and water and continue to cook until liquid is almost totally evaporated, 3 to 4 minutes. Then add cream, slowly bring to the boiling point, and cook until sauce is thickened. Remove from heat, add powdered bay leaves and pepper, and let cool for 1 minute. Strain, pressing solids with a wooden spoon to remove as much of the liquid as possible. Return strained liquid to saucepan, and return saucepan to heat, stirring constantly. Add butter a few pieces at a time, stirring rapidly with a wooden spoon as you do so. Do not let sauce boil. Remove from heat to incorporate butter and to keep the sauce creamy if necessary. Add basil, and heat for a few seconds. Use at once.

Buttermilk, Lemon, and Cardamom Sauce

Makes 1¾ cups

A wonderful complement to desserts or pies.

⅓ cup heavy cream
¾ cup buttermilk
2 tablespoons maple syrup
1 teaspoon finely grated lemon rind
¼ teaspoon ground ginger
⅛ teaspoon ground cardamom

In a medium-size bowl, whip cream with a rotary beater. Mix together all the remaining ingredients in a cup, and gradually add to whipped cream.

Double Orange Cream Sauce with Mint

Makes about 1 cup

Serve this delightful sauce over any fruit.

½ cup sour cream
1½ ounces cream cheese, softened and cut into pieces
1 tablespoon orange-flower water or orange juice
1 tablespoon grated orange rind
2 teaspoons maple syrup or light honey
1 tablespoon finely minced fresh mint

Put all the ingredients except mint into the bowl of a food processor, and blend well. Add mint, and process until sauce is smooth and well blended.

Herbed Yogurt Sauce

Makes 1 cup

An excellent sauce for steamed vegetables or fish.

  1 cup plain yogurt
  2 tablespoons finely minced fresh
      chives
  ½ teaspoon finely minced garlic
  1 teaspoon Worcestershire sauce
2 to 3 drops of hot pepper sauce
  1 tablespoon finely minced fresh
      dill

Mix all ingredients together in a small bowl, and refrigerate for 1 hour to let the flavors blend. Serve at room temperature.

Horseradish and Soy Dipping Sauce

Makes ½ cup

A versatile sauce that can be used on vegetables or seafood. If you use prepared horseradish, place in a small strainer, and press out the liquid with the back of a wooden spoon before adding it to the recipe.

  2 tablespoons grated fresh horseradish
      or prepared horseradish, drained
  3 tablespoons light soy sauce
  3 tablespoons rice vinegar
  ¼ teaspoon light honey

Combine all the ingredients in a small bowl, and let stand for 30 minutes. Serve as a dipping sauce for vegetables, grilled or batter-fried fish, cold seafood, or raw fish.

Honey Mint Sauce

Makes ½ cup

This sauce can be served with lamb at the table or it can be used as a basting sauce that is brushed on the lamb while it's cooking.

  ½ cup finely minced fresh mint
  ⅔ cup light honey
  ⅓ cup tarragon white wine vinegar
  2 tablespoons boiling water

Combine mint, honey, and vinegar in a medium-size heavy saucepan. Bring to a boil, then reduce heat, and simmer for 10 minutes, or until slightly thickened. Add boiling water, and stir. Serve warm.

Low-Calorie Sauce Louis

Makes 1⅓ cups

Perfect for crab, lobster, shrimp, or even tuna.

  1 hard-boiled egg, peeled
  1 cup low-fat cottage cheese
  ¼ cup tomato juice
2 or 3 drops of hot pepper sauce
  1 teaspoon hot mustard
  2 tablespoons finely chopped
      onions
  2 tablespoons finely chopped
      fresh parsley

Put the egg, cottage cheese, tomato juice, hot pepper sauce, and hot mustard into a blender or food processor, and blend until smooth. Transfer to a medium-size bowl, then stir in onions and parsley.

Mint and Cilantro Sauce

Makes 1¼ cups

This sauce will keep for three to four days, covered, in the refrigerator, and it tastes even better when all the flavors have blended. Try it with fish.

- 2 medium-size tomatoes, peeled
- 1 tablespoon finely minced scallions, white part only
- ¼ cup finely minced green peppers
- ½ teaspoon finely minced garlic
- 2 tablespoons finely minced fresh mint
- 1 tablespoon finely minced fresh cilantro
- ⅛ to ¼ teaspoon hot pepper sauce, to taste

Chop tomatoes in a food processor. Transfer to a medium-size bowl, and stir in all the remaining ingredients. Let sauce stand for at least a day in the refrigerator to develop flavor.

Mixed Herbs, Hot Pepper, and Garlic Olive Oil

Makes ¾ cup

Serve this versatile sauce over steamed vegetables or trickle over fish, chicken, or veal before broiling. We always have some on hand for a quick lift to broiled or steamed foods.

- 1 tablespoon fresh rosemary
- 1½ tablespoons fresh marjoram
- 1½ tablespoons fresh sage
- 1½ tablespoons fresh summer savory
- ¼ teaspoon black pepper
- 1 small clove garlic, peeled and crushed
- 2 small whole dried hot peppers, seeded
- ½ cup olive oil

Finely chop fresh herbs in a food processor. Mix with all the remaining ingredients, and let stand overnight at room temperature before using.

Note: To prepare this sauce with dried herbs, use 1 teaspoon of dried rosemary and 1½ teaspoons of each of the remaining herbs.

Mama Leone's Seafood Sauce

Makes 1 cup

This is a sauce that was developed at Mama Leone's restaurant in New York City. It's wonderful with shrimp or crab meat.

- 1 scallion, green part only, finely chopped
- 3 tablespoons chopped sweet red peppers
- 1 tablespoons capers, rinsed and dried
- ½ cup mayonnaise (preferably made with an olive oil base)
- ¼ cup chili sauce
- 1 tablespoon grated fresh horseradish pinch of dried red pepper flakes
- ¼ teaspoon black pepper
- 1 small clove garlic, peeled and minced

In a medium-size bowl, mix together scallions, red peppers, and capers. Stir in remaining ingredients in the order given. Mix well, and let stand for at least 1 hour before serving, or keep in the refrigerator overnight.

Middle Eastern Parsley Sauce

Makes ¾ cup

A versatile sauce for broiled lamb chops or fish, or a tasty dip for raw vegetables.

    2 cloves garlic, peeled
    1 medium bunch fresh parsley
    ¼ cup lemon juice (about 1½ lemons)
    ⅓ cup tahini (sesame butter)
    2 tablespoons water
    ⅛ teaspoon black pepper

In a food processor, mince garlic and then parsley. Then add all the remaining ingredients, and process until smooth. Let stand at room temperature for at least 1 hour to develop flavor. This sauce will keep for 3 to 4 days in the refrigerator.

Mignonette or Shallot Sauce

Makes 1 cup

This sauce for raw clams or oysters is served at the famous Oyster Bar in New York City.

    ½ cup red wine vinegar
    ½ cup tarragon vinegar
    ½ teaspoon minced fresh tarragon
        leaves
    2 tablespoons finely minced shallots
    ½ teaspoon black pepper

Combine all the ingredients in a jar, shake well, and refrigerate. This sauce will keep for several months.

Oriental Ginger and Cilantro Butter

Makes about ½ cup

Try this Orientally inspired sauce with vegetables or fish.

    ¼ pound butter, softened, divided
    1 teaspoon finely minced garlic (about
        1 small clove)
    1 tablespoon grated peeled ginger root
    3 tablespoons finely minced fresh
        cilantro
    2 teaspoons soy sauce
    3 drops of hot pepper sauce

Melt 1 tablespoon of the butter in a small skillet. Add garlic, and saute while stirring for 1 to 2 minutes. Do not brown. Set aside to cool. Place remaining ingredients in the bowl of a food processor, and blend. Add garlic-butter mixture, and blend for a few strokes. Scrape out with a rubber spatula, and serve at room temperature, or form into a roll and chill, slicing off pieces as needed.

Oriental Mayonnaise

Makes ⅔ cup

This recipe uses the same basic principles for preparation and some of the same components as regular mayonnaise—egg yolk and oil. However, the ingredients here give an Oriental twist to this basic sauce. Try 3 or 4 tablespoons with cooked fish, adding one or two minced scallions and 1 teaspoon of minced cilantro for an unusual Oriental fish salad.

    1 large egg yolk, at room temperature
    1 tablespoon Chinese or Japanese rice
        vinegar

½ teaspoon dry English or Chinese
  mustard
½ teaspoon soy sauce
  few drops of hot chili oil or hot
  pepper sauce
2 tablespoons Oriental sesame oil
½ cup peanut or corn oil
1 teaspoon grated peeled ginger root

Put all the ingredients except oils and ginger into a blender or food processor, and blend for about 30 seconds. Combine both oils in a small measuring cup, and while the blender or food processor is running, slowly add oil, drop by drop at first; then, as the mixture begins to thicken, add oil in a slow, steady stream, about 1 tablespoon at a time, processing until all the oil is incorporated. If sauce becomes too thick, add another teaspoon of vinegar or 1 tablespoon of boiling water. Stir in ginger root. Keep refrigerated.

Pesto Genovese

Makes enough for 1 pound of pasta

No book about herbs and spices would be complete without this sauce, one of our favorites. It freezes well and can be used in many ways other than as an accompaniment to pasta. If you do decide to freeze the pesto, do not add the cheese. Add the Parmesan and the Romano when you are ready to serve it.

3 cups loosely packed fresh basil
  leaves
1 cup loosely packed fresh parsley
  leaves

2 or 3 cloves garlic, peeled
    1 teaspoon butter
   12 blanched almonds or
      1 tablespoon slivered
      blanched almonds
   12 walnuts
    1 tablespoon pine nuts
      pinch of dried red pepper flakes
    ½ cup extra virgin olive oil
   1½ cups grated Parmesan cheese
    2 tablespoons grated Romano
      cheese

Very finely chop basil and parsley in a blender or food processor. Remove, and set aside. Then very finely mince garlic, and leave in food processor. Melt butter in a small skillet. Add all the nuts, toss, and toast over low heat for 1 to 2 minutes. Add nuts to garlic, and process until finely minced. Add basil-parsley mixture and red pepper flakes to food processor. Slowly add olive oil while food processor is in motion. Transfer to a medium-size bowl. Stir in cheeses.

As a variation on pesto made with basil, try using 1 cup of dill, removed from the stems, as a tasty substitute. Serve this "dill pesto" as a sauce for shrimp or vegetables.

Steve Thom

Steve's Restaurant
Buffalo, Wyoming

We were filming a documentary about energy out in Gillette, Wyoming, and all through the ten days that we worked at the isolated but exquisite location, we kept hearing about a restaurant that "you folks oughta try, since you write cookbooks." However, the restaurant they were recommending was a 140-mile round trip from Gillette. Nothing is ever close to anything else out there in the West. Finally, on the last night of our shoot, we decided to take the trip. We drove through wild and empty country, where the only signs of life were large herds of antelope, mule deer, and great elk. It was worth the trip to Steve's!

The restaurant sits at the foot of the magnificent, snow-capped Bighorn

Mountains, and its owner is 39-year-old Steve Thom. He was raised in Connecticut, then moved to New Orleans, where he worked at Le Ruth's Restaurant under the tutelage of "an absolute genius, Warren Le Ruth." Eventually, Steve found his way to Buffalo, Wyoming (where the Thom family originated) with his wife, Marcia, and his three children, John, Cody, and Nicholas, and opened his own place. Steve is a great believer in making everything from scratch. Everything. And that includes the bread.

By the way, you can't go wrong with herbs in making bread. Just chop up enough of any fresh herb to make ½ cupful and add it to the dough mix before baking. Then you'll get a tasty, aroma-rich dill bread, basil bread, tarragon bread, or any other kind of herbed bread you like. It's a simple way to add a very special touch.
I believe that restaurateurs have a responsibility to offer the finest and freshest foods available. I use lots of herbs and spices for added dimension; in the summer I have my own herb garden out in back; in the winter I use dried herbs.

Steve avoids using more than two herbs in any particular dish. His basic ingredients are those that are readily available, but he uses them with a different twist.

By different, I don't mean "hummingbird tongues under glass." I just think that the blander foods, like chicken and veal, can be greatly enhanced by the use of herbs and spices. There are many different ways to do it. Here's a favorite of mine: If you're broiling chicken or fish outdoors on a grill, throw some fresh herbs on the coals at the last minute for added flavor and aroma. Be careful to use small leafed herbs; the larger leaves flame up.

I have another easy idea, this time for a dish that uses spices, that anybody can put together in minutes — a chicken breast brushed with a mixture of mustard butter and a little curry powder, then broiled. Effortless and delicious.

People seem to be afraid to use herbs, but they've got to realize that herbs can do wonders for just about any dish. If an herb is new to you and you want to try it without taking a chance with an expensive cut of meat or a prime piece of fish, heat some butter or peanut oil and drop a handful of the fresh herb into the pan. (The heat releases the flavor and aroma of an herb.) Then dip a piece of bread in the herbed butter or oil, and you'll taste the true character of the herb.

Desserts are a big draw at Steve's Restaurant, and he offers a tip that can be used by any cook to add appeal to what some people call "the best part of the meal."

I never make plain whipped cream; I always add a bit of the flavoring that's in the dessert it will be topping — cinnamon for apple pie, ginger for gingerbread, nutmeg for pumpkin pie. It's a nice touch.

Steve's Pesto Fettuccine

4 servings

1 pound fettuccine pasta
1 tablespoon olive oil
2 cloves garlic, peeled and minced
1 cup light cream
¼ cup minced fresh basil
¼ cup minced sorrel
¼ cup minced fresh spinach
    freshly ground black pepper, to
    taste
¼ cup coarsely chopped pecans
¼ cup minced fresh parsley
½ cup freshly grated Parmesan
    cheese

Cook pasta in a large amount of boiling water until al dente, about 10 minutes. Drain, set aside, and keep warm. While pasta is cooking, heat olive oil in a medium-size skillet. Add garlic, and saute for 30 seconds. Stir in cream, and then reduce sauce by one-third. Toss cooked pasta with sauce, basil, sorrel, and spinach. Season to taste with pepper. Serve immediately on warm plates topped with pecans, parsley, and Parmesan.

Piquant Seafood Sauce with Fennel

Makes 1⅓ cups

Use this sauce with seafood or spooned over an avocado.

- ¼ cup tarragon vinegar
- 2 tablespoons hot mustard
- 2 teaspoons grated fresh horseradish
- 1 tablespoon ketchup
  pinch of cayenne pepper
- 1 hard-boiled egg, peeled
- ¼ cup chopped fresh fennel leaves
- ¼ cup chopped scallions
- ½ cup corn oil

In a small bowl, mix together vinegar, mustard, horseradish, ketchup, and cayenne. Finely chop egg in a food processor. Add fennel and scallions to the processor bowl, and finely mince. Then add vinegar mixture. While the processor is running, slowly add oil, and blend until sauce is the consistency of heavy cream.

Puffed Herb Sauce

Makes ½ cup

An excellent sauce for pureed vegetables or fish.

- 1 egg white
- 1 tablespoon mayonnaise
- 1 tablespoon lemon juice
  few gratings of nutmeg
- 1 tablespoon finely minced fresh
  parsley or dill

Preheat broiler.

Beat egg white in a small bowl until stiff. In a small bowl, combine mayonnaise and lemon juice. Fold egg white into mayonnaise-lemon juice mixture. Add nutmeg and minced herb. Spoon over pureed vegetables or fish that have been placed in a shallow, heatproof dish, and place under broiler for 2 to 3 minutes, or until the top is brown and puffed.

Roasted Red Pepper and Borage Sauce

Makes 1½ cups

We first tasted this sauce at the Four Seasons restaurant in New York and then reinvented it at home. It is lovely with fish.

- 1 pound sweet red peppers,
  roasted (page 85)
- ¼ cup olive oil
- 1 clove garlic, peeled and sliced
- 3 shallots, peeled and sliced
- ¼ cup red wine vinegar
- 2 or 3 drops of hot pepper sauce
- 1 fresh borage leaf, shredded

Puree roasted peppers in a blender or food processor. Heat oil in a small skillet. Add garlic and shallots, and saute until soft but not brown. Add to pureed peppers. Deglaze the skillet with vinegar and hot pepper sauce over high heat for a few seconds, and then add to blender or food processor. Blend all ingredients together except borage, and pour into a serving dish. Top with borage.

Note: Borage has a cucumberlike taste. If you do not grow it in your garden, substitute 1 tablespoon of shredded cucumbers.

Ravigote Butter

Makes about ½ cup

This buttery herb-rich sauce goes well with fish, lamb chops, or vegetables.

- 1 tablespoon finely minced shallots (about 1 large shallot)
- 1 tablespoon finely minced fresh parsley
- 1 tablespoon finely chopped fresh chives
- 1 tablespoon finely minced fresh chervil
- 1 teaspoon finely minced fresh tarragon
- ⅛ teaspoon white pepper
- ¼ pound butter, softened

Place all the ingredients into the bowl of a food processor, and process until blended. Scrape out with a rubber spatula, and serve in a small bowl at room temperature.

Spiced Barbecue Sauce

Makes 2 cups

- 1 tablespoon corn oil
- 1 medium-size onion, finely chopped
- 2 large cloves garlic, peeled and finely minced
- 1 tablespoon grated peeled ginger root
- 1 pound tomatoes, peeled and cut into pieces (canned plum tomatoes may be substituted)
- 1 teaspoon dried crushed oregano
- 2 dried hot chili peppers, seeded and cut into small pieces
- ½ cup cider vinegar

- 2 tablespoons light honey
- 1 tablespoon soy sauce
  seeds from 2 cardamom pods
- 2 teaspoons mustard seeds
- 4 whole cloves
- ½ teaspoon coriander seeds
- ¼ teaspoon fennel seeds
- 1 1-inch piece of cinnamon stick

Heat oil in a large nonstick saucepan. Add onions, garlic, and ginger, and saute, stirring often, until onions are wilted. Add tomatoes, oregano, chili peppers, vinegar, honey, and soy sauce, and simmer. Grind remaining spices in a spice grinder, and add to sauce. Simmer slowly, covered, for 1½ hours, or until thickened, stirring occasionally. Strain sauce through a food mill or sieve. Refrigerate and use as needed.

Sage Applesauce for Roast Pork

Makes ¾ cup

- 2 large Granny Smith or other tart green apples
- 2 tablespoons maple syrup
- 1 tablespoon water
  pinch of black pepper
- 1 teaspoon finely chopped fresh sage

Core apples, leaving skin intact. Cut into ½-inch cubes. Place into a medium-size saucepan, add maple syrup and water, and bring to a boil. Lower heat, cover, and simmer for 15 minutes, or until apples are very tender. Force cooked apples through a strainer or strain through a food mill. Discard skins. Add pepper and sage, and let stand at room temperature for 30 minutes to develop flavor.

Tomato and Lemon Thyme Sauce

Makes 1 cup

An easy tomato sauce that is delicate enough to complement the Pork Loaf with Basil, Parsley, and Pine Nuts (page 155), or you might try adding it to cooked brown rice.

    1   tablespoon olive oil
    ¼   cup finely minced shallots
    ½   teaspoon finely minced garlic
    2   cups chopped peeled ripe tomatoes
    ½   dried bay leaf
    1   tablespoon butter
    ⅛   teaspoon black pepper
    ½   teaspoon fresh lemon thyme leaves

Heat oil in a small skillet. Add shallots and garlic, and saute until soft. Add tomatoes and bay leaf, and bring to a boil. Lower heat, cover, and simmer for 5 minutes, stirring occasionally. Remove bay leaf, stir in butter, pepper, and lemon thyme leaves, and blend ingredients thoroughly.

Watercress, Lemon Balm, Parsley, and Chive Sauce

Makes 1¼ cups

A verdant sauce to serve with cold, poached chicken, fish, or seafood. You can also spread it over raw fish or chicken before baking. It goes marvelously with the fried version of Hominy Grits and Shrimp Paste with Lemon Thyme, Parsley, and Chives (page 194).

        1   cup loosely packed watercress
              leaves
        1   cup loosely packed fresh parsley
              leaves
        ½   cup loosely packed fresh lemon
              balm
        ½   cup minced fresh chives
        1   cup mayonnaise
    2 to 3   drops of hot pepper sauce

Put watercress, parsley, lemon balm, and chives into a food processor, and process until fine. Then add mayonnaise and hot pepper sauce, and process until well blended.

Chapter 14

MARINADES & VINEGARS

Cooks in almost every country in the world use marinades to add interest and flavor to their cooking, as well as to tenderize tough cuts of meat by bathing them in some lively combination of oil, acid, herbs, and spices. Even the chefs of ancient Rome used a vast array of marinades. The Romans would marinate a whole lamb or kid overnight in a rather interesting combination of herbs like rosemary, thyme, and savory, along with dates, boiled red wine, vegetable stock, olive oil, and onions. We could use the same recipe today, except for the problem of finding a whole lamb at the supermarket and then roasting it in the average-size oven of an American kitchen!

A marinade enriches and develops flavor by saturation. Essential to this process are the basic ingredients for marinades, which consist of vinegar, wine or citrus, or cultured milk (yogurt or buttermilk), and oil, with the addition of herbs, condiments, and spices. First the acids break down the fibers of the food, then the oil enters, carrying with it the savory flavors of the spices and herbs. Marinades can be a blessing for the cook, since they work equally well with meat, wild game, fish, vegetables, or fruits (though we generally use the word *macerate* when we speak of fruit bathed in citrus, wine or spirits, and spices).

Not only are marinades effective as a precooking device to impart flavor, but they also serve as a basting liquid during cooking, or as a sauce for the finished dish. You can also use marinades to tone down the gamey flavor in the meat of animals such as venison or rabbit, while tenderizing them at the same time.

On the following pages, we give a few basic examples of marinades intended for use with various kinds of meats and game, as well as for fish and tofu. Don't be afraid to experiment, for this is an ancient art that you can use to bring enviable variety to the foods you prepare.

MARINADES

Anise and Vegetable Marinade
(for Duckling or Pork)

Makes 1¾ cups

    1 cup red wine vinegar
    ½ cup water
    2 teaspoons honey
    1 lemon, sliced
    2 dried bay leaves
    2 tablespoons finely minced fresh
         lovage or celery leaves
    1 carrot, cut in julienne strips
    1 large clove garlic, peeled and finely
         minced
    1 large onion, peeled and finely
         chopped
    1 sweet red pepper, finely chopped
    ¼ teaspoon black pepper
    2 tablespoons finely minced fresh
         parsley
    1 teaspoon crushed aniseeds
         chopped orange sections (optional)
         chopped fresh chives (optional)

Mix all the ingredients together in a large bowl. Marinate duckling or pork for at least a day and a night in the refrigerator. Use marinade as the base for a sauce, enriching it with oranges and chives, if desired.

Juniper Berry Marinade
(for Wild Game, Venison, or Beef)

Makes 1¼ cups

    ½ cup red wine vinegar
    ½ cup water
    2 tablespoons olive oil
    1 lemon, thinly sliced
         juice of 1 lemon
    6 crushed green peppercorns
    ¼ cup sliced carrots
    ¼ cup sliced celery
    ½ teaspoon dried marjoram
    1 dried bay leaf
    5 whole juniper berries
    1 large clove garlic, peeled and thinly
         sliced
    1 medium-size onion, peeled and
         thinly sliced

Blend all the ingredients together in a large bowl. Pour over game, and allow to stand from 1 to 3 days in the refrigerator, depending upon the degree of marinade flavor and the gaminess of the meat. Use marinade for basting if meat is roasted or as a sauce if meat is made into a ragout.

Lemon and Cumin Marinade
(for Chicken)

Makes about ⅔ cup

    ⅓ cup lemon juice
    ¼ cup olive oil

1 teaspoon finely minced garlic
¼ teaspoon black pepper
½ teaspoon ground cumin
½ teaspoon dried thyme
    pinch of dried red pepper flakes

Combine all the ingredients in a small bowl. Marinate chicken at least 2 hours or overnight in the refrigerator. Use marinade as a basting sauce if you are baking chicken.

Lime and Soy Marinade (for Seafood, Fish, Tofu, or Chicken)

Makes about ¾ cup

½ cup lime juice (4 to 6 limes)
2 tablespoons corn oil
½ teaspoon finely minced garlic
2 tablespoons light soy sauce
¼ teaspoon hot pepper sauce

Mix all the ingredients together in a small bowl. Marinate seafood, fish, tofu, or chicken in the refrigerator. For broiling chicken, seafood, or fish, use marinade as a basting sauce. For tofu, use it as a cold sauce.

Yogurt and *Garam Masala* Marinade (for Chicken or Lamb)

Makes ½ cup

1 tablespoon finely minced peeled ginger root
1 tablespoon finely minced garlic

¼ cup corn oil
½ teaspoon ground turmeric
½ teaspoon *garam masala* (page 12)
⅛ teaspoon cayenne pepper
½ cup plain yogurt

Mix all the ingredients together in a small bowl. Brush on chicken or lamb, and marinate for at least 1 hour in the refrigerator before cooking.

Yogurt and Mint Marinade (for Lamb)

Makes 1¼ cups

¼ cup finely minced fresh parsley
½ cup finely minced fresh mint
2 to 3 thin scallions, finely minced
1 tablespoon finely minced garlic
½ cup lemon juice
1 cup plain yogurt
¼ cup olive oil
1 teaspoon French-style mustard
¼ teaspoon black pepper

In a medium-size bowl, mix all the ingredients into a slightly thick marinade. Spoon onto any cut of lamb (whole leg, crown, or cubes), making certain that you cover all parts of the lamb completely. Marinate overnight in the refrigerator.

Jimmy Schmidt
The Rattlesnake Club
Denver, Colorado

Jimmy, just barely over 30, is co-owner and chef at The Rattlesnake Club in Denver, Colorado. Even at his tender age he has already made a name for himself in the field of imaginative cooking. Jimmy, who was among the first chefs cited by *Cook's Magazine* for its *Who's Who of Cooking in America* (1984), and who served as executive chef at Detroit's famous London Chop House, actually started out as a student of electrical engineering.

But all that changed when I studied cooking with Madeleine Kamman in France. I worked for her in Boston for 2½ years before going to the London Chop House, where I cooked for 8 years. Then Michael McCarty and I came out here to open our own place.

As in all the fine restaurants, everything served at the Rattlesnake Club is made from scratch—breads, pastas, pastries—and they even age their own meats. Nothing is frozen ("except for the ice cream," Jimmy states), and of course, they use fresh herbs.

The flavor is more definite, and if you handle fresh herbs correctly, they come through—the heat releases the volatile oils and they're just wonderful! We use them for sauces, in soups, with vegetables, for garnishes. Even the stems can be useful. I add herb stems to cream sauces before reducing them because they bring a very nice background flavor to the sauces. The principal part of the herb is reserved for the very end of the cooking time so the fresh flavor and quality of the herb is maintained. In fact, fresh herbs are so important to our idea of good cooking that we spend over $600 a week just for herbs alone!

Jimmy gets his herbs from Maryland, from California, and from two local growers. And, he feels that more home cooks are learning to use herbs.

People are becoming more sophisticated about food. They want better and fresher ingredients. They're eating more fish and poultry. They don't want the old heavy sauces, but they still want the full flavor of the food, and herbs are the key to that flavor.

If you favor basil, as Jimmy does, he suggests you experiment with the many varieties of it, such as lemon basil in fish dishes for its citrus flavor or cinnamon basil to flavor desserts.

One further question: why the name "Rattlesnake Club?" Explains Jimmy:

It's just a name. It gets attention.

It certainly does.

Breast of Chicken with a Medley of Basil

4 servings

4 boneless and skinless chicken breast halves
8 cloves garlic, peeled
½ cup finely chopped fresh basil
½ cup finely chopped fresh dark opal basil
  splash of hot pepper sauce
1 cup white wine, divided
½ cup olive oil
2 cups chicken stock
¾ cup Creme Fraiche (see below)
½ cup fresh basil, cut into julienne strips
½ cup fresh dark opal basil, cut into julienne strips
½ cup fresh lemon basil, cut into julienne strips
1 cup fresh spinach, cut into julienne strips
1 cup Belgian endive, cut into julienne strips
  freshly ground black pepper, to taste
¼ cup unsalted butter

Put chicken into a large bowl. Rub garlic, chopped basil, and chopped dark opal basil over surface of chicken. Splash hot pepper sauce over chicken, and add ½ cup of the white wine. Add oil, and mix well. Allow to marinate for 2 to 4 hours in the refrigerator.

In a medium-size saucepan, reduce chicken stock by three-quarters of its original volume over medium-high heat. Add remaining wine, and reduce by half.

Heat 2 tablespoons of the marinade in a large skillet over medium-high heat. Sear chicken, skin-side down. Turn over, spoon remaining marinade over chicken, and continue to cook. When half done, turn chicken over again.

Meanwhile, add creme fraiche to chicken stock mixture, and continue to reduce to a light sauce consistency. Add strips of basil, dark opal basil, and lemon basil along with spinach and endive. Allow sauce to reduce to proper consistency. Season with pepper. Add butter, and stir constantly to emulsify. Remove from heat to a stainless steel bowl, and set aside. Stir sauce for a few seconds to temper.

As chicken finishes, spoon sauce onto a warm serving platter. Position chicken on sauce, and serve.

CREME FRAICHE

1 part heavy cream
1 part sour cream

In a small saucepan, scald heavy cream over medium heat, and then whisk into sour cream. Maintain cream mixture at a temperature of 110°F for 12 hours. (This can be done by pouring mixture into a thermos bottle.) Refrigerate overnight.

VINEGARS

Borage Vinegar

Makes 1 quart

Borage Vinegar makes an excellent dressing for tomatoes as a change from basil, or you can use it in a sauce for fish.

1   quart white wine vinegar
2   cups coarsely chopped fresh borage leaves
3   peppercorns
    fresh borage blossoms and leaves

Heat vinegar to 150°F in a medium-size saucepan. Do not boil. Place borage leaves and peppercorns into a wide-mouth ½-gallon jar, and pour hot vinegar over them. Cover with cheesecloth, and secure with a rubber band around the neck of the jar. Store at room temperature for 4 to 6 weeks. Strain, and pour into sterilized bottles. Float a borage blossom and a leaf in each bottle.

Dill Vinegar

Makes 1 quart

The raisins, cloves, and orange rind take the acidic edge off the vinegar and mellow the flavor.

1   quart white wine vinegar
2   large sprigs of fresh dill
1   clove garlic, peeled and crushed slightly
1   2-inch piece of orange rind
6   raisins
3   whole cloves
    additional sprigs of fresh dill

Heat vinegar to about 150°F in a medium-size saucepan. Do not boil. In a wide-mouth quart jar, place all the remaining ingredients except additional dill sprigs, and pour hot vinegar over them. Cover with cheesecloth, and fasten with a rubber band around the neck of the jar. Allow to mellow for 4 to 6 weeks at room temperature. Strain, and pour into sterilized bottles. Discard dill, and add a fresh sprig to each bottle.

Herb, Spice, and Garlic Vinegar

Makes 1 quart

2   quarts red wine vinegar
3 to 4   cloves garlic, peeled and crushed
6   peppercorns, crushed
1   teaspoon coriander seeds
2   dried bay leaves
    handful of fresh fennel leaves
5 to 6   sprigs each of fresh thyme, savory, and oregano

In a large saucepan over medium heat, boil red wine vinegar until it is reduced by half. This will take 45 to 60 minutes. Then add garlic, peppercorns, coriander seeds, bay leaves, fennel, thyme, savory, and oregano. Let steep for 2 hours until cold. Strain into a bottle through a funnel lined with cheesecloth.

For a gift to the most discriminating gourmet, steep blue borage blossoms in white vinegar. The blossoms will tint the vinegar a lovely pale blue and give it a slight cucumberlike flavor.

Honey-Mint Vinegar

Makes 1 quart

Try this vinegar with lamb or fruit salads.

1 quart white wine vinegar
1/3 cup honey
1 cup fresh mint leaves
  sprigs of fresh mint

Heat vinegar to 150°F in a medium-size saucepan. Do not boil. Pour honey into a wide-mouth 1/2-gallon jar, add mint leaves, and pour hot vinegar over them. Cover with cheesecloth, and fasten with a rubber band around the neck of the jar. Allow to mellow at room temperature for 4 to 6 weeks. Strain, and pour into sterilized bottles. Add a sprig of fresh mint to each bottle.

Nasturtium Vinegar

Makes 1 quart

This is another example of how flowers and blossoms can be used in everyday cooking — from soups and salads to unusual dressings.

4 cups fresh nasturtium blossoms
1 tablespoon finely chopped shallots
2 cloves garlic
1/4 teaspoon dried red pepper flakes
1 quart white wine vinegar
  additional fresh nasturtium
    blossoms

Fill a wide-mouth gallon jar loosely with nasturtium blossoms. Heat all the remaining ingredients except additional blossoms to 150°F in a medium-size saucepan. Do not boil. Pour over blossoms, cover with cheese-cloth, and secure with a rubber band around the neck of the jar. Let mellow for 4 to 6 weeks at room temperature. Strain, and pour into sterilized bottles. Add a fresh blossom to each bottle for identification.

Opal Basil Vinegar

Makes 1 quart

The color of this pale, rosy vinegar is one that you will not find in a store. Bottled in a clear decorative glass container, it is a unique gift to give to a special cook. The method described below can also be used for other herbs, such as fresh tarragon, thyme, or rosemary. However, the opal basil color is our own favorite.

1 quart malt vinegar
1 cup opal basil leaves
  sprigs of fresh opal basil

Heat vinegar in a medium-size saucepan to 150°F, or until it begins to feel hot to your finger. *Do not allow it to reach the boiling point.* Place basil leaves into a wide-mouth 1/2-gallon jar. Pour hot vinegar over them, cover with cheesecloth, and fasten with a rubber band around the neck of the jar. Let stand for 4 to 6 weeks in a warm place (the top of the refrigerator or near the stove). Strain through a cheesecloth-lined funnel into sterilized bottles. Add a fresh sprig of the herb to each bottle. (The vinegar will have faded all the leaves used for flavoring.)

If you have a bottle of store-bought white vinegar on your shelf (and most of us do), slip a few chive or garlic chive blossoms into the bottle to add a delicate oniony flavor.

Chapter 15

DESSERTS

◄— Poached Maple Pears with Blue Cheese, Walnuts, and Cloves (page 284)

For some people, a meal without dessert is truly like a day without sunshine! Some of our friends even read the restaurant menus from the bottom up, evaluating the desserts before they even begin considering the entrees. This is sure to be their favorite chapter, for there is much that one can do with herbs and spices to create desserts that will surprise and delight even the most jaded lover of sweets.

For example, the muskiness of cardamom and the haunting citrus flavor of lemon balm can add a new dimension to a cheesecake. Fruit sauces blend beautifully with the bite of ginger, and rose geranium leaves marry well with strawberries or fresh rhubarb. The "sweet" spices like cinnamon and mace and allspice can evoke unexpected flavors from pears, plums, and apples.

Vanilla is the flavor that tops every preference survey; it even beats chocolate! This spice adds its subtle appeal to virtually every dessert, from cakes to puddings, from ice cream to cookies. Clove is the sweet-smelling, inimitable flavoring that can transform an ordinary coffee cake into ambrosia.

Don't forget about the classical blends that are commercially available. A combination called apple pie spice (allspice, cinnamon, and nutmeg) is a natural not only for flavoring apple pies, but also for applesauce, dumplings, and strudels. Another popular blend, pumpkin pie spice (cinnamon, ginger, nutmeg, and allspice), is perfect for many other kinds of pies, as well as breads, cookies, cakes, and spice cakes.

On the pages that follow, we provide recipes that open new directions for desserts, fresh ideas you can use to dazzle your dessert-loving friends.

277

Almond Spice Cake with Honey-Cheese Glaze

6 servings

Put together in an unusual manner, the center for this cake is made of puff pastry, which rises to form a central well that holds the honey-cheese glaze and the almond topping.

PASTRY BASE

- ½ cup whole wheat flour
- ¼ cup butter, cut into pieces
- 1 teaspoon cold water

PUFF PASTRY

- ½ cup cold water
- ¼ cup butter
- ½ cup unbleached white flour
- 2 eggs
- ¼ teaspoon pumpkin pie spice (a mixture of nutmeg, allspice, cinnamon, and ginger)
- ½ teaspoon almond extract

GLAZE

- 3 ounces cream cheese
- ⅓ cup honey
- ½ teaspoon grated lemon rind
- 1 teaspoon lemon juice
- ⅓ cup sliced almonds, toasted

To make the pastry base: In a food processor, mix flour and butter together for a few seconds until mixture is the consistency of fine bread crumbs. Sprinkle cold water over mixture, and process only until pastry forms a ball. Press pastry into the bottom of an 8 × 1½-inch round nonstick cake pan. Chill in refrigerator while preparing puff pastry.

To make the puff pastry: Preheat oven to 400°F.

In a 2-quart saucepan, combine cold water with butter. Bring to a boil, then lower heat, and add flour all at once, beating with a wooden spoon until the batter leaves the sides of the pan. Let cool slightly, then transfer to food processor, and add eggs one at a time along with pumpkin pie spice and almond extract. Process until mixture is well combined. The mixture will be thick and sticky. Scoop out with a rubber spatula, and spread over chilled pastry crust. Bake for 35 to 40 minutes. The sides will puff up, forming a center well. Let cool on a wire rack for 10 minutes.

To make the glaze: Beat cream cheese, honey, lemon rind, and lemon juice together in a small bowl, and spoon into the well when the cake has cooled. Sprinkle almonds over glaze, and serve cake slightly warm.

Baked Coconut Bananas with Cardamom

4 servings

- ¼ cup butter
- 4 firm whole bananas
- ¼ cup orange juice
- 1 teaspoon shredded orange rind
- ¼ cup date sugar
- ⅓ cup grated coconut
- ¼ cup slivered blanched almonds
- ¼ teaspoon ground cardamom

Preheat oven to 400°F.

Melt butter in an oven-to-table baking dish large enough to accommodate bananas in a single layer. Roll bananas in melted butter. Pour orange juice over bananas, and sprinkle with orange rind. Then sprinkle evenly with all remaining ingredients. Bake for 10 minutes, basting with sauce. Serve hot.

Green Grapes, Blueberries, and Strawberries with a Gingered Fruit Sauce (page 280) →

Crustless Cheesecake with Lemon Balm and Fruit

Makes 1 9-inch cake

A low-fat cheesecake with a lemony flavor and all the luxurious richness of one made with cream cheese, sour cream, and a butter crust. There's another bonus to this dessert: It's very easy to prepare.

        2 cups low-fat cottage cheese
     ½ cup honey
        3 tablespoons whole wheat flour
        1 teaspoon grated lemon rind
        1 tablespoon lemon juice
        1 teaspoon finely minced fresh lemon
             balm
        2 teaspoons vanilla extract
        4 eggs
     12 seedless green grapes, cut in half
        1 red plum, pitted and cut into
             8 thin slices
        1 sprig of fresh lemon balm (optional)

Preheat oven to 300°F. Spray a 9-inch springform pan with vegetable cooking spray, and set aside.

In a food processor, process cheese until smooth. Add honey, flour, lemon rind, lemon juice, minced lemon balm, and vanilla. Then, while machine is running, add eggs one at a time. Pour into prepared pan, and bake in the center of the oven for 1 hour and 10 minutes. Turn off heat, and leave cake in oven, *without opening the door,* for 1 hour.

Remove cake to a wire rack, and run a thin knife around the outer edge to loosen it. Cool completely, and then chill in the refrigerator overnight. When ready to serve, bring cake to room temperature, and remove sides of pan, keeping cake on the bottom of the pan for support. Arrange grape halves in a circle around the outer edge of the cake, and put plum slices in the center, spreading them from a center point like the leaves of a flower or spokes of a wheel. You can add a sprig of lemon balm if you wish.

Note: This cake should be refrigerated overnight before serving. You may even prepare it 2 to 3 days in advance. It's ideal for dinner parties.

Green Grapes, Blueberries, and Strawberries with a Gingered Fruit Sauce

4 servings

A trickle of honey makes the fruit glisten on this simple, attractive dessert.

SAUCE

        2 tablespoons unsweetened frozen
             pineapple juice concentrate
     5½ ounces apricot nectar
        1 large ripe peach, peeled and
             pureed in a blender
        1 tablespoon grated lime rind
        1 teaspoon finely minced peeled
             ginger root
        2 tablespoons lime juice

FRUIT

     1¼ cups fresh blueberries
        1 pound seedless green grapes,
             removed from stems

Orange Cardamom Cake
(page 282)

½ cup whole fresh wild strawberries
    or sliced regular fresh
    strawberries
  light honey
1 teaspoon finely minced fresh mint
4 sprigs of fresh mint
4 wedges of lime (optional)

To make the sauce: In a small saucepan, combine all the ingredients, and bring to a boil. Lower heat, and simmer for 5 minutes. Let cool, and refrigerate for 1 hour.

To prepare the fruit: When ready to serve, spoon some of the sauce into individual serving plates. Arrange fruit in bands across each plate, so that they form 3 distinctive colors next to one another. Trickle honey over fruit, and sprinkle with minced mint. Decorate each plate with a sprig of fresh mint and lime wedges, if desired.

To add glamour to the punch bowl, freeze sprigs of mint, lemon balm, or scented geranium in a large "ice cube." To make the giant cube, fill a gallon plastic ice cream container loosely with the leaves of washed herbs, add water up to ½ inch from the rim, cover tightly, and freeze. Unmold by placing the container under hot running water. Float the cube in a colorful fruit punch bowl.

Maple Walnut Bars with Allspice

Makes 12 bars

The merest whiff of allspice gives nuance to these crunchy, chewy, extremely easy-to-make cookie bars.

 1 egg
 ¾ cup maple syrup
 2 teaspoons vanilla extract
 ½ cup whole wheat pastry flour
 ½ cup unbleached white flour
 1 teaspoon baking soda
 ⅛ teaspoon ground allspice
 1 cup coarsely broken walnuts,
     toasted

Preheat oven to 350°F. Butter an 8 × 2-inch square baking pan.

In a medium-size bowl, beat egg with a whisk until foamy. Add maple syrup and vanilla, and beat until smooth. In a small bowl, mix together whole wheat pastry flour, unbleached white flour, baking soda, and allspice. Add to maple syrup mixture all at once, and beat well until smooth. Stir in walnuts, pour into prepared pan, and bake for 20 to 25 minutes. The center of the batter should still be soft when removed from the oven. Cool on a wire rack, and then cut into 12 bars.

Orange Cardamom Cake

8 to 10 servings

Sweetened and glazed with maple syrup, this orange cake combines crunchy toasted walnuts and a hint of cardamom for a delicate blend of flavors.

CAKE
 1 cup whole wheat pastry flour
 1 cup unbleached white flour
 1 teaspoon baking soda
 1½ teaspoons baking powder
 ½ teaspoon ground cardamom
 ½ cup butter, softened
 ½ cup maple syrup
 3 eggs, separated
 1 tablespoon grated orange rind
 1 cup sour cream
 ½ cup coarsely chopped walnuts,
     toasted
     thin orange slices (optional)
 3 walnut halves (optional)

GLAZE
 ¼ cup orange juice
 ¼ cup maple syrup
 2 tablespoons butter

To make the cake: Preheat oven to 350°F. Butter a 9-inch springform pan.

Sift together whole wheat pastry flour, unbleached white flour, baking soda, baking powder, and cardamom, and set aside. Cream butter in a food processor. Slowly add maple syrup, processing until creamy and well blended. Add egg yolks, one at a time, and blend well. Add grated orange rind. Alternately add one-third of the sour cream and one-third of the dry ingredients to the food processor, and blend until smooth. Spoon and scrape into a large bowl, and stir in chopped walnuts. In a small bowl, beat egg whites until stiff but not dry, using an egg beater for greatest volume, and fold into cake batter. Spoon into prepared pan. Bake for 50 minutes, or until a cake tester inserted into the center comes out clean. Set cake on a wire rack to cool slightly while preparing glaze.

To make the glaze: In a small saucepan, mix all the ingredients together, and reduce to ¼ cup over medium heat. This takes 10 to 15 minutes. Remove sides of cake pan, keeping cake on bottom of pan, and place it on a serving plate with a rim to catch any drippings. Puncture cake all over the surface with a cake tester, and slowly drizzle with glaze. Decorate cake if you wish with orange slices cut in half and walnut halves.

Rome's entire supply of costly cinnamon was blended with incense and burned at the funeral of his wife, Poppaea, by the emperor Nero.

Poached Cinnamon Apples with Honey-Almond Custard

4 servings

Tart apples are poached in cider with cinnamon sticks and then placed on a bed of almond custard. Simple and very elegant!

POACHED APPLES
    2 large Granny Smith apples
    ½ cup apple cider
    ¼ cup light honey
    1 tablespoon grated lemon rind
    1 4-inch piece of cinnamon stick, broken in half
    2 tablespoons lemon juice

CUSTARD
    2 cups cold milk
    2 tablespoons cornstarch
    ⅓ cup light honey
    ⅓ cup whole blanched almonds, toasted and then very finely ground in a blender (½ cup)
    2 egg yolks
    1 teaspoon almond extract
       sliced almonds

To prepare the poached apples: Peel, core, and quarter apples, and set aside. In a 2½-quart nonstick saucepan, bring cider, honey, lemon rind, cinnamon stick, and lemon juice to a boil. Lower heat to medium, and cook for 1 minute. Add apples, lower heat, cover, and simmer for 5 to 6 minutes, or until apples are tender but still hold their shape. Remove from heat and cool. Transfer apples and liquid to a small bowl, and discard cinnamon stick. Chill apples. While chilling, prepare the custard.

To prepare the custard: Reserve 2 tablespoons of cold milk. Pour remaining milk into a 2½-quart nonstick saucepan, and scald until bubbles form around the edges of the milk. In a cup, mix cornstarch with reserved cold milk, and add to scalded milk along with honey and ground almonds. Stir over low heat for 5 minutes, or until smooth and thick. In a small bowl, beat egg yolks. Add 1 ladleful of hot mixture to egg yolks, beating well with a wire whisk. Return egg mixture to the milk-almond mixture. Cook, stirring constantly, over low heat for 1 to 2 minutes. Remove from heat, and add almond extract. There should be 2 cups of custard.

To assemble, spoon equal amounts of custard on the bottom of 4 glass dessert dishes. Place 2 pieces of poached apple on top of each serving, spoon a bit of the apple syrup over the apples to glaze, and sprinkle sliced almonds over all. Chill before serving.

Prune Souffle with Cottage Cheese and Lemon Verbena

6 servings

The tea permeates the prunes with a smokey flavor, as does the lemon verbena.

½ pound pitted prunes
½ cup strong tea
 1 tablespoon lemon juice
 2 teaspoons finely minced fresh
      lemon verbena
½ cup date sugar
 3 egg yolks
 1 cup low-fat cottage cheese
½ cup sour cream
 5 egg whites
      pinch of cream of tartar
 1 sprig of fresh lemon verbena
      (optional)

In a small saucepan, cook prunes in tea until soft, about 5 minutes. Add lemon juice and minced lemon verbena, remove from heat, and cool for 10 minutes.

Preheat oven to 350°F, and butter a 1½-quart souffle dish.

Mix date sugar and egg yolks until well blended in the bowl of a food processor. Add cheese and sour cream, and blend until well mixed. Then add prunes, and process again until well mixed.

In a large deep bowl, beat egg whites until foamy, using an egg beater to get extra volume. Add cream of tartar, and continue to beat egg whites until stiff but not dry. Fold some of the prune mixture into egg whites with a large rubber spatula. Add remaining prune mixture a little bit at a time, folding into egg whites so that air is incorporated for lightness. Spoon into prepared souffle dish, and place it into a large pan. Pour boiling water into the pan until it reaches three-quarters of the way up the sides of the souffle dish. Bake for 55 minutes. Cool on a wire rack. Before serving, decorate with a sprig of lemon verbena if you wish. This souffle will not deflate; therefore, it can be eaten warm or cold.

Poached Maple Pears with Blue Cheese, Walnuts, and Cloves

4 servings

 4 Bosc, Comice, or Anjou pears,
      peeled and cut in half
½ cup maple syrup
¾ cup water
 3 whole cloves
 4 ounces blue cheese, at room
      temperature
 2 ounces cream cheese, at room
      temperature
½ cup coarsely chopped walnuts,
      toasted
 1 teaspoon lemon juice
      additional whole cloves (optional)

Scoop out centers of pears at their widest part. Place pears in a skillet large enough to accommodate them in a single layer. Mix maple syrup and water together in a small bowl. Add cloves, and pour over pears. Simmer, covered, for 10 minutes, occasionally lifting the lid to baste with the liquid. Test with the point of a knife for tenderness. Comice or Anjou pears, being softer to begin with, take less time to cook than Bosc pears. If using Bosc pears, additional water may need to be added as well.

While pears are poaching, mix both cheeses together in a small bowl with a fork. Mix in walnuts, and set aside. When pears are tender, tilt pan, stir in lemon juice, and simmer until there is a glazed sauce. Spoon some sauce into 4 individual serving dishes. Carefully lift 2 pear halves out of skillet, and set them on the sauce. Put 1 heaping teaspoon of walnut-cheese mixture into each pear hollow, and add a whole clove, if you wish, at the narrow end of the pears to give the appearance of a stem. Serve at room temperature so that the cheese is soft.

Rhubarb Upside-Down Cake with Cinnamon

6 servings

Here is a delicious variation of the traditional pineapple upside-down cake. It's especially attractive when the ruby-red rhubarb is revealed atop the cake, shiny with its honey glaze.

- 2 cups diced rhubarb (¾-inch pieces)
- 1 tablespoon Minute Tapioca
- ⅔ cup plus 3 tablespoons honey, divided
- 1 tablespoon grated orange rind
- 1 teaspoon ground cinnamon
- ¾ cup whole wheat flour
- ¾ cup unbleached white flour
- 2 teaspoons baking powder
- ¼ cup cold butter, cut into pieces
- 1 egg, beaten
- ¼ cup milk
- ¼ cup orange juice

Preheat oven to 350°F. Butter a 9 × 2-inch round nonstick cake pan.

In a medium-size bowl, mix rhubarb with tapioca, ⅔ cup of the honey, orange rind, and cinnamon. Let stand for 30 minutes.

In a food processor, mix together whole wheat flour, unbleached white flour, and baking powder. Add butter, mixing until texture is grainy. In a small bowl, mix together egg, milk, and 2 tablespoons of the honey, and then add to butter and flour mixture. Process only until batter is moistened. Do not overmix. Spoon rhubarb mixture into the bottom of the prepared pan. Spoon batter over rhubarb (batter will be thick), and smooth the surface gently with a spatula. Bake for 25 minutes.

In a cup, mix remaining honey with orange juice, and drizzle it over the surface of the cake. Return to oven, and bake 15 minutes more. Let cool on a wire rack before loosening the sides and inverting on a serving plate. Serve slightly warm.

Fill several small glass vials or vases of different heights with tiny bouquets of individual fresh herbs. Mass them together for a fragrant summer table centerpiece. Add some charcoal to the water to keep it clear and sweet.

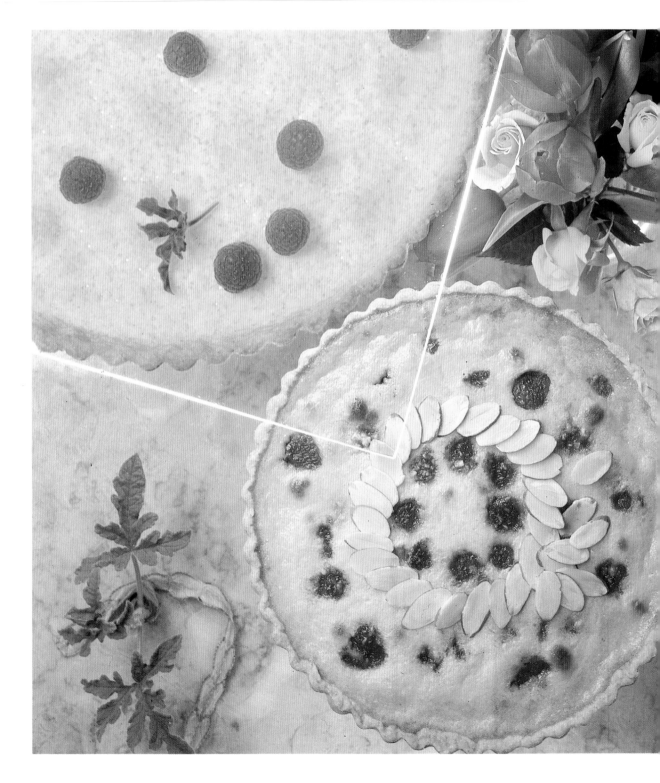

Rose and Almond Dessert with Nutmeg and Cardamom

6 to 8 servings

Rose water adds an exotic touch to this dessert. It can be purchased, along with the concentrated form, rose essence, in Middle Eastern or Indian specialty shops.

 3 tablespoons butter
 6 ounces slivered almonds
 ⅔ cup raisins
 1 quart milk
 ⅔ cup honey
 ½ cup Cream of Wheat
 1 tablespoon rose water or
  ¼ teaspoon rose essence
 ½ teaspoon ground nutmeg
 ½ teaspoon ground cardamom
  rose or rose petals (optional)

Heat butter in a medium-size skillet. Add almonds, and saute until golden. In the last few minutes, add raisins. Remove almonds and raisins with a slotted spoon, put them into a medium-size bowl, and reserve. In a large saucepan, heat together milk and honey. Stir in Cream of Wheat, and bring to a boil. Lower heat, and simmer until thickened, about 5 minutes, stirring constantly. Remove from heat, add rose water or rose essence, and spices, then pour into a fairly flat serving dish or pie plate, and sprinkle top with almonds and raisins. Chill. Serve decorated with a rose or rose petals if you wish.

Shredded Pear Flan with Orange and Lemon Rinds and Mace

Makes 1 9-inch flan

 4 ripe Bartlett pears, peeled and
  cored
 5 tablespoons date sugar, divided
 1 tablespoon grated orange rind
 1 teaspoon grated lemon rind
 ¼ teaspoon ground mace
 2 tablespoons butter, cut into small
  pieces
 3 eggs
 ¼ cup milk
 ¼ cup heavy cream
 1 teaspoon vanilla extract
  a few berries or slices of fruit, or a
   sprig of mint

Preheat oven to 350°F.

Shred pears in a food processor, using the shredding blade. Transfer to a medium-size bowl, and mix with 2 tablespoons of the date sugar, orange rind, lemon rind, and mace. Spoon into a 9-inch nonstick tart pan, and dot with butter. Bake for 10 minutes.

Meanwhile, in a food processor, beat eggs with remaining date sugar. Add all the remaining ingredients, and blend well. Carefully pour over pears, return to oven, and continue baking for 30 minutes more, or until the center is almost set. Let cool at room temperature. Decorate with a few berries, slices of fruit, or a sprig of mint.

← Almond Custard and Raspberry Tart with Rose Geranium Leaves (page 289)

Baked Coconut Bananas with
Cardamom (page 278)

Strawberry Rhubarb Tart with Rose Geranium Leaves

Makes 1 10-inch tart

Basic Pastry (see below)
2   pounds rhubarb, sliced diagonally
       into ½-inch pieces
½   pint fresh strawberries, sliced
       lengthwise into ¼-inch slices
1¼ cups light honey, divided
2   large rose geranium leaves, finely
       minced
1   tablespoon grated orange rind
½   cup Minute Tapioca
2   tablespoons fine whole grain bread
       crumbs
1   large whole rose geranium leaf

Wrap dough with aluminum foil, and press into a flattened disk. Chill for 25 minutes.

In a large bowl, toss together sliced fruit and ¼ cup of the honey. Let stand for 20 minutes, and then drain into strainer over a small bowl for 15 minutes more. While fruit is draining, mix together remaining honey, minced geranium leaves, orange rind, and tapioca in another small bowl, and let them steep to develop flavor. When excess liquid has drained from fruit, combine the contents of both bowls, and add to prepared pastry dough.

Preheat oven to 425°F.

Roll out pastry until it is large enough to overlap a 10-inch tart pan by about 2 inches. Fit pastry into pan, and sprinkle the bottom of the crust with bread crumbs. Add fruit filling, and gently fold the overlap toward the center of the tart, draping it to fit. Bake for 1 hour and 10 minutes, or until pastry is golden and filling is bubbly. Place on a wire rack to cool completely before cutting. While pie is cooling, place whole geranium leaf in the center. The warmth of the pie will release the perfume of the leaf.

Basic Pastry

- ¾ cup whole wheat pastry flour
- ¾ cup unbleached white flour
- 4 ounces cream cheese, cut into small pieces
- ¼ pound butter, cut into small pieces
- 2 tablespoons heavy cream

Put whole wheat pastry flour, unbleached white flour, cream cheese, and butter into the bowl of a food processor, and turn quickly on and off for 10 to 12 strokes. Trickle cream over mixture, which should look crumbly. Use 2 to 3 strokes more to combine. Roll out according to recipe instructions.

Note: This is an unsweetened basic pastry that can be used for all fruit, vegetable, or meat pies in this book.

Almond Custard and Raspberry Tart with Rose Geranium Leaves

Makes 1 10-inch tart

The raspberries are scented with roses, the custard topped with sliced almonds, and the surface crisped for added crunchiness.

Basic Pastry (page 289)
1 cup fresh raspberries

1 large rose geranium leaf, finely minced
2 tablespoons light honey, divided
1 cup half-and-half
2 eggs, well beaten
½ teaspoon almond extract
½ cup finely ground almonds
¼ cup sliced almonds

Preheat oven to 400°F.

Roll out pastry, and fit into a 10-inch tart pan. Prick pastry all over with a fork. Place a piece of aluminum foil, shiny-side up, on crust with foil standing up straight against the rim. Weigh down with pie weights or dried beans, and bake for 10 minutes. Remove foil and weights, and bake for 8 minutes more. Prick areas that may have risen, using a cake tester to release the trapped air, and set aside while preparing the filling.

Lower oven temperature to 350°F.

In a medium-size bowl, mix together raspberries, rose geranium leaves, and 1 table-spoon of the honey, and spread evenly on the partially baked pastry crust. In another medium-size bowl, mix together the remaining honey, half-and-half, eggs, almond extract, and ground almonds. Pour carefully over raspberries, and bake for 30 minutes, or until custard is firm. Arrange sliced almonds on top, and place under broiler for 1 minute, or until nuts are golden. Cool to room temperature before serving.

For all fruit or berry pies: Slip six scented rose geranium leaves under the top piecrust before baking for a mysterious and unexpected pleasure.

Blueberry and Orange Tart with Cinnamon

Makes 1 10-inch tart

     Basic Pastry (page 289)
  5 cups fresh blueberries, divided
  ¾ cup light honey
  ¼ cup Minute Tapioca
  1 cup boiling water
  1 tablespoon grated orange rind
  2 tablespoons orange juice
  2 teaspoons cinnamon
  1 tablespoon butter

Roll out pastry, and fit into a 10-inch tart pan. Prick pastry all over with a fork, and place into the freezer for 15 to 20 minutes to chill.

Preheat oven to 450°F.

Place a piece of aluminum foil on crust with foil standing up straight against the rim. Weigh down with pie weights or dried beans, and bake frozen for 15 minutes. Then, reduce heat to 400°F, remove foil and weights, and bake for 10 to 15 minutes more. If bottom of crust is not completely baked through, bake another 5 minutes. If the bottom begins to puff up, pierce it with the tip of a sharp knife to release the trapped air. Let cool completely on a wire rack before adding filling.

In a medium-size nonstick saucepan, slowly heat 1 cup of the blueberries, honey, tapioca, and boiling water. With a potato masher, crush berries as they cook. Bring slowly to a boil, then lower heat, and simmer for 5 minutes, stirring occasionally. Remove from heat, and stir in orange rind, orange juice, cinnamon, butter, and remaining blueberries. Let cool for 10 minutes. Then spoon into baked piecrust. Let cool completely before cutting.

Peach Walnut Tart with Cinnamon and Apricot Puree

Makes 1 10-inch tart

          Basic Pastry (page 289)
   ½ cup walnuts, toasted and then
            finely ground in a blender
   ½ teaspoon ground cinnamon
   2 pounds freestone peaches
   ¼ cup light honey
   6 ounces dried apricots
   ½ cup honey
   ½ cup water
   1 teaspoon lemon juice
   1 tablespoon butter
15 to 20 walnut halves

Roll out pastry, and fit into a 10-inch tart pan. Crimp edges, and sprinkle bottom of pastry with ground nuts mixed with cinnamon. Place in the refrigerator to keep pastry crust chilled while preparing filling.

Put peaches into a large bowl, and cover with boiling water. Let stand for 2 to 3 minutes to loosen skins. Drain peaches. Slip off skins, remove pits, and cut each peach into 8 slices. Return to bowl, add light honey, stir, and let stand for 15 minutes. When juices accumulate, pour off, and reserve.

Mix apricots, honey, and water together in a medium-size saucepan. Bring to a boil, then lower heat, and cook slowly for 5 to 8 minutes. Cool slightly, and puree in a blender. Pour into a medium-size bowl, and stir in lemon juice, butter, and reserved peach liquid. Set aside.

Preheat oven to 375°F.

To assemble tart, arrange peach slices over nut mixture. Spoon apricot puree over peaches, and bake in lower part of oven for 1 hour. For the last 5 minutes of baking, remove pie, and arrange walnut halves on top of apri-

Turkish Milk Pudding with Rose Geraniums, Pistachio Nuts, and Pomegranates (page 291)

cot puree. Return to oven, and bake until nuts are toasted. Remove pie, and cool on wire rack before serving.

Turkish Milk Pudding with Rose Geraniums, Pistachio Nuts, and Pomegranates

4 servings

Every restaurant in Istanbul displays tiny cups of this pudding. Serve this simple dessert on a black plate for a dramatic presentation.

2½ cups milk, divided
¼ cup light honey
3 to 4 scented rose geranium leaves (depending on size of leaves)
1 tablespoon brown rice, finely ground in a blender
2 tablespoons cornstarch
8 to 12 pistachio nuts and several pomegranate kernels or 4 additional rose geranium leaves and 4 wedges of pomegranate

Mix together 2 cups of the milk, honey, and geranium leaves in a large nonstick saucepan, and heat slowly until tiny bubbles begin to form at the edges of the milk. Combine remaining milk, ground rice, and cornstarch in a cup, and stir until well mixed. Slowly stir rice-cornstarch mixture into hot milk mixture, and cook, stirring constantly, until consistency is thick and rice is tender, about 10 minutes. Remove geranium leaves with tongs, and pour pudding into 4 ½-cup molds that have been rinsed with cold water and left damp. Chill for several hours.

When ready to serve, keep pudding in cups, for the consistency will be soft, but decorate each with 2 to 3 pistachio nuts and a few pomegranate kernels, or present each cup accompanied by a small wedge of pomegranate and a rose geranium leaf.

Note: This dessert can also be served with a sprinkling of ground cinnamon or powdered ginger for a less exotic presentation.

MAIL-ORDER SOURCES

These days, most spices and a great variety of herbs (both fresh and dried) are available locally in supermarkets, specialty food shops, and nurseries. In addition, seeds for do-it-yourself gardeners are also listed in most good catalogs. However, for those who live in isolated areas and those who can't find certain herbs and spices locally, here are the names and addresses of sources for just about everything. All accept mail orders.

Angelica's Herb & Spice Company
137 First Ave.
New York, NY 10003
(212) 677-1549

They carry over 5,000 herbs and herbal products with an emphasis on high-grade wild and organic botanicals. They also list 200 spices and culinary herbs, Chinese herbs, and homeopathic remedies. Write for their catalog.

Aphrodisia
282 Bleecker St.
New York, NY 10014
(212) 989-6440

Billing themselves as "the world's most complete herb store," they stock a large variety of herbs, spices, and essential oils. Their culinary herb and spice section boasts everything from agar-agar to zebrovka. Write for their catalog, which currently sells for $1.

Balducci's
424 Avenue of the Americas
New York, NY 10011
(212) 673-2600

For those living in the metropolitan area of New York, this remarkable store is a treasure house of fresh herbs. In the past few years their selection of herbs has increased substantially, and those that we do not grow ourselves, we buy there. It's also a good out-of-season source.

Caprilands Herb Farm
534 Silver St.
Coventry, CT 06238
(203) 742-7244

They offer a large variety of plants, seeds, dried herbs, and spices, plus some teas. If you're ever in the area of Coventry, Caprilands would make an interesting stop for the family. They serve herb tea, and they celebrate special events such as an Herbal Halloween.

J. A. Demonchaux Co.
827 North Kansas
Topeka, KS 66608
(913) 235-8502

They offer a good selection of annual and perennial herb seeds.

Epicure Seeds Ltd.
P.O. Box 450
Brewster, NY 10509

Epicure sells a variety of herb seeds, including several kinds of basil: dwarf, fine leaf, and opal included. They also stock European varieties, such as Danish and German dill and coriander from France. Send for their catalog.

Fox Hill Farm
444 West Michigan Ave.
Box 7
Parma, MI 49269
(517) 531-3179

This is one of the best sources for herbs. Their catalog ($1) lists a wide variety. Currently they are among the largest suppliers of herbs to Midwest restaurants and gardeners.

Glie Farms
1600 Bathgate Ave.
The Bronx, NY 10457
(212) 731-2130

They sell by mail order to restaurants and the general public. A list of their fresh herbs is available, quoting variety and price.

Hilltop Herb Farm
P.O. Box 1734
Cleveland, TX 77327
(713) 592-5859

Hilltop offers an extensive collection of perennial herb plants, annual and perennial seeds, herb blends, dried herbs, and spices.

Le Jardin du Gourmet
West Danville, VT 05873

This could be called a shopping center for European seeds, mostly with a French accent. They also have a good assortment of "mini-seed" packets containing approximately 30 seeds for about 25¢ each, ideal for small gardeners who want to experiment but don't have the room for huge plantings. A catalog is available.

Nichols Garden Nursery
1190 North Pacific Highway
Albany, OR 97321
(503) 928-9280

They have a large selection of herb seeds, perennial herb plants, dried herbs and spices, herb blends, and tea blends.

Park Seed Co., Inc.
Greenwood, SC 29647
(803) 374-3341

Park stocks a large assortment of annual and perennial herb seeds, and a few perennial plants.

Taylor's Herb Gardens, Inc.
1535 Lone Oak Rd.
Vista, CA 92083
(714) 727-3485

They offer a plentiful assortment of annual and perennial plants, plus a variety of seeds.

Thompson & Morgan, Inc.
P.O. Box 1308
Jackson, NJ 08527
(201) 363-2225

This is an excellent source for all kinds of herbs in addition to the usual vegetables and flowers sold by good nurseries. A catalog is available.

White Mountain Herb Farm
P.O. Box 64
Jefferson, NH 03583

They sell over 60 varieties of perennial herb plants.

INDEX

Page references in **boldface** refer to charts, boxes, or illustrations.